T0291294

Early praise for *Harnessing Digital Disruption*

With this crisp and easy-to-read book, Pascal and Laurent have captured the essence of a successful Digital transformation.

- Paul Cobban, Chief Transformation Officer @ DBS Bank

I really enjoyed the business novel format and the great illustrations.

- Reuben Athaide, Head DevOps and Cloud Transformation, Standard Chartered Bank

Pascal and Laurent bring to life the tools and techniques that enable traditional companies to reinvent themselves.

- Michelle Van Staden, Agile Transformation Leader, Nedbank

A different kind of book: I couldn't put it down.

- Victoria Thompson, Founding member of the London Blockchain Foundation

Full of practical insights, this book is a must read for Senior Executives of traditional companies who need to foster innovation and entrepreneurship in their organization.

- Denis Ricard, Chief Executing Officer iA Financial Group

We were able to apply Pascal and Laurent's approach and methods directly in our business. We were surprised by the results we got and how fast we could realize them!

- Harry Zechman, Chief Operating Officer, Stoner Chemical

Harnessing Digital Disruption

Harnessing Digital Disruption

How Companies Win with Design Thinking, Agile, and Lean Startup

Pascal Dennis
Laurent Simon

Routledge
Taylor & Francis Group

A PRODUCTIVITY PRESS BOOK

First published 2021
by Routledge
600 Broken Sound Parkway #300, Boca Raton FL, 33487

and by Routledge
2 Park Square, Milton Park, Abingdon, Oxon, OX14 4RN

Routledge is an imprint of the Taylor & Francis Group, an informa business

Library of Congress Cataloging-in-Publication Data
A catalog record for this title has been requested

ISBN: 9780367201555 (hbk)
ISBN: 9781138323209 (pbk)
ISBN: 9780429451522 (ebk)

Typeset in Garamond
by Newgen Publishing UK

Contents

Preface vii

About the Authors ix

Asia Pacific Bank's Organization Chart (Main Characters) xi

1   **The Elephant and the Greyhounds** 1
    Asia Pacific Bank is slow, unreliable, and expensive …

2   **Mapping Client Journeys to Grasp the Real Situation** 17
    Learning to think 'outside-in'

3   **Understanding Our Blockers** 33
    Problems are gold

4   **Finding True North with Our Digital Strategy Compass** 51
    What's our aspiration and winning logic?

5   **Fostering Innovation in a Risk-Averse Culture** 71
    What's the journey like and where do we start?

6   **Embracing New Ways of Working** 87
    Hackers, Hipsters and Hustlers working together –
    setting up Asia Pacific Bank's innovation platform

7   **Launching Our First Wave Innovation Projects** 103
    Core business improvement: Bringing tech and
    operations together

8   **Launching Our Second Wave Innovation Projects** 127
    End-to-end flow and a commercial pilot. Can we create
    entirely new digital products?

9 Year-End Review at Asia Pacific Bank.......................**147**
The empire strikes back

10 How Do We Accelerate Our Digital Transformation? **159**
Everybody wants to go to heaven, but nobody wants to die

11 New Digital Ventures **183**
What have we achieved, what have we learned and what's next?

Appendix A – Singapore Places Featured in *Harnessing Digital Disruption* **201**
Appendix B – List of Figures..**207**
Acknowledgments **211**
Index **213**

Preface

Who led the digital transformation of your company?

a) CEO
b) CTO
c) COVID-19

Our world has changed, probably for good. Until now, the shift from brick-and-mortar to the smartphone has been about service, cost, and convenience. Now, it's also a matter of public health.

In some industries, this trend has been evident for some time. But now it's going to accelerate across the gamut of industry. How do we remain relevant in this risky new world? How do we win this uncertain new game? What if ours is a brick-and-mortar organization that depends on face-to-face interaction? Can we learn to harness digital methods, tools, and technologies?

Fortunately, there is a pathway to prosperity. Our story is set in the heady world of international banking, but the prescription, methods and lessons apply equally to manufacturers, utilities, hospitals, insurers, and government agencies.

Harnessing digital disruption entails learning new tools, systems and thinking. Doing so *effectively* requires a sound overall approach based on timeless principles. The more things change, the more they stay the same. But sometimes they look different.

Change your opinions, keep to your principles; change your leaves, keep intact your roots.[1]

---

[1] Victor Hugo, French writer and politician.

About the Authors

 **Pascal Dennis** is a professional engineer, author and executive coach.

Pascal is the President of Lean Pathways and co-founder of Digital Pathways, a firm focused on harnessing technology to enable Digital Transformation.

Since 2000 Pascal and his team have supported leading international firms in a broad range of industries including automotive, aerospace, consumer goods, energy, health care and financial services.

He has authored six books and is a four-time winner of the Shingo Prize for Excellence. Pascal plays guitar and piano and is a dedicated songwriter and performer. He lives in Toronto with his wife Pamela.

www.linkedin.com/in/pascaldennishdd

www.amazon.com/author/pascaldennishdd

Laurent Simon is one the leaders of Datacom's Advisory and the co-founder of Digital Pathways.

Laurent is a recognised thought leader in Agile Transformation and Digital Innovation.

Since 2003, Laurent and his team have supported Financial Institutions, ICT firms and Government Agencies in 1) Protecting their core business with better digital experiences, 2) Igniting new sources of growth with new digital offerings or ventures.

Active contributor to the APAC startup ecosystem, he runs www.FutureFinTech.io, the Open Collaboration platform hosted by INSEAD business school.

Laurent loves anything outdoors: hiking, sailing, skydiving, skiing, rafting... After six years in Singapore, he now lives in Auckland with his wife Eiko-san.

www.linkedin.com/in/laurentsimonhdd

www.amazon.com/author/laurentsimon

Asia Pacific Bank's Organization Chart (Main Characters)

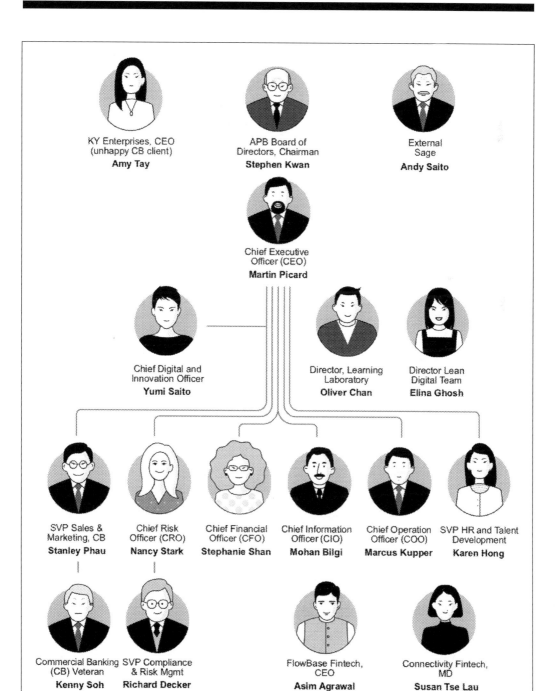

KY Enterprises, CEO (unhappy CB client)
Amy Tay

APB Board of Directors, Chairman
Stephen Kwan

External Sage
Andy Saito

Chief Executive Officer (CEO)
Martin Picard

Chief Digital and Innovation Officer
Yumi Saito

Director, Learning Laboratory
Oliver Chan

Director Lean Digital Team
Elina Ghosh

SVP Sales & Marketing, CB
Stanley Phau

Chief Risk Officer (CRO)
Nancy Stark

Chief Financial Officer (CFO)
Stephanie Shan

Chief Information Officer (CIO)
Mohan Bilgi

Chief Operation Officer (COO)
Marcus Kupper

SVP HR and Talent Development
Karen Hong

Commercial Banking (CB) Veteran
Kenny Soh

SVP Compliance & Risk Mgmt
Richard Decker

FlowBase Fintech, CEO
Asim Agrawal

Connectivity Fintech, MD
Susan Tse Lau

Chapter 1

The Elephant and the Greyhounds

Asia Pacific Bank is slow, unreliable, and expensive …

"It is not necessary to change. Survival is not mandatory."
W. Edwards Deming (American engineer)

Mr. Stork Rooftop Garden Bar, Andaz Singapore Hotel[1]

Amy Tay sits down opposite Martin Picard. "This is one of my favorite places," she says, taking in the panorama. They order lunch and exchange pleasantries.

"Why did we lose your business, Amy?" Martin asks. "We've worked with your family for half a century."

Amy takes a breath. "Asia Pacific Bank (APB) is slow, unreliable and expensive."

Martin looks out across the Central Business District (CBD) and the iconic Marina Bay Sands building. The Strait of Malacca is busy, as usual, with ships pouring in from both the Andaman and South China seas. He has a good relationship with Amy and her father, Kwong Yip, who is

---

[1] https://www.hyatt.com/en-US/hotel/singapore/andaz-singapore/sinaz.

now semi-retired. That's why she's here, he realizes, and being so blunt. She's trying to help.

Martin remembers when their clothing design and retail business, KY Tay International, was just a few stores. Now it's an East Asian powerhouse, a regional dynamo, with hundreds of stores and a striking on-line presence. A dream client for APB's Corporate banking division.

"It pains me to hear that, Amy. It would really help if you can be specific."

"On the commercial side," Amy replies, "getting paid, and paying our suppliers and employees was often a hassle. There were always overpayments, underpayments, and missed payments. On the wealth management side, your advisors were slow, disorganized and expensive. Sometimes, I felt like I was educating them. On the personal side, you even lost my daughter's tuition money a few months ago. She was crying and worried she might lose her place at Oxford. It took several days to fix the problem and you still wanted to charge me!"

Martin has only been CEO for a few months. Profitability is declining, costs are rising, and Martin is counting on growth to solve his problems. Now Amy Tay is saying that three of his core businesses – Commercial Banking, Wealth Management and Retail Banking – are lousy. Have I accepted a poisoned chalice, he wonders?

"I don't mean to be disrespectful," Amy continues. "You know how important relationships are to our family. But we have other alternatives now, and your service isn't getting any better."

"What kind of alternatives?" Picard asks.

Amy holds up her smartphone. "Look Martin, digital methods help me manage design, sourcing, inventory, sales, and warehousing. We're hoping digital can also help manage our complex logistics and Trade Finance. You know what our bottleneck is? *Asia Pacific Bank* – working with you is like going back in time. Forgive me for speaking severely."

Picard listens quietly, Amy's words reverberating: *slow, unreliable, and expensive…*

"Amy," he says finally, "what do we have to do to get better?"

"You have to wake up, Martin."

Martin lingered after Amy Tay left. He looked out again toward the Port of Singapore, one of the world's biggest and most successful. You'd think they'd stand pat, thought Martin. But the Republic was betting big on unseen long-term trends. The massive TUAS port expansion project to the west would *triple* the port's size. And it would be a 'Smart' port, with digital technology, sensors, automated cranes, driverless vehicles, drones to inspect equipment, and a smart grid. The executive team was committed to seamless and efficient port clearance. "We want to cut turnaround times in half," the port's Chief Operating Officer had told him. "Nobody wants to wait."

But Asia Pacific Bank clients have to wait for everything, thought Martin. They wait for accounts to open, payments to clear, loans to be approved, and for APB to fix the many transaction errors. Delay, errors and hassle, that's us, thought Martin. Can we learn to apply technology the way the Port of Singapore – or Amy's company does, he wondered? Can we become a *digital* bank? And is Technology alone the answer? A respected colleague told him transformation was fundamentally about *culture*.

Martin was a business guy, primarily interested in strategy, budgets and technology, and less so in the 'soft stuff' like culture. He was well aware of the so-called Fintech disruption, but had believed the threat was overblown **[See Figure 1.1]**. We have *trust*, Martin had told himself, and in banking that's the most important thing. Our retail customers, business clients and regulators trust us with money and information. We also have scale, resources, a banking license and matchless marketing muscle. How can the Fintechs compete with that? On the other hand, Fintechs, not banks, seem to be doing most of the hiring.

And now here is Amy Tay, he thought, telling us we're dinosaurs. Have I been a bozo? If this is how Amy feels, what chance do we have with her children and the next generation of entrepreneurs?

Revenue was flat, cost was rising, and Cost-to-Income ratio[2] continued to worsen, which meant that investors didn't like what they saw either. Martin was feeling old and tired, but he had never lacked courage. Maybe we can turn this threat into an opportunity, he thought. Maybe APB can learn from Fintechs and technology firms in general, and thereby improve our capability, operations and current offering. And that's when he decided to call Yumi Saito.

---

[2] The cost-to-income ratio is a key financial measure in valuing banks. To get the ratio, divide the operating costs (administrative and fixed costs, such as salaries and property expenses, but not bad debts that have been written off) by operating income. The ratio gives investors a clear view of how efficiently the firm is being run – the lower it is, the more profitable the bank will be.

Figure 1.1   What Is Fintech?

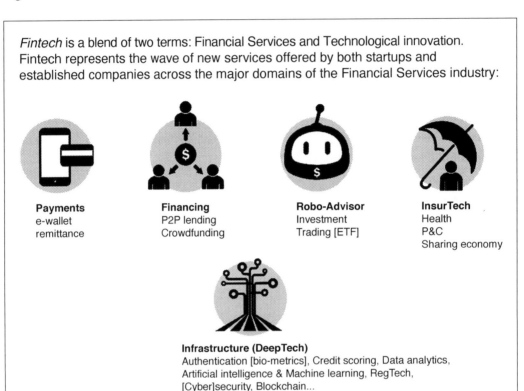

Fintech is a blend of two terms: Financial Services and Technological innovation. Fintech represents the wave of new services offered by both startups and established companies across the major domains of the Financial Services industry:

Payments
e-wallet
remittance

Financing
P2P lending
Crowdfunding

Robo-Advisor
Investment
Trading [ETF]

InsurTech
Health
P&C
Sharing economy

Infrastructure (DeepTech)
Authentication [bio-metrics], Credit scoring, Data analytics,
Artificial intelligence & Machine learning, RegTech,
[Cyber]security, Blockchain...

Source: FutureFintech.io

For both corporate clients and individual customers, the best Fintechs offer services and products that are *cheaper, faster*, more *convenient*, and more *transparent* than those of traditional financial institutions. They're compelling banks, insurers, and Financial Services regulators around the world to revisit their overall approach and activities.

"Hello Yumi-san, it's Martin," he said. "Long time no see... Listen, I want you to come back to Asia Pacific Bank!"

After a moment, Martin heard a familiar laugh roll out of his cell phone. "Martin Picard, subtle as always! I heard about your promotion: CEO of Asia Pacific Bank – congratulations!"

"Thanks, Yumi. But I'm serious, we need you back. I'm not so sure about this place anymore."

"You haven't changed at all, Martin-san. How are Monique and the kids?"

"The family is great. The boys are finishing high school, and Monique is back at work. Life is good. Business-wise, we're in trouble, Yumi-san.

I feel a typhoon coming. I'm afraid it's going to be worse than the Global Financial Crisis."

Martin told Yumi what Amy Tay had said, what losing a key client like KY Tay international meant for APB and all that he'd learned since becoming CEO. "I want you to help me transform our business, Yumi. I want to learn and apply the latest and greatest technologies. I want to learn from Fintechs and technology firms in general, and maybe even partner with them. I want to change our culture. I intend to create a new senior position for you and to give you all the resources you need."

🦒

Martin Picard had spent his first three months as CEO talking to clients, employees, suppliers, and partners of Asia Pacific Bank's core businesses: *Retail Banking, Commercial Banking, and Wealth Management*. He met with APB leaders at all levels and with front-line employees. He talked to regulators, competitors and pundits. He read books, watched videos, and attended lectures.

Fintechs were sprouting up all over Singapore and the Asia Pacific region. They seemed to be full of creative, motivated young people doing interesting things. Their mantras seemed to resonate with people. *'Think big, start small, scale fast'* and *'Build products your customer wants'*.

Martin's feelings were mixed. Fintechs were direct competitors with cutting edge technology and few regulatory constraints. There were worrisome presentations on Fintech's potential effect on APB's business **[See Figure 1.2]**. As Jamie Dimon put it: *"Hundreds of startups with a lot of brains and money are working on various alternatives to traditional banking. They all want to eat our lunch. Every single one of them is going to try."*[3] **[See Figure 1.3]**

On the other hand, thought Martin, maybe we can *learn* from Fintechs – not just their technology, but also how they work. Maybe they can help us reassess our offering, channels and how *we* work.

To Martin's chagrin, few established Fintechs had any interest in working with APB. "Waste of time," one startup leader told him, not knowing who he was speaking with. "On-boarding took almost a year, wrestling with Procurement, Legal and the rest. We then spent three months on a

---

[3] JP Morgan CEO, in JPMC 2014 Letter to Shareholders/.
[4] Prototype can also be called 'Proof of Concept' [PoC].

Figure 1.2   Potential Impact of Fintech on APB's Overall Business

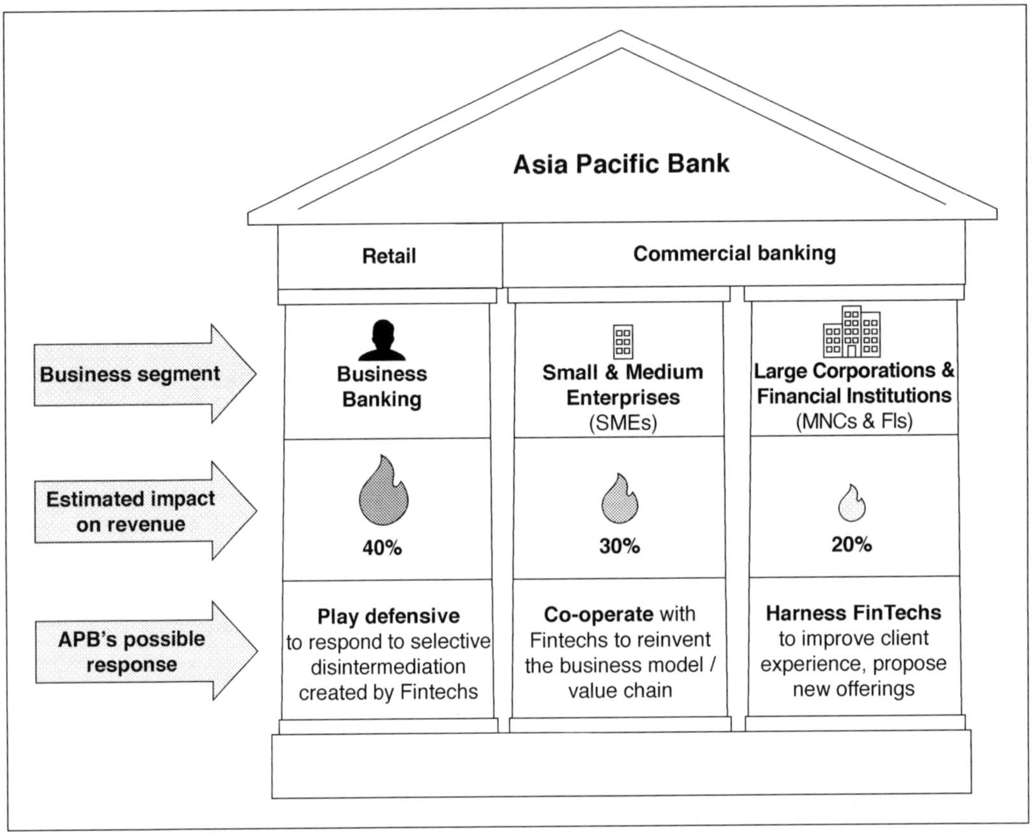

Source: Singapore Fintech Festival (iso Singapore Fintech Festival)

prototype[4] – and proved it would work. But APB did *nothing* with it. We felt trapped in prototype hell. Never again!"

APB had set up its own 'innovation lab', but most people considered it to be a 'marketing and PR exercise'. Some even used the term *Innovation Theatre*.[5] The lab's employees, though obviously talented and dedicated, seemed disconnected from APB's core business. Even when the Lab developed a great product with a good, scalable business model, it faced significant resistance from the parent company. Furthermore, few people could articulate the lab's overall purpose or expected contribution to APB's

---

[5]   Expression first coined by Steven Blank to emphasize the issues associated with corporate innovation programs.

Figure 1.3 Impact of Fintech on APB's Payment Business

APB prices are 6x more expensive...
Sending $10,000 from Singapore to Hong Kong, in SGD

	Fee	FX margin	Total
TransferWise	50	0	50
Asia-Pacific Bank	83	225	308

... putting 84% of transfer revenues at risk
APB revenue from international money transfers ($m)

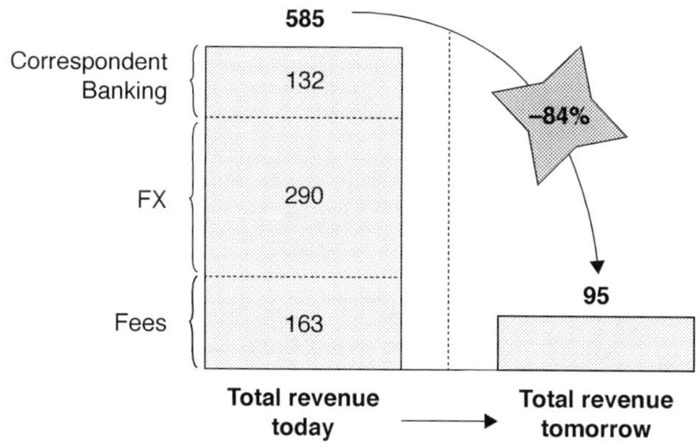

585
Correspondent Banking 132
−84%
FX 290
95
Fees 163

Total revenue today → Total revenue tomorrow

Source: Digital Pathways (inspired by a real-life situation)

strategic agenda. Even fewer people could tell Martin how many projects were in progress or provide examples of tangible business impact. It was all for show, he realized.

The regulators he spoke with at the Monetary Authority of Singapore (MAS) also told a dispiriting story. "Martin, what's going on at APB? You have entire departments focused on ensuring compliance, and yet we keep finding significant infractions."

Martin was a Montreal boy who had moved his family to Singapore almost two decades ago. He missed the Montreal Canadiens hockey team, but not the Canadian winter. He didn't mind Singapore's hot and humid weather, or the often-present rain. He loved Singapore's energy and creativity, the wonderful food and spicy stew of cultures – Chinese, Indian, Malay, English, French, Japanese... Above all, Martin valued stability and prosperity. He'd experienced economic hardship as a kid in Montreal in the 1970s and 1980s when businesses were closing down or leaving Montreal for Toronto and Calgary. He remembered the unspoken dread in the family home. Would papa lose his job? Would we lose our home?

Martin made his name at APB during the Great Financial Crisis (GFC) when it looked like the bank might go under. The crisis triggered Martin's dormant anxieties and he worked like a man possessed. He helped to stabilize the Corporate banking division, developed the organization and processes that satisfied the demanding new regulatory and compliance framework. The human cost was heavy – a lot of people lost their jobs. APB got its house in order and returned to profitability quicker than most other banks. This made Picard a hero and put him on the fast-track. He rode the ensuing East Asia growth wave into the C-suite.

Picard's right hand at the time, a young Japanese-American woman named Yumi Saito, had led the GFC process improvement teams. Yumi was an ace and APB had big plans for her. But after APB regained its balance, Yumi resigned and joined a niche coaching and consulting practice that focused on Lean and Digital transformation in Financial Services.

Yumi had always dreamed of changing the world for the better. She felt that she had somehow failed, and that her knowledge and skills had contributed to the mass layoffs. "I can't do this, Martin," she told him. "I want to help grow something."

"You're being hard on yourself," Martin had told her. "At least we saved some of the jobs." But it wasn't enough to persuade Yumi to stay.

Yumi had grown up in Nagoya and Kentucky and had studied engineering, technology and business. She loved solving complex problems and large technological organizations fascinated her. She inherited from her father, Andy Saito, a retired Toyota senior executive, a solid understanding of Lean operations and management systems.[6] She also inherited a love of jiu-jitsu and aikido, which she practiced at Singapore's Japanese Association.

---

[6] Please refer to *Andy & Me and the Hospital – Further Adventures on the Lean Journey* (New York: Productivity Press 2016). *Andy & Me – Crisis and Transformation on the Lean Journey* 2nd Edition (New York: Productivity Press 2011). *The Remedy – Bringing Lean Out of the Factory to Transform the Entire Organization* (New York: John Wiley & Sons 2010).

Yumi's unique knowledge and experience made her invaluable to financial institutions navigating the digital transformation journey. She was one of the first to combine Lean and Digital thinking. That's how Martin had first met Yumi, during a break-through event at SIBOS[7] in San Francisco.

Yumi Saito had a unique perspective, and, in Andy, a rare coach. In fact, Andy kept an apartment in Singapore and frequently worked with Yumi and her team on what they came to call 'Lean Digital' innovation projects. Over time, Andy and Yumi adapted the Lean planning and execution system called *Strategy Deployment,*[8] to help Financial Institutions ensure their Digital strategy was properly deployed and executed across and throughout the hierarchy. The approach was also a great help in visually tracking overall progress, as well as, the results of individual innovation initiatives.

※

"You're right to be concerned, Martin," said Yumi. "The Fintech disruption is real. I'm honoured by your offer. But I'm not interested in another down-sizing gig. I want to help create something that lasts, something that focuses on growth and creates prosperity. And that means we'd have to rock the boat pretty significantly. Are you really ready for that?"

"I want those things too," said Martin. "I want us to bring Asia Pacific Bank to the Digital Age. As I said, I want to learn from, and if need be partner with, Fintech and Tech companies as a whole. I think there might be some synergy **[See Figure 1.4]**.

"I want to reinvent what we sell to our clients and the way we work," Martin went on. "Will there be job loss? I imagine so. But if we get ready now, I think we can *save* a lot of jobs. And if we reinvent ourselves, maybe we can create some jobs too."

This surprised Yumi, who had resigned herself to never working for a big bank again. Could this be something different? She knew Martin was a straight shooter. "Do you have any idea what the obstacles are, Martin-san?"

"I'm beginning to understand them," Martin replied. "But I'd like to hear your thoughts. You've spent the past decade working in our industry. What have you learned?"

---

[7] Annual banking and financial conference organized by the Society for Worldwide Interbank Financial Telecommunication (SWIFT) in various cities around the world.

[8] Also known as Policy Deployment (*Hoshin Kanri* in Japanese); a proven method for ensuring that a company's strategic goals and activities are aligned at every level. Hoshin Kanri focuses on alignment, deployment, and execution, while providing senior leaders and the Board with a reliable, consolidated view of what's really happening across the organization. For more information please see *Getting the Right Things Done – A Leader's Guide to Planning and Execution* (Cambridge MA 2006, Lean Enterprise Institute) by Pascal Dennis.

Figure 1.4   Collaborating with Fintech – Why It Makes Sense on Paper

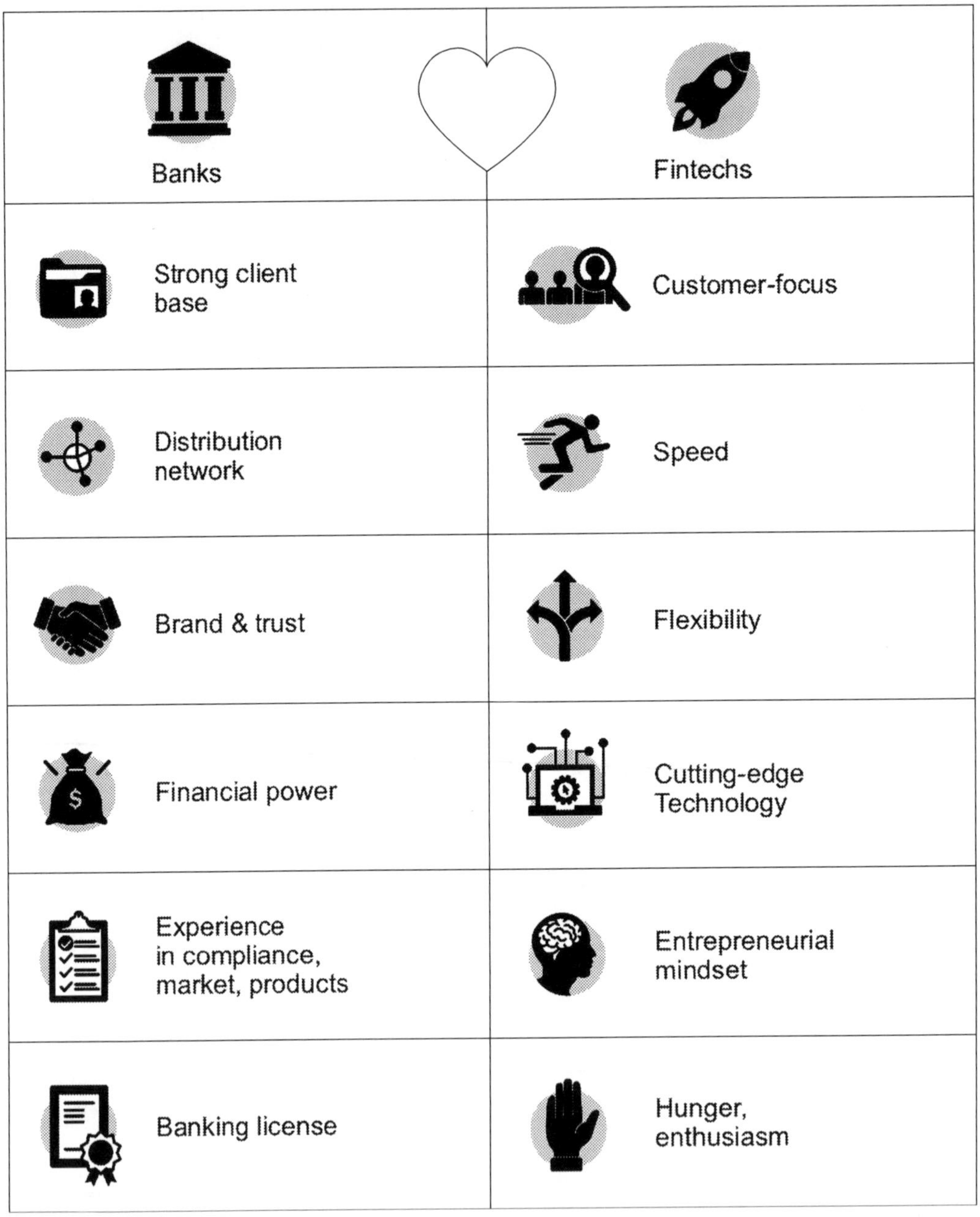

Banks		Fintechs	
	Strong client base		Customer-focus
	Distribution network		Speed
	Brand & trust		Flexibility
	Financial power		Cutting-edge Technology
	Experience in compliance, market, products		Entrepreneurial mindset
	Banking license		Hunger, enthusiasm

Source: Digital Pathways

"How much honesty can you handle? "

"Give it to me straight, Yumi-san."

"Okay," said Yumi. "With all due respect, when I think of big banks, the following words come to mind: *Siloed, rigid*, and *out-of-touch* with both business clients and individual customers. I would add *risk-averse* and *change-averse*. You're right about Amy Tay's children – to Millennials, Asia Pacific Bank is increasingly irrelevant. Let me elaborate:"

"Silos – there are so many, deep silos that few banks can see, let alone understand, the end-to-end client experience. Silos mean fragmented teams, processes, IT systems, and data models. People focus on their own function and local optimums, instead of on what the client needs. You all are addicted to hierarchy and top-down control. Staff and Management tend to hide problems from you. All this makes APB slow and not terribly bright.

"You're also out-of-touch with your employees, who are disengaged and uninterested in improving the business. In fact, if they challenge the *status quo*, they know they risk punishment. And all this makes big banks risk- and change-averse."

Martin drew a long breath. "All this is pretty much what our clients are telling me."

"Transforming Asia Pacific Bank entails rewiring not just how we work," Yumi went on, "but how we *think*. Don't even start unless you're in it for the long haul, ready to take some risk, and ready to learn from failure. You say you want to work with Fintechs? Well, they are APB's polar opposite. Currently, APB looks like an elephant competing with greyhounds in a coursing game. Fintechs are agile: they're focused, flexible and fast. They are creative, non-hierarchical and have deep empathy for their customers and clients. To work with Fintechs, you will have to give up some control." **[See Figure 1.5]**

"Whoa, that's a lot for me to take in," said Martin, "I'd want some control of our transformation."

"Well, you can't control it, Martin. We don't know the questions yet, let alone the answers. We have to *discover* them by running experiments, we have to *learn* our way to countermeasures. To deal effectively with the current level of uncertainty, we need different *ways of working*. Some call it Agile, others call it Design Thinking, and still others, Lean Startup. In fact, it's all three, and a good deal more. In the past 5 years, my team and I have developed a structured innovation process that integrates all we've learned.

"We call it 'new ways of working'" [NWoW] and have had good success with smaller banks and insurers.

But will our methods work in a major international bank, with all the blockers I described? I just don't know."

Figure 1.5   Collaborating with Fintech – Why It Is Difficult in Practice

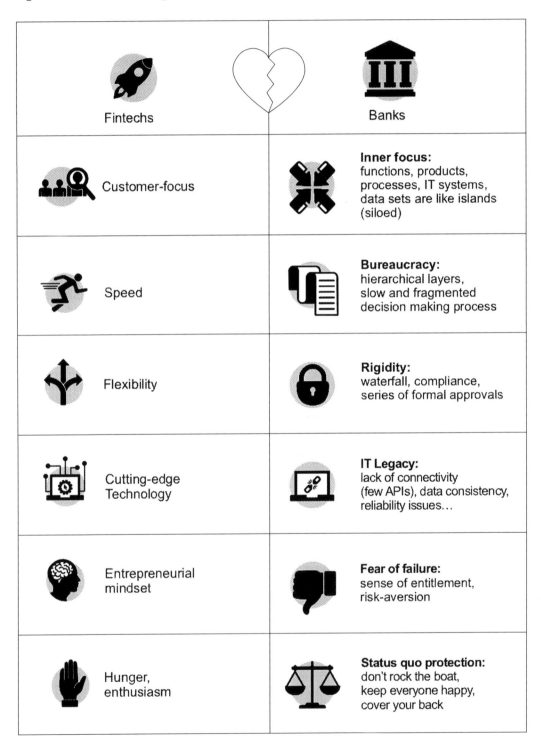

Fintechs	Banks
Customer-focus	**Inner focus:** functions, products, processes, IT systems, data sets are like islands (siloed)
Speed	**Bureaucracy:** hierarchical layers, slow and fragmented decision making process
Flexibility	**Rigidity:** waterfall, compliance, series of formal approvals
Cutting-edge Technology	**IT Legacy:** lack of connectivity (few APIs), data consistency, reliability issues…
Entrepreneurial mindset	**Fear of failure:** sense of entitlement, risk-aversion
Hunger, enthusiasm	**Status quo protection:** don't rock the boat, keep everyone happy, cover your back

Source: Digital Pathways

"I'm ready to try," Martin said. "I don't want to be a caretaker CEO, managing APB's slow decline. I want to create something new."

It was Yumi's turn to be silent. "Before I respond," she said, "I need to talk to my family."

Yumi poured green tea into her father's cup and then into her own. "Asia Pacific Bank's new CEO is offering me a big job, *Otou-San*."[9]

"Are they good people?" Andy asked. "Can you trust them?"

"The CEO is a good man," Yumi replied. "He tells me he wants to reinvent what APB sells to clients and how they work. I believe he is sincere, but I don't think he understands how far behind they are or what the journey requires."

"What does the journey require, Yumi-chan?"

"A new way of working and thinking for financial services companies. It's all based on what you've taught me since I was a child, translated for a digital world. It's about agility and high-velocity learning, defining and testing hypotheses quickly, and thereby getting closer and closer to client value. It's like that movie you enjoy – Oceans 11. Autonomous teams come together fluidly. The small core team pulls in experts as needed. Once the problem at hand is solved, the team dissolves again – until the next challenge. The great industrial companies can do it, but it's a huge stretch for banks.

"An excellent model," said Andy, "but very difficult. You'll need to maintain two very different business models in parallel – a 'zero-defect' culture in the core business, and an experimentation-driven culture in the emerging digital business. To deploy new ways of working and drive experiments alongside the Bank's core business, you'll need strong, sustained commitment and support from APB's Board and senior leadership team."

"I agree, Otou-San." Yumi said. "Otherwise it'll be digital lipstick. Technology-enabled innovation is all about learning by doing. We've had great success with our clients, but they're largely startups – young, flexible, digital natives or small-size banks and insurers. They know our methods

---

[9] Daddy in Japanese.

well and are comfortable with them. With APB, the problem statement is different: How do we teach a major multinational bank to be quick, flexible and client-centric? APB's training, culture and mind-set are exactly the opposite of what we need to develop."

"You've been looking for the opportunity to test your ideas at scale," said Andy. "This would be a severe test."

"Whether we succeed or not, there's likely to be significant job loss."

"The banking industry is changing very fast, Yumi-chan. If you succeed, I believe you can save some jobs and maybe create some new ones."

"There are so many blockers, *Otou-San*. I'm afraid of failing."

Andy took a sip of tea. "I know you are, but I have absolute confidence in you. At the very least, you are going to learn a great deal. And I believe you have every possibility of success."

Yumi called Martin back a few weeks later. "Okay, Martin, I'm in – with the following conditions. Three-year contract, mutually cancellable. I'd like you to create a new position for me – Chief Digital and Innovation Officer, on a par with COO and CIO. I report directly to you and I get to pick my team. We have to be ready for major resistance, and for at least some degree of 'organ rejection'. If you're not serious or back away from tough decisions, I'll quit and you have to pay me a big severance."

"Fair enough," said Martin.

"To transform this company, we have to: (a) reconnect with clients, (b) build digital innovation capability, and most important, (c) change how we think. Later, we'll likely need a broad workforce re-skilling plan. We need to move quickly; I'll personally assemble and lead APB's first Lean Digital team – a cross-functional *SWAT* team comprising ten people to start. Over time we'll likely add 'fellowship' positions, wherein people join for a period, and build their skills before returning to their home divisions."

"Done," said Martin.

"We want to demonstrate how a team comprising three very different personas – business people, software engineers, and designers[10] – can

---

10   Chapter 5 addresses so-called 'hustlers, hackers, and hipsters'.

deliver breakthrough innovation. We want to show what can happen when you connect and align silos. We'll have to agree on specific business outcomes and timing, of course, and on how we bring new products, services, business models into APB's core business.

"We need to learn by *doing*," Yumi went on, "which means developing new processes, products and eventually, new *businesses*. Good governance will be essential. We'll need to set up an *Innovation Council*[11] to ensure new technology-enabled initiatives both contribute to our strategic agenda and have the resources and space to scale. This is essentially a senior level steering committee that meets regularly to plan, check and adjust transformation activities. The Innovation Council will manage the innovation portfolio and deliver metered funding to promising innovations – much like an internal Venture Capital firm.

"Members will be senior leaders committed to changing APB's culture and processes to get needed business results. You have to be Chair, and I'll be Vice-Chair. You need to lead this thing – and be seen as leading it. To get over all the obstacles and blockers, we'll need strong, visible sponsorship."

"Agreed," said Martin.

"Another thing," said Yumi. "My dad, Andy, is my coach and I'll be relying on him for advice. He's a retired senior executive and keeps an apartment in Singapore. You don't have to pay him, but you may see him around from time to time."

"Free advice from a top executive – sounds like a good deal for Asia Pacific Bank," said Martin. "I'll check with the Board, but I don't imagine it's going to be a problem."

"With respect to style," Yumi went on, "I'm not going to pull any punches. I'll be respectful, but we haven't any time to waste."

"Crack on, Yumi-san," said Martin.

"Last thing," said Yumi, "the overall approach and methods I'm going to teach you have deep roots and a long history of success. But it's like mountaineering. I'll guide you up the mountain, but you and the senior leadership team have to fully commit to the journey. You all have to walk and carry your own pack. If you don't, we'll fail, and it's on you."

---

[11] Also known as a 'Growth Board'.

CHAPTER 1 – STUDY QUESTIONS

1. Martin suggests that big banks face digital disruption related to Fintechs and evolving client preferences.
   a. Do any other industries face a similar threat?
   b. What threats do you see in your organization's horizon? What's at stake?
   c. Is the potential disruption wide recognized in your organization? How is your organization preparing for it?
   d. Any observations, stories or reflections?

2. The COVID-19 pandemic is expected to accelerate the trend away from 'brick and mortar' and toward remote (e.g. smartphone) interactions.
   a. What are the implications for your organization?
   b. How is your organization preparing?

3. Yumi suggests that most big banks are rigid, siloed, out of touch with clients, and risk- and change-averse.
   a. Are these characteristics unique to financial institutions? Explain your answer.
   b. Any stories, observations, experience, or personal reflections?
   c. What product or service offerings do your clients see as stale or outdated?

4. Yumi suggests that the following are strategic priorities for APB: (a) reconnect with clients, (b) build digital innovation capability, and (c) change how we think.
   a. What are your organization's strategic priorities? How is your organization approaching them?
   b. What are typical pitfalls in major corporate transformations?
   c. Any observations, stories, or reflections?

5. Yumi mentions she'll assemble and lead a cross-functional SWAT team comprising different profiles (business people, software engineers, and designers).
   a. Why are these three profiles important for the SWAT team? Are any other personas, unique to your industry, required?
   b. What kind of benefits can such cross-functional teams provide? What can hinder such teams?
   c. Any observations, stories, or reflections?

Chapter 2

Mapping Client Journeys to Grasp the Real Situation

Learning to think 'outside-in'

"Innovation starts by closely observing your client."
Jeremy Gutsche (Canadian businessman)

Martin Picard's office, Asia Pacific Bank Place, 37th Floor

Teak, leather, antique screens. Yumi walks over to a glass case containing blue and white pottery. "Ming vases," says Martin, "part of our collection. The rest are in the Asian Civilizations Museum."

"An old ice hockey player surrounded by priceless antiques," says Yumi. "What could go wrong?"

"Welcome back to APB, Yumi-san," Martin says, grinning. "Let me set the tone for our coaching sessions. Like any old hockey player, I like to keep things simple. If I don't get something, I'll say so and I'll keep asking questions until it clicks. Sound okay?"

Yumi nods. "I'll be asking questions too. My father calls it 'respectful inquiry', and it reflects a new way of working APB needs to learn."

Martin gives Yumi a thumbs up.

"Strategy is our first topic," Yumi says, walking to the whiteboard. *"Where are we now? Where do we need to go? What is preventing us?*

These are the big questions. Let's focus on the first: where are we now, Martin?"

"*Slow, unreliable, and expensive,*" Martin says. "That's a direct client quote. Here's another: *Working with you is like going back in time…*"

"A vivid summary," says Yumi. "Let's dig in. What are the specific pain points in each client journey? And how do our processes, technology and mindsets contribute to each pain point?"

"Client journeys are like the voice of the client, right?" Martin asks.

"Voice of the Client on steroids," Yumi replies. "My father calls it 'understanding our mess'. That's not being negative. Life is messy. We start by mapping our most important client journeys, then linking each pain point to internal gaps. Then we report the entire mess to the Board. Should create a sense of urgency, no?"

"Why don't we start with KY Tay International?"

"You're reading my mind," says Yumi.

Martin rubs his forehead. "Should I brace myself?"

"Yes, I believe so."

Asia Pacific Bank Place, 33rd Floor, Transformation Lighthouse

Yumi got off to a brisk start. Working with APB's head of Human Resources, she began putting together APB's Lean Digital team. Yumi looked internally to start, seeking people who understood the bank's clients, technology and operations, and who were also open to innovation and not afraid to fail. Over time she developed activities like hackathons and internal TED-like talks to identify executives who embraced innovation and change. Later she would look for outside talent, tapping into Singapore's thriving Fintech ecosystem.

Yumi's first recruit was Elina Ghosh, a young software engineer from Gurgaon who had trained in Bengaluru's vibrant tech scene. She'd had success implementing Lean and Agile in parts of APB's labyrinthine Information Technology (IT) system. Elina wasted no time setting up the 'Lighthouse',[1]

---

[1] Inspired by the Japanese Obeya (Big Room) concept. The Lighthouse comprises a dedicated, easily accessible room whose purpose is to dissolve silos and foster communication and alignment. Visual management and cross-functional standup meetings help teams monitor progress, understand blockers and problems, and devise countermeasures. Obeya has been likened to the bridge of a ship, command center, and even the 'shared brain of the team'.

a large, open and convivial space which would serve as APB's digital transformation hub and the Lean Digital team's abode.

Yumi invited Martin for an introductory tour. "Innovation begins with how we work," she began. "This is our so-called Transformation Lighthouse, whose purpose is to inform, engage and align people. **[See Figure 2.1]** You can think of it as our control tower, cockpit, or command center. The Lighthouse tells our story: *What are we trying to do? Are we winning or losing? Where are the hot spots? What are we doing about them?"*

"Hold on," said Martin, "isn't this top-secret stuff? How can we leave our Lighthouse open like that?"

""To pull this off we have to engage everybody," said Yumi, "and that means being transparent.

We'll be prudent, of course, but strategic secrecy makes little sense in our situation."

Martin rubbed his forehead. "Okay."

"We'll tell our story," said Yumi, "on three walls:

■ **Wall 1 – *Aspiration* (True North)**
  • What are we trying to achieve, and how are we doing right now?
  • Goals, Metrics, and Targets
  • Expected outcomes (Revenue and Cost improvements)

■ **Wall 2 – *Initiatives***
  • Annual (macro) plan – winning logic, key initiatives
  • Weekly sprint

■ **Wall 3 – *Roadblocks*** and Root Cause Problem Solving (RCPS)
  • Roadblock causes and consequences
  • Propose countermeasures, expected outcomes and responsibilities
  • Status and impact of countermeasures

"Digital transformation requires *radical* collaboration, which runs contrary to banking culture. How do you break down silos? You co-locate people from the Business, Sales, IT, Legal, Risk, and from Singapore's Fintech ecosystem and turn them into a *cross-functional, self-directed* team. You teach visual management, hold daily stand-up meetings and practice RCPS. With time and practice, team members internalize these new ways of

Figure 2.1 APB's Transformation Lighthouse

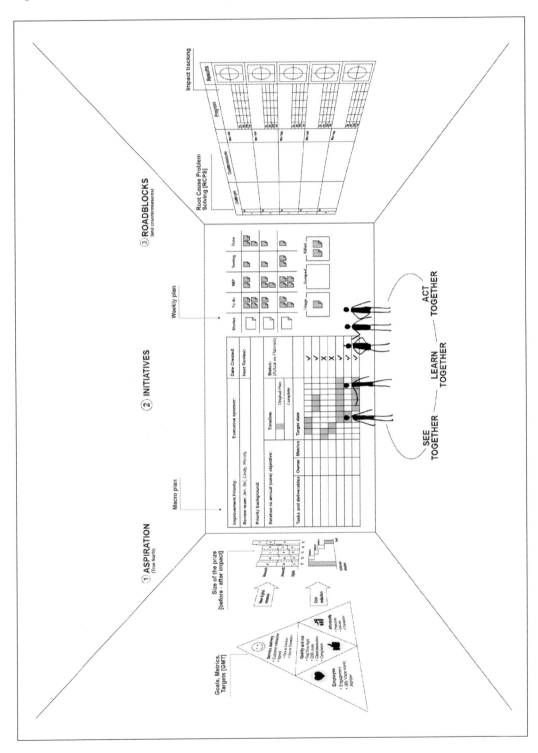

working. Our Lighthouse expresses how we want to work going forward. It's our 'shared brain', if you will, and the key to speed, alignment, and accountability."

Martin absorbed this in silence. "I think I get it," he said finally, "but we're going to need a lot of coaching. On a related note, I want the Board and Senior Leadership team to understand our 'mess' as you put it. I want them to see just how out of touch we are with clients – and how big the opportunity is. Can you give me a timeline?"

"Of course," said Yumi, "here's the plan for the next month:
[See Figure 2.2]

Step 1. Build a Shared Understanding (consensus) based on the data: Align internal stakeholders on what clients, products, journeys, goals and assumptions we need to test.

Step 2. Draft client journey map(s): Start with the Bank's perspective and map selected client journeys to our internal processes and technology. We'll interview teams involved in the process, analyze the current IT landscape and baseline our performance. Typical performance metrics include: Speed (Turn-Around-Time, as a proxy for client service), number of touchpoints (to measure client friction), client satisfaction, number of employees involved (Full Time Equivalent or FTEs), % of transaction needing rework (% First Time Right transactions, as a proxy for quality), and unit cost per transaction. In short, we will be digging inside APB to conduct internal research and generate a first draft, hypothesis-based, journey map.

Step 3. Final client journey map(s): Hear client stories to better understand what it's like to bank with us. We call this ethnographic research because we literally *walk their journey*. Our goal is to understand the client's 'jobs to be done', and the context, while watching them navigate the journey. Such field observation is critical to validating client journey maps. We'll supplement this work with a competitive analysis, looking not only at other banks, but also Fintechs and other industries. We will synthesize key findings in a visually compelling way, highlighting the biggest pain points, possible root causes and improvement opportunities. Result: a fact-based, client-validated journey map.

Step 4. C-Suite Deep Dive: Help the Board experience the client perspective – grasp how painful doing business with us can be. Understand improvement opportunities and possible 'size of the prize'. The goal here

Figure 2.2 Yumi's First 30 Days Plan

	1. Build consensus	**2. Draft client journey map**			**3. Finalize client-validated journey map**		**4. C-suite deep dive to decide way forward**
STEPS	Stakeholders' alignment	Internal research [bank's perspective]	Hypothesis-based journey map	External research [client's perspective]	Fact-based journey map		
ACTIVITIES	• Define the scope and goal of journey mapping initiative (personas and scenarii) • Engage and educate key stakeholders	• Interview various teams [roles] involved in product / service delivery • Visualise current state: process + IT • Baseline performance	• Gather existing research on clients and competitors • Visualise client experience, every step of the journey • Identify gaps [in order to focus external research]	• Conduct ethnographic research [interviews, observations…] • Fill research gaps • Validate or invalidate assumptions @ 1st draft journey map	• Visualize client experience, based on data and anecdotal evidence gathered • Identify pain points and possible root causes • Prioritize improvement opportunities		
OUTPUTS	• Core team and sponsors aligned around shared goals • Priority journey selected • Client persona	• Value Stream maps + IT landscape • Key metrics: inventory of touchpoints, waiting time…	• First draft of the client journey map • Key insights include: most critical interactions	• Synthesis of qualitative client research [understand why]	• Final client journey map, emphasizing key insights: pain points and proposed countermeasures		

Source: Digital Pathways

is to agree on direction and get a mandate and the resources to reinvent ourselves as fast as we can.

Does all this make sense?"

Martin nodded and took a deep breath. "What's a Deep Dive meeting?"

"A Deep Dive meeting," Yumi answered, "brings together the Senior Leadership Team (SLT) and the broader Digital Transformation team. It takes place in the Lighthouse and usually lasts for half a day. It's a key milestone in any transformation journey. We want to collectively develop a deep empathy with our clients. We want to experience what they really value and what APB currently provides. By understanding the biggest gaps and pain points, we can begin to understand the size of the prize."

"Okay, how is this different from normal meetings with the SLT?"

"A Deep Dive meeting is *interactive* – a platform for feedback and shared insights. It's not a one-way presentation – there are multiple presenters and perspectives. We use simple and hopefully compelling visuals and multimedia – no PowerPoint junk allowed. This represents a major cultural shift for APB, from 'happy talk' to evidence-based management." **[See Figure 2.3]**

Figure 2.3   Senior Leader's Deep Dive – Rules of Engagement

- **Fully immersive:** Make it visual – show and tell
- **Non-judgmental approach:** Open questioning, listen first, seek to understand before speaking.
- **Sincere Teamwork (flat hierarchy):** leave your 'rank' at the door, build on what others are saying (say 'and' instead of 'but')
- **Problems are gold:** Make them visible – we're looking for root causes, not culprits
- **Honesty & humility:** No sacred cows, no silver bullets, no magical thinking
- **Evidence-based management:** Test and validate hypotheses, use data to support your claim (no 'happy talk')

Source: Digital Pathways

"What can the Board and SLT expect to see in a good Client Journey map?"

"Here's a good template," Yumi replied. **[See Figure 2.4]**

Martin absorbed this. "All this will help answer *'Where are we now?'*, and *'What's preventing us?'* But how do we answer *'Where do we want to go?'*"

Figure 2.4   Client Journey Map – Core Elements

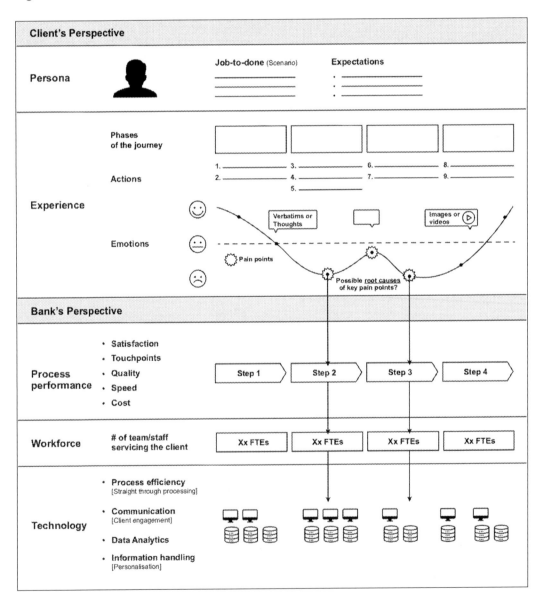

Source: Digital Pathways

"Banking's future is a blank sheet, and anything is possible," Yumi said. "And so, I suggest we defer answering that question. Once we better understand Fintech, maybe we can harness it. And maybe constraints will turn into opportunities."

"Would it make sense to start with Commercial Banking?" Martin asked. "It's a major Line of business with high visibility, and it's where I come from. I know the strongest leaders and the teams that would give us a higher probability of success."

"Commercial Banking would be a good choice," Yumi said. "Pilot area teams will have to be strong, as you suggest, and willing. We'll triage based on client satisfaction scores and client volumes. We could begin with a simple journey, say, an existing client needing to open an account in a new market to support business expansion. Next, we could tackle Business Lending, say SME loans. That would help build our confidence and ability to handle the more complex challenges in Corporate and International Banking."

Akane Restaurant, Japanese Association Singapore[2]

Bowing, Yumi offers the flower arrangement to her friend – orchids in a delicate bamboo vase. "Thank you for coming, Amy-san."

Amy Tay bows in return. "Thank you for such a lovely gift, Yumi-san. It is my pleasure to be here. How long have we been ikebana[3] classmates?"

"Three years at least," Yumi answers. "You are very kind to support our work at Asia Pacific Bank. I know your experience was not the best."

"APB is acknowledging the need for change and trying to improve. I respect that. And Martin Picard is a family friend. Please let me know what I can do."

"Martin has asked me to help him transform Asia Pacific Bank," Yumi says. "My title is Chief Innovation Officer, and my focus is client experience. We've decided to start in Commercial banking. Important clients tell us we are *'difficult to do business with'*. We want to understand why. We want to put ourselves in our clients' shoes, map their journeys, understand the most critical interactions (so-called 'Moments of Truth'), and sources of positive and negative emotion. We call this ethnographic research. And so, with

---

[2] http://www.jas.org.sg/.
[3] Ikebana (living flowers) is the Japanese art of flower arrangement.

your permission, we would like to observe your operations and interview key people in your team, including yourself."

"You have my full support," Amy says. "I'll connect you with the right people, and I'm happy to answer your questions. I wish APB had done this five years ago."

"Thank you, Amy-san," says Yumi. "Martin tells me that APB took forever to open accounts in new markets to support your geographical expansion. I'd like to ask you about your experience if I may…" **[See Figure 2.5]**

Preparing for the Deep Dive Meeting

Transformation Lighthouse, Asia Pacific Bank Place, 33rd Floor

Yumi and the Lean Digital team held a planning session in preparation for the Deep Dive. They organized their work as follows **[See Figure 2.6]**:

Yumi's team led the work streams, in collaboration with representatives from key functions including Sales, Risk, Compliance, Legal, IT, Data Management, and Management Information Systems. Elina Ghosh focused on external research, mapping the journey of selected key clients, and gathering intelligence on the competition, and especially new Fintech entrants. Martin asked that they benchmark APB vs. best-in-class Banks, as well as, leading Fintechs.

Three weeks into it, Yumi gave Martin a call. "Can you meet me in the Lighthouse? I'd like to share our work to date."

Martin got there early to get the feel of the Lean Digital team's abode. High ceilings, exposed ductwork, long wooden desks, small kitchen, and whiteboards everywhere. He helped himself to a cappuccino and took in the whiteboards. *Purpose, Process, Current Status, Biggest Problems*…each team was evidently trying to tell its story using shared guidelines. Visual management, he thought, it seems okay.

Yumi arrived a few minutes later and led Martin to the Client Journey team wall. "Here are the results of our ethnographic research," she began. "As you can see, we have pictures, videos and verbatim quotes to give Board members a gut level understanding of our gaps. Let's have a look at an important KY Tay client journey map – opening a CaSA in Hong Kong. **[See Figure 2.7]**

Figure 2.5   Client Persona – CEO of Tay International Retail Group

Singapore-based client willing to open a Current and Saving Account (CASA) in Hong Kong [KY Tay International, key Commercial Banking client]

Job-to-be-done [scenario]

Amy TAY's [persona]

As... CEO, I'm in charge of developing our business internationally

I need to... open a new account with simple products such as cash and trade finance

So that... we can do business in new markets

You might hear Amy say

"We've been a client of APB for 19 years! To open a new account, we need to fill 40+ pages and provide 12 sets of documentations. Why waste our time asking for things you already have?"

"We need be ready to transact in about a week. I expect APB to commit to a deadline."

"I am not always confident that APB can setup our account on time. It feels like no one is accountable for meeting our deadline. And there is no simple, digital way to track the progress of our application."

"The instructions provided by APB did not suffice to setup the account in our system. Due to that error, were could not transact immediately."

Overall Satisfaction: 5/10

☆ ☆ ☆ ☆ ☆ ☆ ☆ ☆ ☆ ☆

Expectations

    Convenience

• **First Time Right**: Reduce number of touchpoints to the minimum [<5], no back and forth (Ask Once)
• **Speed**: < 7 days to open new account [you already know me]. <10 to send / receive $

    Agility

• **Straightforward information**: concise, plain English docs
• **Clarity**: regular updates on my requests and transactions (progress and results)
• **Ease**: Accessible from different devices, anytime, anywhere

    Personalization

• **Customised propositions**: leverage my data and provide incentives [reward my loyalty]
• **Value for money**: competitive pricing plan, special deals [discount on volume]

Source: Digital Pathways

Figure 2.6   Three-Week Work Plan to Wow APB's C-Suite

WorkStream	Key insights for the Senior Leadership Team
Customer Experience	• Customer Actions and emotions, for each phase of the journey • Main causes of pain points: analyze customer complaints, identify detractors and reasons for dissatisfaction • Prioritized list of customer pain points: lowest moments in the journey, mapped to underlying process and technology
Metrics (performance baseline)	• Efficiency: # customer touch points, Turn Around Time, Value-Add ratio[1] • Effectiveness: Conversion rates (across process / product, by channel), Unit cost of transaction (Cost per channel / cost to serve), Customer satisfaction (linked the main causes of NPS detractors, complaints)
APB Processes APB Technology[2]	• Process pain points, integrated with overall journey map • List of priority processes to focus on, using three criteria: touch the highest number customers, cause most complaints and are APB's most costly (i.e. heaviest workload, largest headcount) • Technology pain points, integrated with overall journey map • List of priority IT enablers to focus on and/or digital capability to build fast

[1] VA ratio is frequently analyzed through Process Cycle Efficiency (PCE = Time taken by VA activities / Total Time spent in the process).

[2] Technology assessment focuses on the following capabilities: Process efficiency (Straight-Through-Processing), Analytics, Customer interactions, Information handling.

Source: Digital Pathways

Figure 2.7   Client Journey – KY Tay International Retail Group

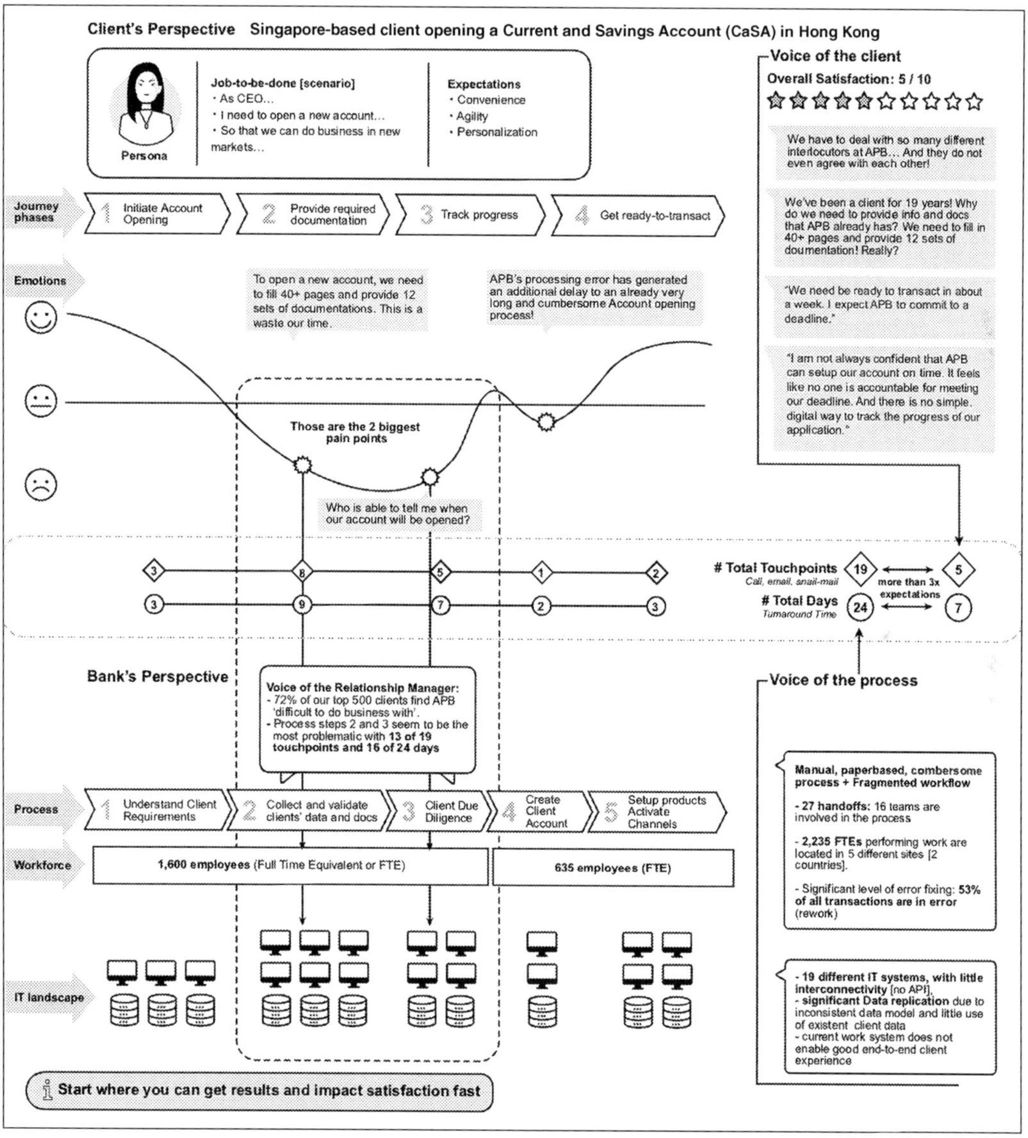

Source: Digital Pathways

"It's pretty clear why Amy Tay was so unhappy," said Yumi. She had a bad experience at the most critical interactions.[4] Overall, there's a big gap between what she expected and what we delivered. Here are some specifics:

■ **Speed**: Amy expects to be 'ready to transact' in less than seven days, but APB takes *24* days
■ **Friction**: She expects us to use existing information and 'ask once'. But Amy experiences an endless back-and-forth amounting to *19* touchpoints.

"The biggest pain points coincide with process steps 2 and 3 – *Collect and validate client data and docs*, and *Client Due Diligence* (CDD)." These look like low hanging fruit. Starting here, we can score some quick wins and build momentum".

"Good lord," said Martin, "24-day Turn-Around-Time (TAT), 19 client touchpoints, 53% defect rate – all for an existing client who wants to enter a new market. What's best in class?"

"For big banks, best-in-class TAT is *seven days*. Some Fintechs claim to on-board new clients in less than a day," Yumi replied. "Best-in-class Digital onboarding entails 10% defect rates, and a much better client experience and lower unit transaction cost. Our other client journey maps tell a similar story."

Martin was silent for several moments. "I didn't realize things were this bad," he said finally. "What really hurts is we're employing over 2200 FTEs to achieve this lousy level of service. No wonder our Cost/Income ratio is deteriorating."

"Would you like to hear what Process and Technology teams are finding?"

Martin shrugged. "Why not?"

"Here are some initial insights," said Yumi, walking to the Process board. "APB processes are *not* designed around the client. Each team tends to operate like an island, often working in different locations, and unconcerned about what happens downstream. We process a lot of paperwork manually. Client issues cross multiple teams and are often lost in all the hand-offs. Lean Banking fundamentals like visual management, standardized work, and Root-Cause Problem Solving (RCPS) are weak or

---

4 Also known as 'touch points' and 'moments of truth'.

non-existent. These terms may not mean much to you right now, but you're going to learn about them in our executive coaching program."

Yumi then moved to the Technology board. "We're mapping IT systems to client journeys," she said, "and assessing the underlying digital capability. Our IT systems appear to mirror our processes. They're slow, error-prone, and disconnected – from one another, and from the outside world. We're just scratching the surface. I'd like to talk about our blockers in depth now."

"Can we please defer that discussion?" said Martin. "I need time to fully absorb all this. To be honest, it's painful, but I appreciate the effort and skill that's gone into it. Please thank Elina and the Lean Digital team on my behalf. See you next week."

CHAPTER 2 – STUDY QUESTIONS

1. What are the benefits of having a *Transformation Lighthouse* and *Deep Dive meetings?*
   a. What kind of culture is needed for these to be effective?
   b. Are such meetings possible for teams that are geographically dispersed? How do you enable such meetings virtually?
   c. Please describe any related experience you've had. What are your learning points or reflections?
2. What are your organization's most important client personas?
   a. How well does your organization understand them?
   b. How can you better understand what clients value versus what they actually experience?
3. What are the most important client journeys in your organization?
   a. How well does your organization understand them?
   b. What can your organization do to better understand your client journeys?
   c. What is meant by the client's 'jobs to be done'?
   d. Select a handful of client journeys and identify the most important jobs to be done.
   e. What data does your organization currently have regarding client needs, jobs to be done, preferences and habits? How might your organization improve?
4. What are your most important clients' pain points?
   a. What causes these pain points?
   b. How might you reduce this pain and hassle for your clients?
   c. How can you distinguish between 'low hanging fruit' and 'high hanging fruit'?

Chapter 3

Understanding Our Blockers

Problems are gold

"If I had an hour to solve a problem and my life depended on the solution, I would spend the first 55 minutes determining the proper question to ask... Once I know the proper question, I can solve the problem in less than five minutes."

– *Albert Einstein*

Downtown Singapore, early evening

Yumi leaves Asia Pacific Bank Place and makes her way northwest along Marina Blvd. She's heading to Brasserie Gavroche in the Duxton Hill neighborhood and a catch-up dinner with her father, who is back from Japan.

Yumi loves early evening walks in the old neighborhoods. Chinatown, Little India, Kampong Glam, Joo Chiat, Katong, Panjong Pajar, Tiong Aahru ... even the names exude mystery, magic, and all the romance of the Malay peninsula.

There's the Fullerton Hotel, its grey granite colonnade turning orange-pink in the falling light. There's the Merlion, symbol of the city, streaming water from its jaws, and the elegant Esplanade Bridge, which provides the best nighttime views of the city.

Yumi turns left at Raffles Quay, passing Lau Pa Sat Food Hawker Center, which is beginning to fill up. She turns right on Boon Tat Street, and then left on Telok Ayer.

She walks past Yu Huang Gong Temple of Heaven, Al Abrar Mosque, and the lovely, restored Chinese Methodist Church. Telok Ayer Park is full of young families – Malay, Indian, Chinese, Indonesian, Japanese, English, French – out for their evening stroll.

Old folks sit on benches surrounded by lush trees and gardens. The setting sun is turning everything pink and violet.

Yumi turns onto Tras Street, finds Gavroche and walks through a pink and white door, past the walnut bar and brass wall sconces, to the table at the back beneath the sky light where her father is waiting.

Andy greets his daughter warmly, "So good to see you Yumi-chan."

They order dinner and chat about family, life, Singapore and eventually, APB.

"We're starting to understand our blockers, Otou-san," says Yumi, "and they're as formidable as we expected."

"Are senior leaders giving you their commitment and support? How about the Board?"

Yumi takes a sip of Chablis. "We're going to find out very soon."

Asia Pacific Bank, 33rd Floor, Digital Transformation Lighthouse

Martin and Yumi were concluding a Lean Digital executive coaching session. Today's topic was Lean and Agile team huddles. Yumi gave Martin his homework and asked for questions.

"I'm ready to hear about our blockers," said Martin. "Please help me understand what's preventing us from moving forward."

"Let's walk over to the corresponding whiteboards," said Yumi. "This discussion is also likely to be difficult. We can pause whenever you'd like."

"Give it to me straight up, Yumi. I'll absorb as much as I can. We'll no doubt have repeated discussions."

What's Preventing Us?

Understanding Our Blockers

"We've grouped blockers," said Yumi, "under the following categories:
[See Figure 3.1]

Figure 3.1   Understanding APB Blockers through Three Systems

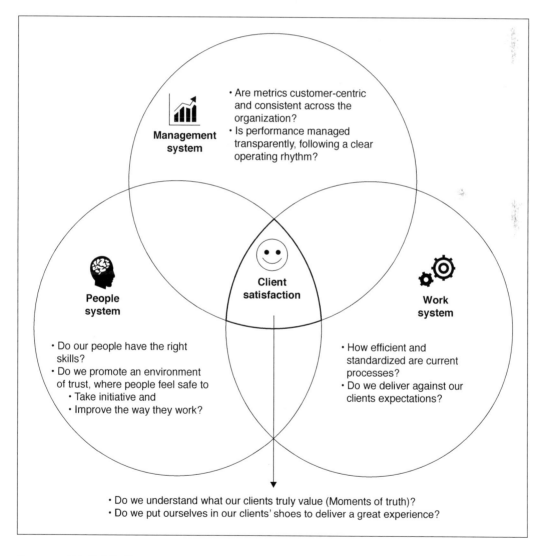

Source: Digital Pathways

1. People system
   a. Skillset
   b. Mindset and behaviour (culture)
2. Work system
   a. Process
   b. Technology
3. Management system
   a. Metrics used to measure performance
   b. Cascading process and management cadence (Operating Rhythm)

A clear story is emerging: *APB has yet to have its 'Copernicus*[1] *moment'*. We talk a good game, but the client is in no way the center of our world."

"Why group the blockers in this way?" Martin asked. "How do we benefit?"

"For change to stick, you have to level up all three systems," Yumi answered. "I've learned this the hard way. Most transformations fail because companies neglect one or more of them, usually the People system. And so, it's a helpful lens through which to view our activities."

"Makes sense," said Martin. "My sense is we have serious challenges in all the three systems."

1. People System *(Skills, Mindset, and Behaviours)*

Skills Gap

"Let's begin with the capability of people," Yumi continued. "Clearly, we have broad knowledge gaps around Lean fundamentals like visual management, standardized work, and quality in the process. As for advanced methodologies like Flow and Strategy Deployment, we don't understand them at all.

As a result, leaders at all levels have a hard time developing and managing solid processes. That's why Lean fundamentals are an important part of our executive coaching curriculum."

"I want to understand this stuff," said Martin, "and I want the senior team to understand it too."

"Only four of twenty-six teams interviewed have regular daily stand-up meetings," said Yumi. "That's a big problem because team huddles are the lifeblood of a management system. As a result, few teams can clearly

---

[1] Nicolaus Copernicus was a Renaissance-era mathematician and astronomer who formulated a model of the universe that placed the Sun rather than the Earth at the center of the universe.

articulate client needs, the current condition or their biggest problems. Zero of twenty-six teams interviewed are doing meaningful Root-Cause Problem Solving. We saw a lot of band-aids.

"The absence of solid processes, daily huddles and problem solving means we have a hard time developing new employees. It's a classic downward cycle – the more we scramble, the worse we get, and the more we have to scramble..."

"How are we getting things done?" Martin asked.

"In effect, we're buffering with capacity. When you don't understand the work, you don't know how many people you need." "And so, you just ask for more and more people."

Martin massaged his forehead. "That's our story the past ten years. Keep on adding people to cover up for lousy processes. We got away with it because the market was growing so fast. But now growth is levelling off while our costs are still rising..."

"Now let's look at the skills required to support a Digital Transformation," said Yumi. "These include Data Analytics, Design Thinking, Agile, Growth Marketing, and Lean experimentation. With help from Karen Hong and the HR team we've done a corresponding employee survey. On a voluntary and confidential basis, we asked employees to evaluate current versus required capability levels across a range of skills. And you know what? Our employees are open and eager to share and learn. Here's what they told us. **[See Figure 3.2]**

"As you can see, we have big knowledge gaps. Our digital literacy is low – few people understand mainframes, Application Program Interfaces (APIs), microservices, Cloud or Big Data. Few people understand Design Thinking or Agile. And even fewer know how to develop good processes, let alone automate them. On the plus side, our people are keen to learn. We need to invest in them and empower them. It's not luck or magic."

The Culture Gap *(Mindset and Behaviours)*

"Culture is *what we do when nobody's watching*. As you know, it's informed by our core beliefs or 'mental models' about how the organization works. Mental models, in turn, are informed by our experience, temperament, training and upbringing. With HR's help, we also conducted an Employee Engagement survey. More than 500 people replied in less than a month. So, what are the core beliefs of Asia Pacific Bank employees?"

"I may need a drink after this," Martin said.

Yumi smiled. "Here are some core themes:

Figure 3.2   Understanding APB Skill Gaps (People System)

Competency	Market 1				Market 2			
	Senior leaders	Managers	Frontline supervisors	Staff	Senior leaders	Managers	Frontline supervisors	Staff
New Ways of Working (nWoW) -Data Analytics -Design Thinking -Agile product dvpt -Growth Marketing -Lean experimentation								
Skills summary #1	◔	◔	◑	◔	◑	◔	◑	◔
Business -Customer orientation -Lean-digital services -Strategy execution -Visual management -Data-driven decision making								
Skills summary #2	◑	◑	◕	◔	◕	◑	◑	◑
Leadership -Direction setting -Effective comms -Role modeling -Team building -Coaching								
Skills summary #3	◔	◔	◑		◑	◔	◑	

Source: Digital Pathways

■ Don't take any risks. Avoid failure at all costs
■ We're good at reacting to client complaints, but not so good at fixing them
■ It's not safe to share work-related issues and concerns
■ You can never do too much analysis
■ There's not much an individual can do to change the system
■ Always defer to the *HiPPo* (Highest Paid Person's opinion)
■ Client focus has one of the lowest scores

And here are some other highlights." **[See Figure 3.3]**

"You'll agree," Yumi continued, "that all this is antithetical to Lean-Digital ideas like *Build-Measure-Learn, make problems visible,* and *fail fast, cheap, and often.* Another concern is that it appears leaders dedicate little time or attention to coaching and talent development. That's not going to help us bridge our capability gaps."

Figure 3.3   Surfacing APB Core Beliefs (People System)

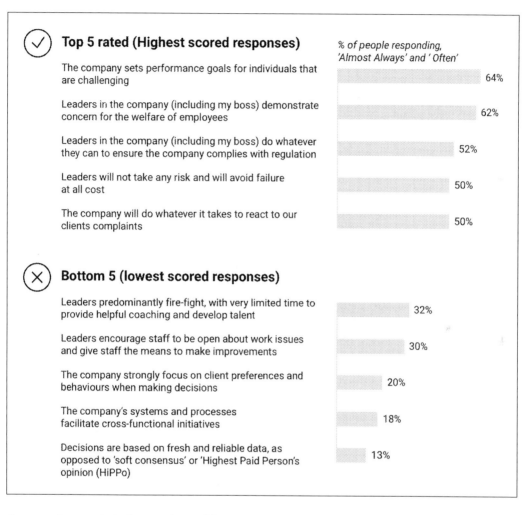

Source: Survey jointly conducted by HR Talent Development and Yumi's team. The percentages account for the people answering 'almost always' and 'often'.

Martin looked out the window. "This is hard to take, but I can't say I'm surprised. It's partly our industry, but mainly it's us, and the way we've conditioned people."

"It takes a big person to say that," said Yumi.

"I guess I'm through the Denial phase," said Martin, "and into Depression..."

"We can hit the Pause button, if you'd like," said Yumi.

"No, please continue," said Martin. "We have to understand our blockers."

"The net effect of our culture and management system gaps," said Yumi, "is a lack of *rigor*. Most of our work is shallow, showy, and ultimately meaningless. Our so-called Innovation Labs are a good example. This is an expensive and highly visible program, but nobody can answer the most basic questions about it:

- What's the purpose of our Innovation Labs and how does it align with APB's overall purpose and strategy?
- What's their current condition and overall contribution so far?
- How many PoC projects are in progress?
- What is the status of each project?
- What have we achieved and learned so far?"

Martin looked out the window some more. "We're good at window dressing, but not so good at evidence-based management."

2. Work System (*Organisation, Process and Technology*)

"Now let's talk about our *Work System*, which comprises our process and technology capability," said Yumi. "Here's a sketch by one of our team members. It's quite compelling, no?" **[See Figure 3.4]**

Martin pondered the image for several minutes. "Are our processes really this bad?" he asked finally.

Yumi shrugged. "Our people have never been taught how to design a good process. It's never been important, the way it is in other industries."

Process Capability Gap

"In any event, our processes are *not* designed around the client," Yumi went on. "A senior director told me, '*We don't make money off the client ; we make money off money*'. Imagine that. He's not a bad person, he's just expressing the attitudes he's learned.

"Teams tend to operate like islands, indifferent to what happens downstream. For example, only seven out of the twenty-six Commercial Banking teams we interviewed have output metrics aligned with their downstream (internal) client. Only two of these teams have regular meaningful feedback sessions with their downstream clients.

"Most APB processes are manual and poorly defined. Only three of twenty-six teams have what we would call 'standardized work'. By this, I mean simple, easy-to-understand summaries of how to do the work.

Figure 3.4   Understanding APB Process and IT Landscape (Work System)

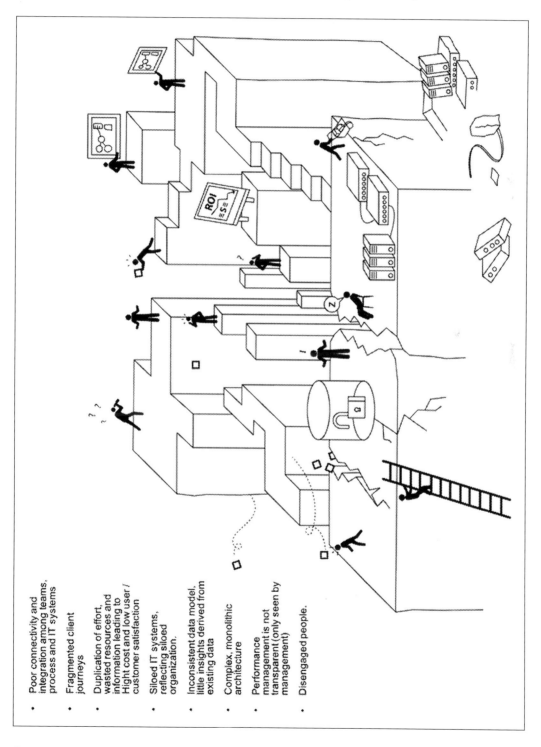

- Poor connectivity and integration among teams, process and IT systems
- Fragmented client journeys
- Duplication of effort, wasted resources and information leading to Hight cost and low user / customer satisfaction
- Siloed IT systems, reflecting siloed organization.
- Inconsistent data model, little insights derived from existing data
- Complex, monolithic architecture
- Performance management is not transparent (only seen by management)
- Disengaged people.

Source: Yumi's team member (who prefers to remain anonymous...)

Instead, we have lengthy, confusing 'Standard Operating Procedures', which are largely ignored. As a result, training is haphazard and usually amounts to 'sink or swim'. And so, people do things their own way and don't share their knowledge. Poor work standards mean high error rates despite a large QA[2] department. Reducing defects would require building in-process checks into our standardized work."

Martin took a deep breath. "No wonder we keep getting fined by the Regulator."

"And so," said Yumi, "APB processes are full of waste.[3] Our value-add ratio[4] is far below 1%. Our activities create very little value - they just add cost. Let me hit the Pause button. Any questions?"

Martin thought about all the Jeff Bezos videos he'd seen. *The client is at the center of everything we do.* Bezos always talks about value in very concrete terms, thought Martin. *Amazon exists to create value for customers and clients.* It's not just happy talk, Martin realized. Bezos *means* it. And what's APB's mantra? *We don't make money off clients, we make money off money.*

"The truth at last," Martin said. "I have to say I'm stunned. I had no idea…"

Technology Gap

Yumi then moved to the Technology board. "We've also mapped client pain points to IT systems." **[See Figure 3.5]**

"*Nineteen* of our twenty-three major IT systems affect client on-boarding and they share the following features:

- Little interconnectivity (few API or bus connections),[5]
- Significant Data replication (caused by a weak and inconsistent data model), and
- Little use of existing client data.

---

[2] Quality Assurance.

[3] Typical examples of waste in APB's processes: rework to fix cases in error, duplication of effort, numerous handoffs (siloed workflow), switching among IT systems to cut and paste data, demand-capacity mismatches (bottlenecks)…

[4] A common measure of process capability, which entails measuring value-added time and dividing by the total process time.

[5] Application Program Interface. In general terms, a set of clearly defined methods of communication among various components. A good API makes it easier to develop a computer program by providing all the building blocks, which are then put together by the programmer.

Figure 3.5   Understanding APB Technology Platform (Work System)

Digitization - Area of performance	Maturity level (1 = low ; 4 = high)			
	1	2	3	4
Information handling: showing client you know him/her → personalize products and services		O		
Process efficiency: Straight-Through Processing → automate mundane tasks @ single platform		O		
Analytics: understand behaviours / predict needs → anticipate & correct issues faster		O		
Communication: proactively engaging with clients on different channels → ability to rapidly adapt to changing situations		O		

Source: Yumi's team, diagnostic conducted alongside client journey mapping

Our IT landscape mirrors our organization structure in that regard. Our systems lack external API connections which will hinder Fintech collaboration.

"Our mainframes aren't bad, by any means. They're robust workhorses that accurately process an enormous number of transactions each second. Availability, speed and security are excellent. They just haven't been configured to interact with other systems, and especially not with the Fintech ecosystem."

"I keep hearing that we have to blow up our legacy systems," said Martin, "and move everything to the Cloud."

"Not true," said Yumi. "Today's mainframes are open for collaboration and API-friendly. And contrary to all the hype, Cloud Computing is not the answer to everything. We have to be smart and find the mainframe, server and Cloud mix that works for us in each of our businesses. We have to play chess, and not just push wood around the board."

"Our Sales and Marketing people tell me our IT systems are hopeless," Martin said. "They complain that they can't produce much client insight."

"That may be true," Yumi replied, "but it's not because our hardware is bad, or because our people are stupid. There's a deeper reason why Mohan and the IT team are not investing in APIs and microservices. We just haven't found it yet, and so far, Mohan and his team are keeping their heads down.

"With respect to efficiency, there is little automation or self-service. Clients have to push a lot of paper and pester our staff to get the most basic service. With respect to Data Analytics, an advanced capability admittedly, we collect data at each stage of the journey, but we don't leverage it. So it's hard to show our clients that we know them, and are working to make their lives easier (e.g. with prefilled fields). We don't understand what our clients buy, how often, or why. Our most advanced competitors, by contrast, engage their prospects in a compelling way, offer personalized advice, and can predict their appetite for specific services and products."

"They say data is the new oil," said Martin.

"Data is more like air," Yumi replied, "all around us, everywhere. And every day we create more of it. We have to learn to map and understand the data we have, our so-called data lake. Then we have to organize it into data warehouses from which we can start to glean insight. Data science is a splendid field we're going to have to master. The challenge is to balance the client's desire for a bespoke experience, with the Ethics of privacy. Our most important asset is Trust, after all."

3. Management System Gap

"What do you mean by *management system*, Yumi-san," Martin asked.

"Our management system determines how we *run* the business, and how we *improve* the business," Yumi replied. "It's a practical and proven way of aligning and connecting our silos, and of engaging our people. It defines how information flows up and down the organization, and how we connect teams to one another, and to our Aspiration. We're borrowing a page from the great industrial companies. Here's a one-pager that illustrates the key elements." **[See Figure 3.6]**[6]

"We're trying to align *horizontally* across client journeys," Yumi continued, "and vertically across organization layers. Information flows up, support with blockers flows down. Visual management is a core enabler. Each Tier holds regular stand-up meetings or 'huddles', at a predetermined

---

[6] Interested readers are referred to *Getting the Right Things Done – A Leader's Guide to Strategy Deployment* (Lean Enterprise Institute: Cambridge MA 2006) by Pascal Dennis.

Figure 3.6   Enabling Effective Strategy Execution at APB (Management System)

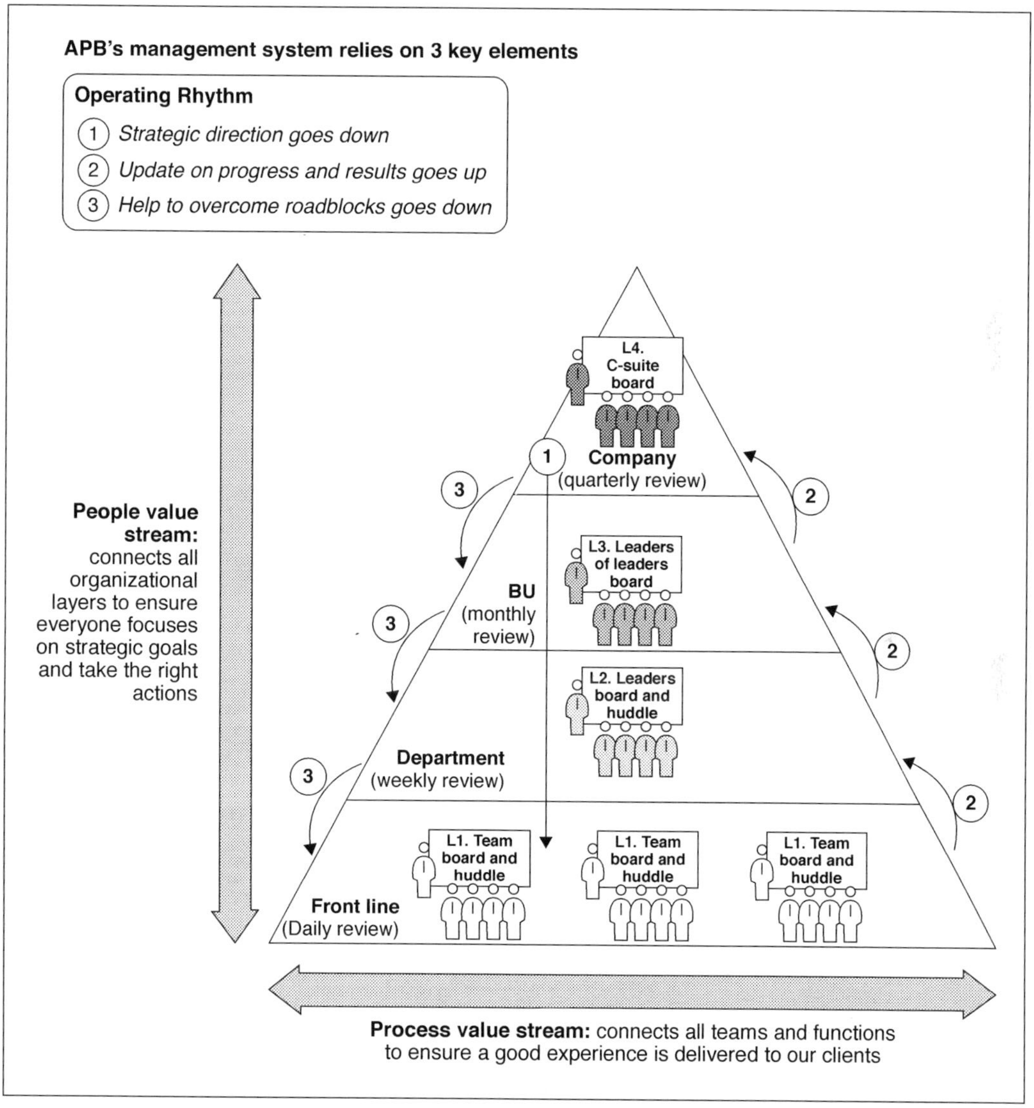

APB's management system relies on 3 key elements

Operating Rhythm
1. *Strategic direction goes down*
2. *Update on progress and results goes up*
3. *Help to overcome roadblocks goes down*

L4.
C-suite
board

1. **Company**
(quarterly review)

L3. Leaders
of leaders
board

BU
(monthly
review)

L2. Leaders
board and
huddle

Department
(weekly review)

L1. Team
board and
huddle

L1. Team
board and
huddle

L1. Team
board and
huddle

Front line
(Daily review)

People value stream: connects all organizational layers to ensure everyone focuses on strategic goals and take the right actions

Process value stream: connects all teams and functions to ensure a good experience is delivered to our clients

Source: Digital Pathways, inspired by Strategy Deployment methodology (Hoshin Kanri)

frequency, and in front of whiteboards organized around their purpose, process, current status, and biggest problems. We want teams at every level telling their story in a simple and visual way."

"Tier 1 meetings usually happen every morning, Tier 2 meetings are usually held weekly, and Tier 3 meetings bi-weekly or monthly. These

'Operating Rhythms', or core routines, are the heartbeat and nervous system of the organization. Each team solves its own problems. When they can't, they pull on the help chain."

"This looks very much like a nervous system," said Martin.

Yumi nods in agreement. "That's a good metaphor. Our management system also entails broader governance items like organizational structure, how we make decisions, how we decide what to fund and who gets promoted. But let's stick to the basics for now."

"Tiers 1 and 3 reflect the front line and senior leadership and make intuitive sense," said Martin. "Help me understand Tier 2."

"Tier 2 is focused on end-to-end Flow and is difficult in siloed organizations like ours. Tier 2 requires that somebody *own* the entire client experience. Metrics typically include turn-around-time, errors, and client satisfaction. At APB, nobody owns end-to-end client experience. The great industrial companies have solved this problem by explicitly organizing for end-to-end flow, usually in the form of product platforms. Toyota facilities, for example, are organized around platforms like Corolla, Camry, and Lexus. At the end of each day, platform teams gather round a whiteboard to review end-to-end results and make necessary countermeasures."

Martin absorbed all this in silence. "So this is how we run and improve the business," he said finally. "So, what's the management system gap?"

"As I said earlier, only four of the twenty-six Commercial Banking teams interviewed have regular huddles. Only 5% of core value streams reviewed have Tier 2 (end-to-end) governance. All of which begs the question: *Who at APB owns end-to-end results?*"

Martin rubbed his forehead. "Nobody owns it," he said, "which is why we lost KY International. As I said, we're good at window dressing but not so good at evidence-based management. And yet, Yumi-san, we have smart people…"

"Smart people in a bad system," Yumi said. "And they're scared Martin. They know our results are bad and what that means. We have to give them something to believe in."

Martin was silent for a full minute. "Thanks for the excellent work, Yumi," he said. "I'd like to reflect on this for a few days, and then share it with our Chairman, Stephen Kwan. After that, let's have our Deep Dive with the Board."

Yumi nodded. "We need to build a coalition. Mr. Kwan's support is an essential first step."

"Stephen was a Deputy Minister of Finance for over two decades," said Martin. "He's a good man, and a patriot above all. Stephen believes Singapore's future prosperity depends on financial services and technology."

Discussion with the Chairman

Lean Digital Transformation Lighthouse, Asia Pacific Bank, 33rd Floor

A few days later, Yumi and Martin took Stephen Kwan through the Client Journey, Technology and Process boards, followed by a deep dive on 'what's preventing us?'.

"Our Deep Dive meeting should be interesting," said Stephen. "Please let me know how I can help."

"Your thoughts on the likely stance of key participants would be valuable," said Yumi.

"In confidence, I expect Information Technology will be a big challenge," Stephen replied. "They're our biggest and most powerful Division. Nothing happens without Mohan Bilgi's support. As you said, we have *twenty-three* major IT systems and hundreds of applications – which don't talk to one another very well.

"Mohan is a nice man, but it seems that IT exemplifies all APB's cultural hang-ups: top-down control, fear of failure, little inter-connectivity among systems and weak feedback loops. To be fair, Mohan and his team have to manage complex legacy systems, which can't be easy. Our systems are temperamental. We're lucky to do a single code release per month – a major handicap that hinders our sales and growth efforts.

"Many people talk about Agile and DevOps but we plod along with the traditional waterfall approach. And yet, I'm pretty sure that Mohan considers IT innovation to be his baby. I understand that he wants to develop a new system internally. I'm told he'll be presenting his budget and recruitment plan to you very soon."

"With all respect to Mohan, creating a new system may be a bridge too far, at least right now" said Yumi. "And buying would be way too expensive. So, we likely need to partner with somebody."

"I hear you loud and clear, Yumi," Martin said. "Don't worry, I'll have a word with Mohan. Please continue, Stephen. Any other insights?"

"Richard Decker is head of Compliance," Stephen went on. "He's a well-connected lawyer with deep ties to Singapore and the 'City' of London. In confidence, I understand that Richard can be a bully. He is all about top-down control and maintaining silos, which he claims are necessary to protect the bank. Many improvement ideas come to an end with the question, *'But what about Legal?* He will not like your *Build-Measure-Learn* motto, Yumi, and certainly not *Make Problems Visible.*"

"Richard Decker and I have crossed paths," said Martin. "We have a shared understanding – we don't like each other. In my opinion, Richard is a Zebra – Zero Evidence but Really Arrogant. But he's well-connected, as you say, especially with our regulator,[7] so we have to be careful. Beware Yumi – he'll likely see you as my proxy and may try to embarrass you."

"He can try, Martin-san."

"Nancy Stark, SVP of Risk and Compliance, and Chief Risk Officer, is Richard's boss," Stephen added. "She's an Aussie from Melbourne, and of Greek descent, I believe. I find Nancy to be fair and reasonable. If Richard becomes a problem, we may be able to appeal to her."

"How about the rest of the senior team?" Martin asked.

"Stanley Phau is SVP of Sales and Marketing," Stephen answered. "I believe you know him, Martin."

"Stanley and I go back a long way," said Martin. "He's a Hong Kong native and a terrific salesman. Stanley is a very concrete guy. Just give him good products and point him at a market. He knows improving client experience makes selling easier, but he won't care how we do it. Motivation may be an issue though. Stanley is only five years from retirement, and I know he wants to slow down."

"How about Karen Hong, our SVP of Human Resources?" Yumi asked. "This transformation is all about people."

"I don't know Karen well," said Stephen. "She has extensive experience at General Motors and Wells Fargo. She's a noted expert in labor relations, and compensation and benefits. Is she up to the people development challenge in a major transformation? I don't know."

"I'd like to work closely with Karen," said Yumi.

Martin nodded. "Let me know if you need support."

"We have some new blood," Stephen continued. "Marcus Kupper, COO, is an interesting fellow. He combines Swiss formality, with an impatience with bureaucracy. He's had success in Europe breaking down silos and elevating client experience. Stephanie Shan, CFO, is an accountant and Singapore national who began her career at a world class Toyota facility, where she learned Lean management. Then she joined a Venture Capital firm in California. I imagine her experience at both will be helpful. She is a 'show me the money' type. You'd better have good data though."

---

[7] The Monetary Authority of Singapore (MAS).

"Both Marcus and Stephanie are potential allies," Stephen went on, "but we'll need to get results fast. We have to prove that our Lean Digital innovation approach works. As for our broader management team, Procurement is probably the biggest concern. They like 200-page contracts and have a *'I'll get back to you in six weeks'* mindset. They've alienated a number of Fintechs."

Yumi listened in silence. She respected Mr. Kwan's insights, but knew it was far too early to judge Mohan, or Richard, or anybody else.

CHAPTER 3 – STUDY QUESTIONS

1. Describe the *three systems* Yumi and Martin use to categorize APB's blockers?
   a. How are these helpful and why is it important to think in such terms?
   b. Please describe any related experience you've had.
   c. What are your learning points or reflections?
2. *People System*: How do *skill* and *culture* gaps relate to one another?
   a. What are the most important skills gaps in your organization?
   b. What are the most limiting core beliefs in your organization?
   c. What are the root causes of these gaps?
   d. What can your organization do to improve?
3. *Work System (1/2)*. Describe your organization's process landscape. (E.g. Are processes clearly defined, visible, well understood and consistently applied? Who develops processes? How are they taught to new employees?)
   a. What are the most important *Process capability gaps* in your organization?
   b. Where are they located?
   c. What are the root causes of the biggest process gaps?
   d. What can your organization do to improve?
4. *Work System (2/2)*. Describe your organization's IT landscape[8] to the best of your understanding. (E.g. Hardware and software landscape, flexibility, robustness, legacy systems, knowledge, and capability)
   a. What are the most important technology capability gaps in your organization?
   b. Where are they located?
   c. What are the root causes of these technology gaps?
   d. What can your organization do to improve?
5. *Management System*: Describe the *People* and *Process* value streams in Figure 3.6. How do these relate to one another?
   a. Describe your organization's management system. What are the most important gaps?
   b. What are the corresponding root causes?
   c. What can your organization do to improve?

---

[8] A detailed description, though not necessary here, might also include hardware, software, 'connected things', application landscape, mix of on-premise versus outsourced, legacy IT systems, security processes and measures, data platforms, data lakes and warehouses, data technologies, relative strengths and weaknesses, and how all these are configured to support your business.

Chapter 4

Finding True North with Our Digital Strategy Compass

What's our aspiration and winning logic?

"Impossible is a word to be found only in the dictionary of fools."

Napoleon Bonaparte

Maison Ikkoku,[1] *Bugis,*[2] *Singapore*

Martin, Yumi, and Andy settle into their chairs and take in the cool, high-ceilinged bar. Late afternoon light streams through the window. They look out on Arab Street and the golden domes of the Hajjah Fatimah Mosque. Bugis, one of Singapore's spiciest neighborhoods, is coming alive.

"There's no menu," says Martin. "The bartender makes bespoke cocktails, based on what you like and how you're feeling."

"They have some fine bourbon," says Andy, eyeing the bottles on the wall.

"I want to talk more about strategy," Martin says. "I have a good idea of where we are and what's blocking us. And I'm developing a picture of where we need to go. But I don't know how we're going to get there."

---

[1] http://www.ethanleslieleong.com/.
[2] https://en.m.wikipedia.org/wiki/Bugis,_Singapore.

"We have to dig a little deeper to confirm our understanding. Then we have to define our *winning logic,* and *where we'll play,*" Yumi answers. "Then we have to explain how we're going to deal with our blockers and gaps: *What capabilities do we need to develop? What management systems do we need to develop?*"

"You have done a good presidential analysis," says Andy. "And I understand APB did a detailed diagnosis last year."

Martin nods. "We hired a big consulting firm to analyze and benchmark our business results by market segment, product and service mix, technology and competition. It was helpful, but their recommendations were unconvincing and sounded canned."

The drinks arrive, marvelous creations that reflect each patron's mood and taste.

"We want bespoke countermeasures," says Yumi, "like these cocktails."

They click glasses, and look out on the streets of Bugis, pondering the days to come.

Deep Dive Meeting with the Board

Asia Pacific Bank Place, Level 33, Transformation Lighthouse

Did you know...?

The Lighthouse was filling up with Asia Pacific Bank's senior leadership team and Board members. Martin welcomed them as they arrived. Body language varied widely. Some people seemed open and relaxed, others closed and guarded. Stephen Kwan, elegant and cheerful, made the rounds greeting and chatting with everyone. Richard Decker and Mohan Bilgi arrived together and seemed to be enjoying a joke, Decker making droll faces at all the visuals.

"*Did you know,*" Yumi began, "that to open a simple current and savings account, a new-to-bank Commercial Banking client will need to:

- Provide 12 document sets
- Fill in a 46-page Account Opening pack, and a 7-page Channel Activation form, and
- Wait for 24 days (if they use the on-line portal) or 31 days (if they use e-mail)

"Did you also know," Yumi went on, "that from APB's point of view, this 'simple' process will:

■ Involve 16 teams, located in 5 different locations (in 2 countries),
■ Use 19 different IT systems, that do not easily talk to one another, and
■ Entail a great deal of manual work including data replication, data flow back, and error correction, amounting to roughly 2000 FTEs

"Fifty percent of all transactions will need rework," Yumi said. "Our productivity rates and turn-around-times are in the bottom quartile of our industry."

Yumi then compared APB's performance with best-in-class banks and FinTechs. Some attendees responded with shock, as Martin had. Others questioned the accuracy of the data.

"I'm not sure these numbers are accurate," said Mohan. "Many of our processes are best in class."

"We need to confirm this data," said Stephanie. "If accurate, it puts us in a bad light."

"You're very new here, Yumi," said Richard, "and may not be aware of all our data sources. But don't worry, we'll help you get up to speed."

"I wish our results were an anomaly, Richard," said Yumi. "But the voice of the client is very clear. Let's walk over to the Client Journey board and you'll see what I mean."

After a concise overview, Yumi passed the microphone to Elina Ghosh and the Lean Digital team, who mapped client journey pain points to gaps in Capability (Process and People), Technology, Management System, and Culture. "We haven't quite finished this work," said Elina, "but the direction and implications are clear."

Each report triggered debate, and in some cases, challenge and denial. Yumi, Elina and team handled challenges dispassionately, with examples and facts. From time to time, Martin and Stephen Kwan shared supporting personal experiences. As the meeting progressed, a grudging, though incomplete, understanding of Yumi's core thesis emerged: APB's deteriorating business results were rooted in poor client experience, which in turn was caused by the gaps the Lean Digital team had discovered and illuminated.

"A powerful presentation, thank you," said Stephen Kwan. "I believe that we now have a shared understanding of APB's condition. To Martin and the senior team, I ask *What is your strategy?* How will Asia Pacific Bank restore profitable growth and create prosperity for our clients, employees, shareholders and community? Please reflect deeply and report back as soon as practicable. And remember that our decisions will affect thirty-two thousand people and their families."

Martin called Yumi after the meeting. "Well, what do you think?"

"I'd say 50-50," Yumi replied. "Half the Board and senior leadership team are open; the other half are not. Right now, APB is all about management by *optics*. Nobody has decent data, so people just say whatever they think. It's another example of *Zebra* management – *Zero Evidence But Really Adamant*."

"You know what Andy-san told me?" said Martin, "Management here is just a *hobby*."

Martin, Yumi, and the Lean Digital team spent the next month preparing their answer to the Chairman's question. They pulled in Martin Kupper, Stephanie Shan and other senior leaders whenever they could. They used the consultants' reports and went back several years looking for patterns, trends, and root causes. Martin shared Yumi's mountaineering metaphor. The plan was to confirm the strategy with the senior team, before presenting it to the Board. Gradually, they illuminated their complex and murky chessboard and developed a coherent strategy.

Senior Leader Strategy Presentation[3]

Asia Pacific Bank Place, Corporate Boardroom, 37th Floor

Martin welcomes Commercial Banking's senior leaders: Marcus Kupper, Stephanie Shan, Mohan Bilgi, Stanley Phau, Karen Hong, Richard Decker, and Yumi Saito.

"Thanks to the Lean Digital team and to your support," Martin begins, "we've developed solid answers to the *Big Strategy Questions:*

---

[3] This chapter draws on *Playing to Win – How Strategy Really Works* (Cambridge MA: Harvard Business Review Press, 2013) by A.J. Lafley and Roger Martin, and *Getting the Right Things Done – A Leader's Guide to Planning and Execution* (Cambridge, MA: Lean Enterprise Institute, 2006) by Pascal Dennis.

1. Where are we now?
2. *Where do we want to be?*
   - *What's our winning logic?*
   - *Where will we play?*
3. How do we get there?
   - *What's preventing us?*
   - *What capabilities do we need to develop?*
     i.   *People System: Skillset, Mindset, and Behaviours*
     ii. *Work System: Process and Technology*
     iii. *Management System: Performance Management and Organization*

By now you've all seen our analysis of our current condition – there's no need to repeat it. I'd like to focus on questions 2 and 3 today. My goal is to develop a shared understanding in advance of our presentation to the Board."

What is Our Aspiration?

Digital to the Core

"We're in deeper trouble than I imagined," Martin continues. "I thought our competition was Asian banks and small specialized Fintechs – but I was wrong. In fact, our competition is Big Tech and the great e-Commerce platforms – Alibaba, Tencent, Baidu, and before long, Amazon and Google. To give you a sense of what we're up against, here's the cost per transaction differential in Retail banking:

- Brick and Mortar: $4.00;
- ATM $0.85;
- On-line: $0.17;
- Mobile phone: $0.08

It all adds up to one thing: we have to become *Digital to the Core* – which means we have to learn new ways of working."

Richard sighs. "With respect, Martin, we're a bank, not a tech company. Your aspiration runs counter to all our traditions and culture."

"I agree with you Richard," says Martin, "but I believe we have no choice. We change or we die."

The words hang there, both threat and challenge. The air is thick with unspoken thoughts. *Richard's right – we're a bank, not a tech company. Can this possibly work? If not, can I ride it out till retirement? Do I want to be associated with failure? What if it works and I'm not on board?*

"It's still early, but the data suggests that digitizing client journeys brings enormous benefits," says Stephanie, breaking the tension. "Higher revenue and less cost per client, and higher engagement levels. It's a big stretch for us though, given all the gaps we're learning about."

"A good summary, Stephanie," says Martin. "And that's why our Aspiration is to become *Digital to the Core*. Now I'd like to ask Yumi to present our winning logic."

"To achieve our Aspiration," says Yumi, "we need to (a) Digitize key client journeys, (b) simplify and modernize our IT and data architecture, and (c) deploy new ways of working. We call these our Pillar Statements." **[See Figure 4.1]**

Yumi then presents the rationale behind each pillar statement in detail.

- Pillar One: Digitize Key Client Journeys [**See Figure 4.2**]
- Pillar Two: Deploy New Ways of Working [**See Figure 4.3**]
- Pillar Three: Simplify & Modernize Our IT & Data Architecture [**See Figure 4.4**]

The senior team absorbs Yumi's presentation in silence. The logic is compelling but there are practical problems. Are these expected outcomes realistic? What does 'digitize key client journeys' really entail? What does 'new ways of working' really mean?

"Can you tell us more about Pillar One?" Marcus asks. "In particular, what client journeys will we focus on, and why?"

"We'll focus on journeys that can give us quick wins in client experience and productivity," Yumi answers. "And we'll start with simpler projects to build our capability and confidence. For the KY Tay journey this likely means fixing the two hot spots: client document and data collection, and client due diligence. As we get stronger, we'll take on, say, *end-to-end* client on-boarding, in other words the entire journey. With time we'll further expand our scope to client on-boarding across different products and client segments."

"Are we really this desperate?" Richard asks. "We've had a good decade. And despite a slow down in the past few years, we're still making money. And the data around digital clients are not convincing. Yes, revenues appear to be higher, but correlation is not causation. It could simply mean that early adopters are wealthier."

Figure 4.1   Our Winning Logic

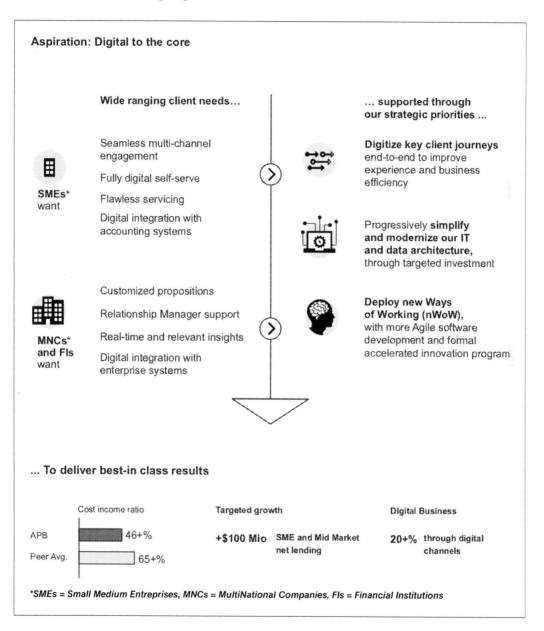

Source: *Digital Pathways*

Figure 4.2   Strategic Pillar One: Digitize Key Client Journeys

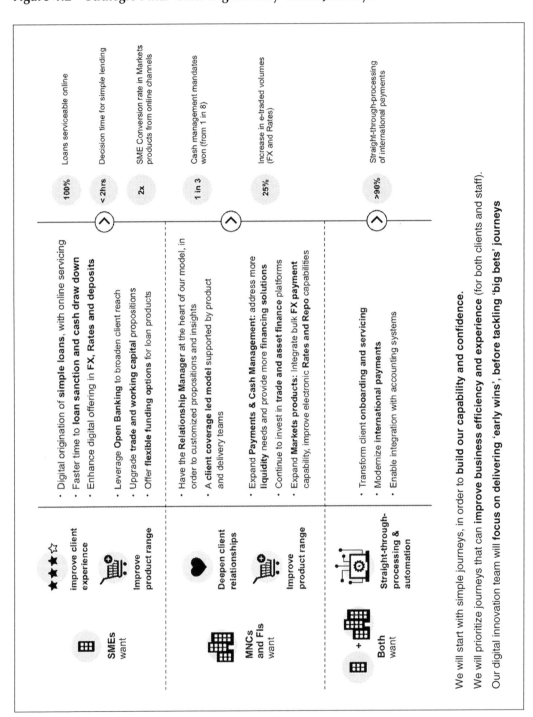

Source: Digital Pathways

Figure 4.3   Strategic Pillar Two: Deploy New Ways of Working

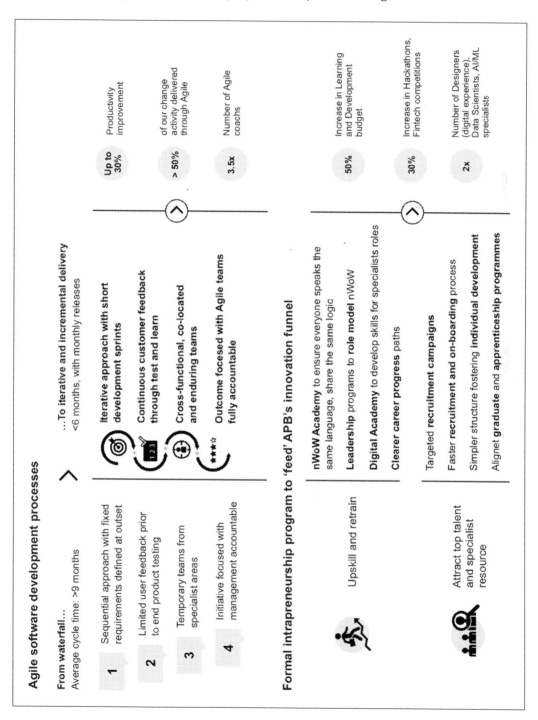

Source: Digital Pathways

Figure 4.4   Strategic Pillar Three: Simplify & Modernize Our IT & Data Architecture

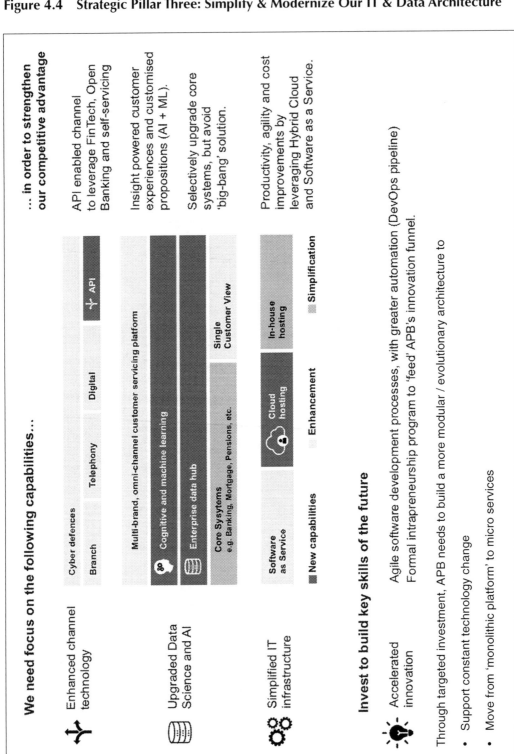

"This is a huge investment – and a huge risk," says Mohan. "We'll have to open up our systems and connect with potential partners using APIs.[4] But we have to do so without crashing existing systems. We have to keep the lights on. I repeat, it's a huge risk."

"Touché, Mohan," says Richard. "Openness is a fine buzzword, but *compliance* trumps everything. Since the GFC, we haven't had any significant data breaches. The regulator likes us, and I'd like to keep it that way."

"Our people are not digital natives," Karen Hong says. "We'll also need a big investment in training and development. Experiential learning is the best, and that means a lot of boot camps. We'll also need an on-line learning management system. There are good ones available, but will our people use them?"

"The ASEAN plus Six[5] nations are booming," says Stanley. "My team believes we can greatly expand our mobile service offerings in these markets. Home internet may be unreliable, but *everybody* has a cell phone."

"Let's continue," says Martin. "To achieve our Aspiration, we need to develop a portfolio of innovation projects. Fortunately for us, in her previous life Yumi developed her *Digital Innovation Compass* process, which we'll use to develop our innovation portfolio. Yumi, if you please..."

Developing Our Digital Strategy Compass

"When I was a young engineer," says Yumi, "my father Andy taught me a powerful planning and execution system called *Hoshin Kanri*.[6] I've translated its core principles for our digital world. It's all about navigating disruption, identifying and cultivating potential sources of growth early on, and creating the structures needed to sustain them. [**See Figure 4.5**]

"To succeed, we'll need to manage two different strategic objectives in parallel:

---

[4] Application Program Interface – a set of clearly defined methods of communication among various components. APIs help the enterprises open individual components in well-documented services so that the internal developers and partners can rapidly iterate new features.

[5] The Association of East Asian Nations comprises Indonesia, Thailand, Singapore, Malaysia, the Philippines, Vietnam, Myanmar, Cambodia, Brunei, and Laos. 'Plus Six' refers to China, Japan, South Korea, Australia, New Zealand, and India.

[6] Also known as Strategy Deployment, or Policy Deployment. The interested reader is referred to *Getting the Right Things Done – A Leader's Guide to Strategy Deployment*, (Lean Enterprise Institute: Cambridge MA 2006) by Pascal Dennis.

Figure 4.5 Our Digital Strategy Compass

1. Where are we now?		2. Where do we want to be?	3. How do we get there?
Disruption map	**Capability map**	**Investment thesis**	**Balanced initiatives portfolio**
What is the nature of disruption? • Social, regulatory trends • Emerging Technologies: Big Data, AI, Blockchain, IoT… • Changes in customer behaviour? **Interesting moves from competition** • New digital products / services? • New New business models? • Notable start-up collaboration (partnerships, commercial pilots, Joint-Ventures)? **What is the impact on our business?** • Shifts in our Value Chain? • Revenue pools at risk?	**Client experience breakdowns** • Major value streams / Client journeys • Moments of Truth, level of customer effort (friction), Satisfaction level, major pain points and opportunities **Capability gaps identified** How do we assess our current maturity? • **People system:** mindset, skillset and behaviours • **Work system:** process, technology, organisation • **Management system:** transformation Lighthouse, visual management and operating rhythm	**Strategic aspiration** • Where do we believe industry is going? • What sort of businesses will succeed? • What's preventing us (blockers)? **Investment thesis** • Attractive 'Value spaces'? (Seek intersection of changing customer behaviour and new technology) • Where will we play – and not play? 　• What areas of our current business should be digitized? 　• Which digital products/services are missing from our portfolio? 　• What areas should be abandoned? • Where to compete / collaborate? • *Consistency: Does our Digital investment thesis support our overall strategy?*	**What's our winning logic?** • How can we turn constraints and threats into opportunities? • How will we address blockers, and in particular, capability gaps (build, rent, or buy?) • Strategic priorities (focus areas)? **What is our way forward** • Is our transformation roadmap realistic and compelling? • Is our portfolio of initiatives balanced? 　• How will we protect our core business (efficiency innovation), 　• While igniting new growth engine (sustaining and disruptive innovation)? • How do we create synergy and build on learning? (Mutually reinforcing moves) • Who's accountable, for what? • How do we measure progress and results?

Source: Digital Pathways

- *Protect our core business*: (play the game better)
- *Create new sources of growth:* New digital offerings and/or business models (change the game)

We can map all this as follows." **[See Figure 4.6]**

Figure 4.6 Aligning Innovation Projects with Strategic Objectives

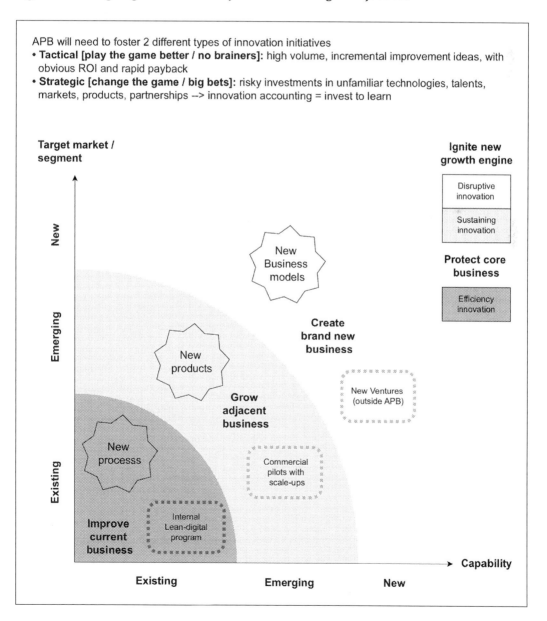

Source: Digital Pathways

Three Types of Innovation

Efficiency Innovation

"There are three types of innovation," Yumi resumes, "and in a healthy company they build on one another. *Efficiency innovation* protects our core business. We use Lean Digital methods to reduce waste and hassle in existing value streams. The time horizon is shorter, and we seek projects with obvious and rapid ROI. Often, they involve process redesign with smart automation, advanced analytics and Machine Learning with the ultimate goal of digitizing key client journeys.

"Efficiency projects will comprise *most* of our innovation work during the next few years. Executed well, such projects free up cash and people, and create capacity that can be redeployed to build the momentum in other parts of the business. Any questions?"

"Efficiency innovation is sometimes called *kaizen*, no?" Marcus asks. "And I believe we're all going to learn Lean Digital methods, correct?"

Yumi nods in agreement. "The great industrial companies involve and develop their people through efficiency innovation. And this in turn enables broader improvements. It's a core element of their culture, and with time, hopefully ours too. And yes, we're deploying a Lean Digital curriculum across Commercial Banking."

Sustaining Innovation

"*Sustaining* innovation helps us grow," Yumi says. "It has a medium-term horizon and entails (a) making existing products better, or (b) creating new digital offerings. A good example would be growing our adjacent business in, say, Small and Middle Enterprise Lending or Trade Finance, perhaps through collaboration with established Fintechs. To really ignite our growth engine, though, we need to create *new business models*."

Disruptive Innovation

"And that's what Disruptive innovation is all about," Yumi continues. "Such projects entail disrupting *ourselves*, rather than waiting for competitors to do it. They have a longer time horizon and entail working with unfamiliar technology, products and markets. Disruptive innovation might involve Open Banking, such as creating a full digital bank, or creating a digital platform and an ecosystem of clients and suppliers.

"Disruptive initiatives are very different from 'protect the core business' work. We're trying to 'break the bank ourselves' and that means working in unfamiliar areas, engaging with unusual people with unusual talent, and untried partners. To reduce the risk and properly assess progress, we'll need to supplement conventional accounting with so-called Innovation Accounting."

"Hold on," says Stephanie. "I need to understand any new valuation methods. I understand that ROI may not be the best metric for Disruptive innovation. But if our books are dodgy, I'm the one that goes to jail."

"It all sounds dodgy to me," says Richard.

"Yumi, please engage Stephanie and her team regarding Innovation Accounting and related governance issues," says Martin. "We need full alignment here, and I'm sure Stephanie's VC experience will be helpful."

Yumi nods in agreement. "Innovation Accounting is based on so-called options math," she says. "I have a number of corresponding papers, which I'll share with you all. The basic idea is to provide *metered* funding to PoC teams based on their ability to reduce market risk. We fund only those PoCs that meet agreed upon goals. By doing so, we are buying the right to purchase the innovation at a discounted price, as in a conventional option. By culling losers quickly, we protect our innovation budget so that we can invest in big winners. In effect, we're purchasing profit insurance."

"Sounds interesting," says Stephanie, "but I need to know more."

"Let me hit the Pause button here," says Yumi. "Any questions?"

"If Disruptive innovation is about 'breaking the bank ourselves'," says Marcus, "how can we possibly deploy it? Won't business line leaders shut it down?"

"Touché, Marcus," says Richard Decker. "Really, Yumi, are you really suggesting that we ask business leaders to put themselves out of business? These people have spent their careers developing their teams, products and businesses. Give them a so-called Disruptive innovation and they'll bury it. That's what I would do."

"These are excellent questions," Yumi replies, "that companies around the world are struggling with. There are a number of different approaches, which we can explore at another time. At the very least, we're going to require an Innovation Council, chaired by the CEO and comprising the most senior leaders to help make decisions about what kind of innovation we pursue and how we deploy it while balancing the needs of our employees, shareholders, clients, and community."

"For the record," says Richard, shaking his head, "I believe we are greatly exaggerating the Fintech risk, and seriously underestimating our strengths. Beware throwing the baby out with the proverbial bathwater."

"Your concerns are noted, Richard," Martin says. "At the end of the day, Asia Pacific Bank has to get better at protecting our core business and growing new business and that means learning and applying what Yumi is teaching us."

"As I understand it," says Stephanie, "the outcome of our Digital Strategy work will be a balanced portfolio of innovation projects. What will that look like?"

"The Lean Digital team," Yumi replies, "together with your senior leaders, are reviewing our existing portfolio. We're trying to identify so-called *value spaces* by answering questions like:

- Which emerging digital products and services are missing from our portfolio?
- What kind of products/services are clients likely to demand?
- Which offerings and elements of the existing operating model should be digitized or fully reengineered to improve client journeys?
- What offerings and areas should be abandoned?

The output will be a Value Space map, which we'll share as soon as possible. Achieving a balanced portfolio will require assessing opportunities according to innovation type, blockers, needed capabilities and overall strategy. That's where the Innovation Council comes in.

"One final point, our Digital Strategy Compass will help us fill our innovation pipeline *today*. In the long term, however, we'll need to fill our innovation pipeline *internally*, which means developing homegrown *intrapreneurs*. But that's a story for another day."

They go on like this for several more minutes, Martin encouraging difficult questions and frank discussions. Finally, he brings the meeting to a close. "Thanks for an excellent discussion. See you all at next week's Strategy presentation to the Board."

View from the Front Line

Kenny Soh was a veteran front-line leader in Commercial Banking. He had led teams in virtually every CB department and was widely liked and respected. Kenny told great stories about his childhood in a traditional kampung[7] village. He and Martin went back a long way. In fact, he had taken Martin under his wing when Martin first joined Asia Pacific Bank.

Martin sought out Kenny one late afternoon. "I need a favour," Martin said. "We're embarking on a business transformation here, and I don't know how it's going to turn out. Between you and I, I'm a little scared. I don't want to lose sight of our people, Kenny. From time to time, I'm going to ask you how we're doing. I'd like you to keep me honest. Can you do that for me?"

"I'd be happy to, Martin," Kenny replied, "and I'm honored that you'd ask."

Martin shrugged. "Okay then, how are we doing so far?"

"Well, the so-called Lean Digital team seems to be everywhere, asking questions, taking measurements, and doing analyses. They seem like a bright and positive group. I met Yumi and she seems very capable. They've started doing Lunch & Learns, which are pretty interesting so far. They always give us homework, which I don't mind. I understand we're also going to do so-called Process Improvement Events."

"So far, so good then?"

"Well, there *is* something bothering me," said Kenny. "We're starting to hear about our Aspiration and winning logic. *Digital to the Core* is scary for a lot of people. What if you're not tech savvy?"

"We all have to learn and grow, Kenny," Martin answered. "If we're going to survive, we have to learn Digital methods. There's no way around it. Lunch & Learns and PIEs are just the beginning."

"Digital means fewer jobs, Martin. Everybody knows that. I'm close to retirement, so it doesn't affect me so much. But what about younger people?"

"My personal pledge," said Martin, "is that everybody will have a chance to learn and grow. People whose jobs disappear because of Digital will have ample retraining opportunities or generous retirement packages, if that's what they want."

Kenny absorbed this. "That seems fair," Kenny said finally. "Everybody knows we're in a difficult spot. Please feel free to drop in. It means a lot to people."

---

[7] A traditional Malay village usually comprising houses with thatched rooftops, built on stilts because of periodic flooding. Kampung villages are noted for their community spirit and culture of helping each other.

CHAPTER 4 – STUDY QUESTIONS

1. According to Yumi and Martin, the first Deep Dive meeting with the C-Suite was only partially successful in aligning the senior team.
   a. What do you think Yumi saw that told her this?
   b. What are the dynamics in your own Deep Dive meetings?
   c. What are common reasons that senior leaders fail to engage with or support a major business transformation?
   d. What are possible countermeasures for each reason?
2. Andy suggests that management at APB is a 'hobby'.
   a. What do you think he means by this?
   b. Define *Hippo* and *Zebra* management.
   c. Describe decision-making under such management.
   d. What kind of culture does such management encourage?
   e. Any personal experience or anecdotes?
3. What is APB's Aspiration?
   a. Does it resonate or should APB have chosen another theme? Does this phrase apply to products as well as services?
   b. How might the following technologies affect product-focused industries:
      i. Internet of Things
      ii. Artificial intelligence
      iii. Data Analytics
      iv. Robotics
      v. Drones
      vi. Three-D printing
      vii. Augmented reality
      viii. Virtual Reality
4. What is APB's winning logic?
   a. Do the three pillars proposed by Martin and Yumi make sense?
   b. What would you change, and why?
5. What is *your* organization's Aspiration and winning logic?
   a. How are these communicated and how effective are these channels?
   b. How well are these understood? (Ask ten people.)
   c. Describe your organization's approach to developing and deploying digital strategy. What's working well, and what can be improved?

6. Define the *Digital Strategic Compass* process.
    a. What are disruption and capability maps? Why do they matter?
    b. What is an 'investment thesis'? How does it help APB?
    c. What does 'balanced initiative portfolio' mean? What are *value spaces*?
    d. Any personal experience or anecdotes related to strategy execution?
7. APB needs to pursue two strategic objectives in parallel: *Protect the core business* and *Ignite new growth engines*. Provide examples of each strategy from your experience.
    a. What challenges are entailed in supporting these differing strategic objectives?
    b. What does 'two-gear organization' mean?
8. Define Efficiency, Sustaining and Disruptive innovation
    a. Describe any current examples of each in your organization
    b. What's working well, and what can be improved?
9. Kenny Soh, veteran front-line leader in Commercial Banking, expresses core concerns about digital methods.
    a. What do you think of Martin's response and why?
    b. How might a digital transformation change needed skills and resources in your organization?
    c. How should organizations address the promise and risks posed by digital methods?

Chapter 5

Fostering Innovation in a Risk-Averse Culture

What's the journey like and where do we start?

"If you want to build a ship, don't drum up the men to gather wood, divide the work and give orders. Instead, teach them to yearn for the vast & endless sea."
– Antoine de Saint-Exupéry (French aviator and writer)

Straits Clan Cafe, Singapore

Morning light bathes the art deco floor. Martin and Yumi order breakfast and take in the flowers, artwork and bustling Bukit Pasoh Road. Yumi walked here through the streets of Chinatown, admiring the old peranakan[1] homes and gaily colored facades. Lee Kwan Yew[2] grew up here. She loves the old shophouses and brickworks, now restored, and the mishmash of styles – traditional, transition, and art deco.

"This used to be the New Majestic Hotel," says Martin, "and this street was known as the 'street of clans'."

---

[1] Singaporeans of mixed descent, usually Chinese and Malay.
[2] 'Founding father' and Prime Minister from 1959 to 1990.

"Singapore is an immigrant city," says Yumi. "The so-called clans were about unity and kinship and helping people in need."

"Immigration is hard," says Martin, "even for a spoiled brat like me. I love Singapore but I'll always miss Montreal."

"What did you want to talk about?"

Martin takes a sip of kopi. "Before I go to the Board for resources, and before I reach out to our employees, I need to understand the nature of the journey."

"Let's start with our overall approach," Yumi answers. "We call it *Lean Digital*, as you know."

"We went through our 'Lean' phase about ten years ago," says Martin. "Is it still relevant?"

"A long-lasting foundation requires good quality cement. The great industrial companies have achieved unmatched levels of quality and productivity. Agile, Lean Startup, DevOps, and the like are all based on their ideas. The key is to translate them for a digital world."

"What kind of fruit can we expect from Lean Digital?" Martin asks.

"New processes, new digital offerings, and if we stick with it, new ventures and business models."

"These correspond to Efficiency, Sustaining and Disruptive innovation, correct?" Martin asks.

Yumi nods in agreement. "In fact, to make it easier, we're going to start calling them diamonds, coins and stars, respectively. Diamonds are about protecting the core business; coins and stars are about *growing* the business."

"Can you tell me about 'new ways of working'?" Martin asks, tucking into a fruit salad.

"It's kind of like your fruit salad," says Yumi, "melon, kiwi and pineapple, all working together. To fix client journeys we need to engage disparate characters with complementary skills. This also helps to dissolve our silos and shift our culture."

"Everybody talks about cross-functional teams," says Martin.

"But how many actually do it?" Yumi asks.

They continue like this through breakfast, parsing themes they'll return to repeatedly.

"What's our ask of the Board?" Martin asks.

"A place to stand," Yumi answers, "and the space to innovate."

Martin's weekly 2-hour coaching session usually began in the Transformation Lighthouse. Each session built upon the last, and comprised pre-reading, a practical lesson and a 'go see' walk in the 'gemba'.[3] Coaching sessions included videos, computer simulations and/or tabletop demonstrations of key concepts. Lessons concluded with a Q&A session and homework (usually another go see). Yumi emphasized the importance of learning by doing, and by engaging early and often with your staff and clients.

Yumi and the Lean Digital team were also coaching Martin's direct reports, whose understanding would be crucial to APB's journey. Senior leaders were expected, with time, to teach the concepts to their own direct reports. "The leader's job is to learn and to teach," Yumi told them, even though such ideas drew sighs and blank stares. The cultural gap remained a chasm, and a thorn in Martin's side. Nonetheless, green shoots of change began to appear.

The Lean Digital Road Map

If you digitize bad processes, you just get garbage faster.

"I'm beginning to understand the nature of the journey," said Martin. "I'm ready for a more detailed road map."

Yumi handed Martin a one-pager. "Here's a more detailed road map, which'll take time to fully absorb. As you can see, there are four main phases:

1. Prepare for the journey
2. Start, lay the foundation
3. Survive, build momentum, and
4. Thrive and scale

We're trying to practice 'smart sequencing', which means each phase lays the foundation for the next phase. A common failure is jumping ahead before you're ready." **[See Figure 5.1]**

Martin absorbed the image for several minutes. "There's a great deal here," he said finally. "I get your point about not jumping ahead too quickly. I'd love to be launching new digital ventures, but I doubt we're ready for it."

---

[3] Japanese: the 'real place' where work gets done.

Figure 5.1   Lean-Digital Transformation Road Map – Think Big, Start Small, Scale Fast

Lean-Digital transformation roadmap:
Think big, start small, scale fast

Ignite new growth engine
- Disruptive innovation
- Sustaining innovation

Protect core business
- Efficiency innovation

Prepare for the journey
- Explore context
- Define true north and way forward (Digital Strategy Compass)
- Setup the transformation infrastructure
- Train the core team on Design Thinking, Agile, Lean startup

Start, lay the foundations
- **Lean-Digital Pilot** in selected area (Learning Lab to showcase new Ways of Working are real and deliver results)
- Process Improvement Events (PIEs) and Lean IT to remove waste fast
- **Design thinking** to focus on Job-to-be-done and 'Client journeys'

Crossing the chasm

Survive, build momentum
- **New Digital offerings**
- **Lean-Digital journeys:** end-to-end pilots across departments & divisions to improve customer experience on *Moments of Truth*
- Standardised transformation approach is expanded (16-week waves)
- **Agile software development:** Tech & Ops platforms

Thrive and scale
- **New digital ventures**
- **More Digital offerings**
- **More Lean-Digital journeys**
- Lean-Digital is Not a program any more but 'the way we work here'
- The aspiration of becoming digital to the core is become real and is know by the wider innovation ecosystem.
- **Regular Lean experimentation** to enable data-driven investment decisions (metered funding)
- **DevOps and Cloud migration:** faster, scalable prototyping platform

Key activities

Target audience

Advocates
- **C-suite**
- **innovation team**
- Engage with Senior Business Leaders to find early adopters (possible entry point)

Early adopters
- C-suite: visible, frequent sponsorship
- Business: X-team #1 in selected area
- First collaboration with insurtechs [~5]

Early majority
- C-suite sponsorship
- CoE + first Intrapreneurs
- Business: 10-20% (more BUs, functions)
- More insurtechs [~50]

Late majority
- C-suite sponsorship
- Broader Intrapreneurs Community
- Business: 20-40% BUs
- Full innovation ecosystem [100+ partners]

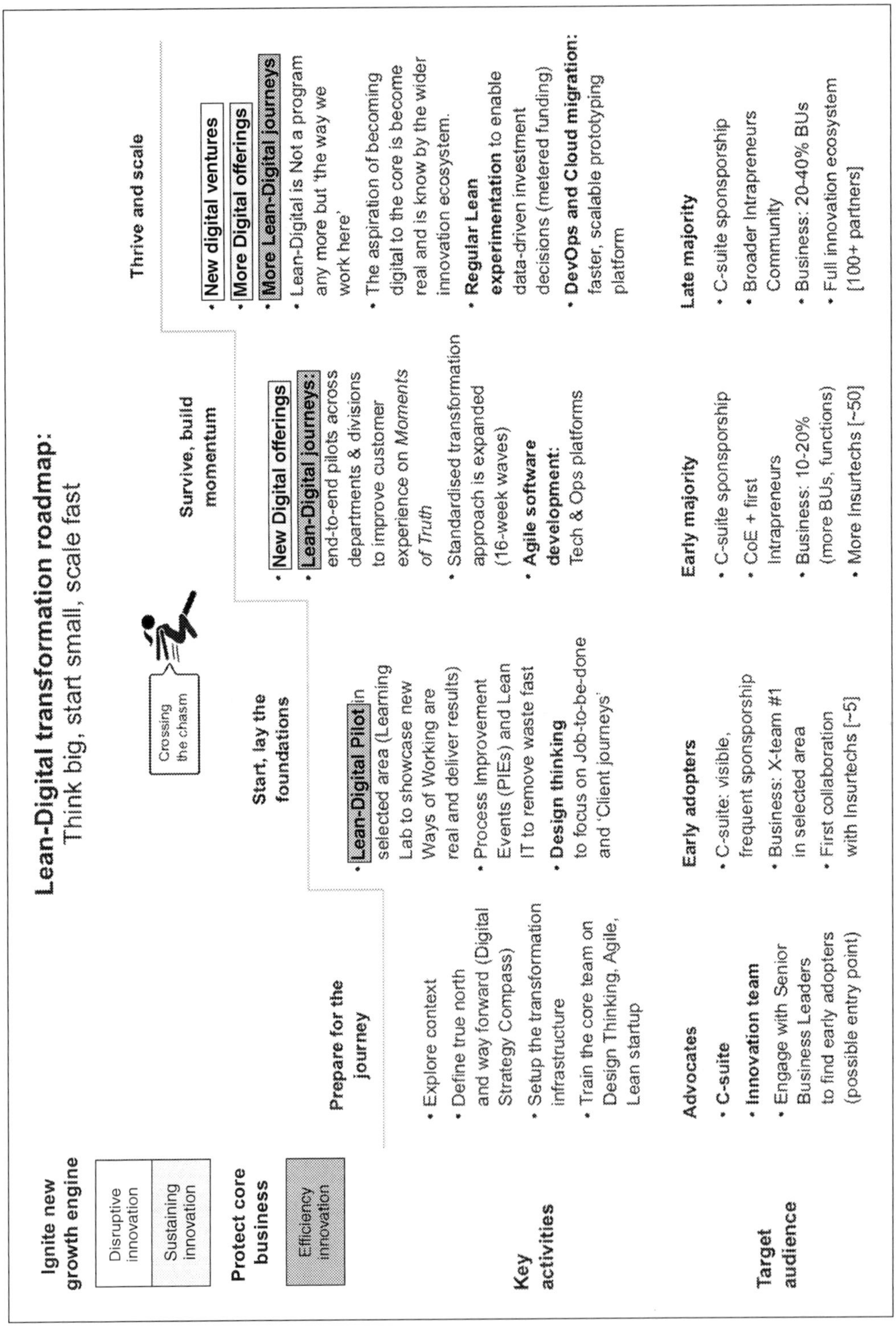

Source: Digital Pathways

Yumi nodded. "New digital offerings and ventures are built on sound processes, technology, management systems and people. Going 'Digital to the Core' means shoring up our work, management and people systems. That's what our strategic pillars are all about."

Martin rhymed them off. "Digitize key journeys, deploy new ways of working, and level up IT infrastructure. Our Digital Strategy compass is also an example of smart sequencing, correct?"

"That's correct," Yumi answered. "Another common failure is jumping to innovation projects without considering how each one fits into the bigger picture."

"Got it," said Martin. "That's why Aspiration, Winning Logic and Digital Compass are all part of 'Prepare for the Journey'. Seems to me we're through phase 1 and into phase 2 – laying the foundation."

Yumi nodded in agreement. "Process Improvement Events (PIE) an essential early step. If you digitize bad processes you just get garbage faster. Our employees are learning to take waste out by applying Lean fundamentals including:

- Standardized Work
- Visual Management
- Quality in the Process
- Principles of Flow, and
- Root Cause Problem Solving

A solid foundation requires solid processes."

"If you digitize bad processes, you just get garbage faster," Martin repeated. "I like that. Tell me more about PIEs."

"They're intense, cross-functional three-day sprints, typically, aimed at a concrete goal. We'll likely do hundreds of them - that's how much opportunity there is. Our initial focus is Client Due Diligence and Credit, both major client pain points. Pilot area turn-around-times and productivity are already over 20% better."

Martin raised an eyebrow. "That represents real money."

"We also measure progress in terms of *client-hours saved*," Yumi continued. "Our goal is to save 10 million hours[4] over the next twelve months."

---

[4] A tip of the hat to our colleagues at DBS, named 'the world's best digital bank', whose work informs this chapter, and to our friend and colleague, Paul Cobban, Chief Transformation Officer, for many fruitful discussions.

"Ten million client-hours saved…how do we measure that?"

"Let's pick a client journey," Yumi replied, "say, replacing a lost credit card. Suppose it takes 72 hours at present – and 24 hours after we fix the journey. That's a savings of 48 hours, multiplied by the total number of incidents per year. Our client journey work has uncovered countless similar opportunities."

"I've dropped in on a number of PIE teams," said Martin. "They really enjoy the process."

"PIEs teach important lessons," said Yumi. "Such as, *everything can be improved. Individuals can make a difference. Small daily improvements add up. Small regular experiments teach you a lot. The problem is usually in the process, and not with the people.* These contribute to culture, and lay the foundation for our Lean Digital experiments."

"People think digitization is a magic wand," Yumi added. " In fact, it's extraordinarily expensive and time-consuming. Suppose we have a ten-step Commercial Banking process, and only three steps provide value. Why would you want to digitize the whole mess?."

"What do you mean by *Lean IT?*" Martin asked.

"Lean IT involves the extension of Lean principles, like those noted above, to Information Technology. There are many similarities between IT, and say, manufacturing. For example, each requires process and value stream development, demand management, quality control, security, and so on. Lean fundamentals apply equally well to IT."

"But everything in IT is invisible," said Martin. "How do you know if you've taken out the waste?"

"That's why Lean IT is essential," Yumi said. "The key is making IT waste *visible*. Our IT PIE teams have found tons of waste already. This too, is foundational stuff. Thereby, we free up time and energy for strategy Pillar 3: *simplify and modernize our IT and data architecture.* We have big IT challenges ahead, believe me. In fact, our strategic pillars are another example of smart sequencing. Pillar 3 may be our biggest challenge."

"I believe you," said Martin. "Let me change gears. I think I understand road map phases 1 and 2. Phases 3 and 4 are still abstract to me. One comment though, I see us moving from Efficiency to Sustaining and Disruptive Innovation, in other words, from diamonds to coins and stars."

"Each level supports the next one," said Yumi, nodding. "We build our innovation muscles thereby. Waste-free processes support digital journeys, which support new digital offerings, which support new digital ventures. Except for PIEs, these are abstract, but they're going to come to life very soon."

Martin put his hands on his head. "I'm beginning to see the big picture. Thanks, Yumi. I'd like to change gears now, and talk about Pillar 2 and *how* we're going to work. Can you help me understand 'Lean and Agile' methods? I get that it's about cross-functionality, but why is that a big deal? We've been talking about it for years."

Lean, Agile and Oceans 11

Yumi handed Martin a one-pager. **[See Figure 5.2]** "Lean and Agile methods involve replacing rigid hierarchy with what my father calls 'Ocean 11' management," Yumi said. "Remember the movie? A small, stable core team, George Clooney and Brad Pitt, lead the way. They summon experts when needed, and the now broader team works together fluidly to solve a specific problem.

"There is no hierarchy or chain of command – just a clear objective and a capable team leader who enables cooperation. They break the project down into small parts, and check in frequently. Each member reports progress and key problems to be solved. They iterate to solutions and adjust fluidly to hassles as they arrive. When the job is done, the team dissolves, until the next job. And what's the benefit? Much shorter project times, better decision-making and engagement, fewer mistakes, and quicker solutions, closer to the client and better productivity. You'll notice the Oceans 11 team is much smaller than the big batch or so-called 'waterfall' approach team."

"And why is this a big deal?" Yumi went on. "Because very few organizations actually do it. We all talk a good game, then retire to our silos. The most obvious evidence is our messed up, convoluted, wasteful client journeys and IT systems."

Martin absorbed this in silence. "You're right," he said, finally. "We talk a good game, but our silos rarely share their people or power. For senior leaders, promotion is all about expanding your empire and jealously guarding your resources."

"Touché, Martin-san," said Yumi, "and that's probably our biggest cultural challenge. PIEs are cross-functional by design, and thus a good starting

Figure 5.2   Lean and Agile Ways of Working

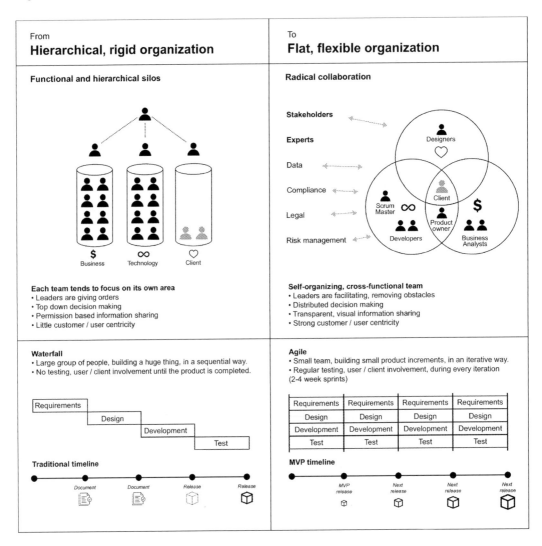

Source: Digital Pathways

point. But as we'll see, sustained digital innovation requires mental, as well as, physical cross-functionality. For example, hackers have to learn to think like designers and business people, and vice versa. I'll hit the Pause button there. More to come."

"Okay, let me change gears again," Martin said. "We've talked about the importance of linking our innovations with our Aspiration and strategy. With that in mind, can you please take me through our Value Spaces map?"

APB Innovation Value Spaces

Yumi handed Martin another one-pager. "Our Digital Strategy Compass has helped us identify a number of possible projects. We're in the process of prioritizing them based on alignment with our Aspiration and Winning Logic, ease and impact, and business team readiness."
[See Figure 5.3]

"Smart sequencing is important," Yumi went on. "We want to pick projects that not only cash out, but naturally lead to higher level innovation. Fixing Client Due Diligence, for example, not only reduces hassle and cost for clients like KY Tay International, it also opens the door to developing entirely new *digital* journeys."

"In other words," said Martin, "we want to play chess, and not simply push wood around the board."

"Good metaphor," said Yumi. "We need to think several moves ahead, and make sure our sequence gets us to where we want to be."

Martin absorbed the map. "What do you mean by 'business team readiness'?"

"I mean, does the team have the authority, budget and motivation to do it?"

"I have a culture question," said Martin. "Clearly, we need a zero-defect culture in our core business, and an experimentation-driven culture in our innovation work, correct?"

Yumi nodded. "We want to run the business and at the same time, innovate like crazy."

"So how do we avoid corporate schizophrenia?"

The Ambidextrous Organization

"We want to become ambidextrous, and not schizophrenic," Yumi answered. "We have to get good at both coins and stars. Fortunately, coins lay the foundation for stars. And we'll pull in Fintech partners to help us."

"How are we going to find viable Fintech partners?"

"The Innovation Festival is very soon," said Yumi. "I want to introduce you to the local talent."

Martin took a deep breath and looked out the window. "Thanks, Yumi, this has been very helpful," he said. "I have a better grasp of our road map,

Figure 5.3   APB Innovation Value Spaces

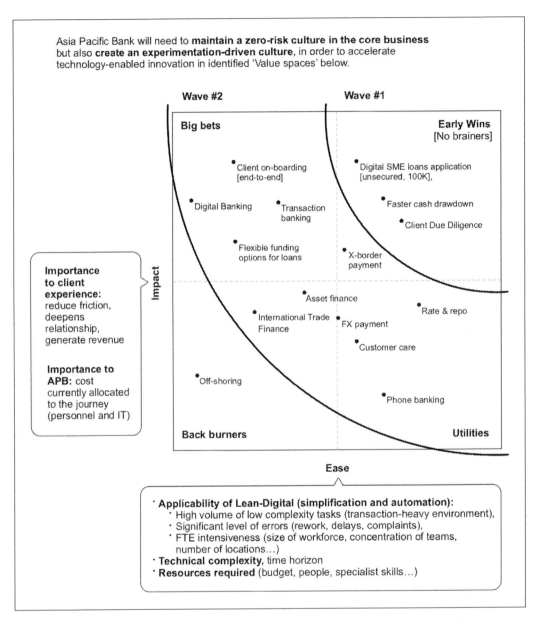

Source: Digital Pathways

value spaces and how we're going to work. Here's my last question for the day. What's our transformation model? We're a thirty thousand person multinational corporation. There are so many moving parts. How are we going to *sustain* all this activity?"

Three Swimlanes for a Sustained Transformation

"We're going to apply the Three Swimlane model," Yumi replied, "which my consulting team and I developed". **[See Figure 5.4]**

1. *Leadership development*
   a. Executive coaching – Lean Digital for Senior Leaders
   b. Boot Camps and/or Fintech challenges (learn by doing)
   c. Innovation accounting
   d. Role of the Leader
2. *Pragmatic Innovator Network*
   a. Lean Digital 101
      i. Design Thinking, Agile, Lean Startup
      ii. Tiered management system,
      iii. Innovation Accounting
   b. Intrapreneurship 101
3. *Focused Innovation* in selected pilot areas
   a. Innovation Portfolio aligned with corporate strategy
   b. project selection and Fintech partnering
   c. Growth Hacking – getting up the hockey stick curve

"We validated the model in a number of industries," Yumi continued. "We have a detailed curriculum for each swimlane."

"What's the underlying rationale?" Martin asked.

"Our spearpoint is *focused innovation* aligned with strategy," said Yumi. "To support and sustain it, we need *capable intrapreneurs*, and *senior executives* who understand and support them. The model's greatest benefit may be scalability. We can deploy and scale it in any division. We simply adjust the content of each swimlane based on the blockers."

"Please tell me more about the diamonds, coins and stars," said Martin.

"As you know, these represent Efficiency, Sustaining, and Disruptive innovation projects," said Yumi replied. "Diamonds will represent at least 80% of our innovation portfolio. We assess diamonds using traditional accounting metrics like ROI."

"Process Improvement Events are diamonds, correct?" Martin asked

Yumi nodded in agreement. "Diamonds lay the foundation for coins, which do the same for stars. Each prepares us for the next challenge."

"Coins represent new digital products which help us grow, correct?" said Martin.

Figure 5.4   Three Swimlanes for a Sustained Transformation

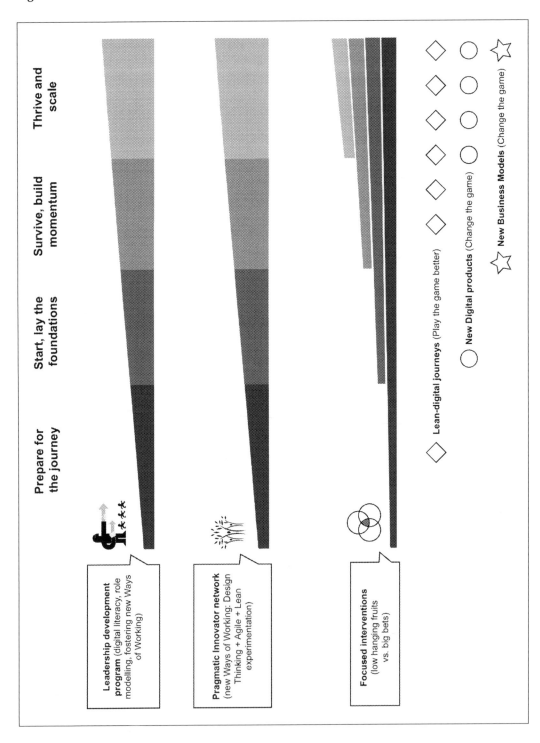

Source: Digital Pathways

Yumi nodded again. "And our overall approach here entails learning through lean experimentation. And because coins represent *new* products and services, we need to change how we measure progress. Instead of traditional accounting, we use Innovation Accounting."

Martin took a deep breath. "And that's because traditional accounting metrics would all be zero – for both coins and stars, correct?"

"You got it, Martin," said Yumi. "Stars, lastly, represent Disruptive innovation, game changers that often take the form of beta businesses or joint ventures."

"What does beta business mean?"

"New venture, challenger mindset, and rapid experimentation," Yumi answered. "Those are the key elements. Our challenge, as I mentioned earlier, is to sustain both zero-defect and experimentation cultures."

"The ambidextrous organization," said Martin. "Here's a question for the future. Do we build our Breakthrough Innovations inside or *outside* the organization?"

"It's a complex question," Yumi answered. "In fact, there are two other possibilities. You can build inside, then move it *out*. Or you can build outside and move it *in*. As you suggest, let's defer the discussion for now."

"So let me read all this back to you," said Martin. "Our transformation model comprises three swimlanes: *focused innovation* aligned with strategy supported by *capable intrapreneurs* and *leaders* who get it. Our innovation portfolio comprises diamonds, coins and stars – representing Efficiency, Sustaining, and Disruptive Innovation. The former is focused on waste reduction and is measured using traditional metrics like ROI. The latter two are focused on growth, are measured using Innovation Accounting, and entail rapid experimentation toward new offerings or new businesses. Lastly, diamonds lead to coins, which lead to stars."

"Crack on, Martin," said Yumi.

Next Deep Dive Meeting with the Board

What is your ask of us?

"A detailed strategic overview – thank you, Martin, Yumi and team," said Stephen Kwan. "I like your Aspiration. *Digital to the Core* will resonate with our clients and team members. And your winning logic makes good sense:

1. Digitize key client journeys
2. Deploy New Ways of Working
3. Simplify and modernize our IT and Data architecture

I especially like how you have put the client in the center of everything we do. Now comes the big question: What resources do you need to implement this strategy? In other words, *what is your ask of us?"*

Yumi looked over at Martin, who nodded imperceptibly.

"Dear Mr. Kwan and Board members," Yumi began, "we're grateful for your support. Here's what we need to get started. As we scale our activities, we will likely need to augment our request:

1. *A dedicated budget for Digital transformation.*
   a. Purpose
      i.   To close the critical gaps we've identified in Process and People Capability, Technology, Management System, and Culture
      ii. To fund our Learning Laboratory and innovation projects
      iii. To fund additional activities as our transformation expands
2. *Space for our Learning Lab* – We would like to have the entire floor of a building, but not in the central business district. We need space, light and the freedom to play, unencumbered by our current culture.
3. *A Learning Lab support team*, comprising a Director, and a core team of ten people to start. We'll work with HR to find people with the right qualities. Over time, we'll need to add an additional ten rotating positions. People will join the Learning Lab for, say, six months or a year, and then return to their regular jobs as certified *intrapreneurs*. They become part of a growing network of pragmatic innovators who help us sustain and expand our transformation.
4. *Executive sponsorship*: Strong, visible and consistent support. We're going to need air cover, especially when the blockers counterattack, as they will.
5. *Delegated authority* to overcome technology and process barriers. Our team must have the right to be an 'exception' to outdated or ill-defined rules.

In summary, we need a place to stand, and the space to innovate."

CHAPTER 5 – STUDY QUESTIONS

1. Describe the phases of Asia Pacific Bank's planned transformation journey.
   a. How does each phase support the next phase?
   b. Why not simply jump to advanced activities like DevOps?
   c. Why not simply 'digitize everything'?
   d. Does such a phased approach make sense in your organization? What are the risks and benefits of such an approach?
2. What are the main blockers to APB's transformation?
   a. How do these compare with blockers in your organization? Any reflections or learning points?
   b. Are there unique blockers to digital transformation in your organization? Describe them.
3. What does 'Oceans 11 management' mean?
   a. What are the prerequisites for such a fluid management approach?
   b. What would an Oceans 11 innovation project look like in your organization? (Make a 'movie' in your mind.)
   c. What are the obstacles to Oceans 11 management in your organization?
   d. What would it take to make Oceans 11 management a normal part of your business?
4. Describe the Three Swimlane Model
   a. Describe your organization's transformation support model, if any.
   b. Describe other transformation support models you are familiar with.
   c. What are their strengths and weaknesses?

Chapter 6

Embracing New Ways of Working

Hackers, Hipsters and Hustlers working together – setting up Asia Pacific Bank's innovation platform

"We are what we repeatedly do. Excellence, therefore, is not an act, but a habit."

– Aristotle

Tower Club, 64th Floor, Central Business District

Martin Picard looks out past the Marina Bay Sands Hotel, to the Strait of Malacca and the churning armada of container ships. It's another hot, humid day. Martin thinks of the St. Lawrence River and Montreal, now in the depths of winter and half-frozen.

Yumi, Stephen Kwan, and Marcus Kupper arrive for their weekly check-in. They exchange pleasantries and begin.

"The Board understands that we have embarked on a long-term journey," Stephen begins, "but we would also like to see some quick wins."

"I asked Stephanie Shan to scour our financial statements," says Martin. "She found very significant savings."

"Good news," says Stephen. "This will buy us time."

"Our PIEs have saved almost two million client-hours to date," Marcus says, "which is freeing up a lot of people."

"Client pain points correspond to heavy headcounts," Yumi adds. "Rather than fix the process, we throw people at it."

Stephen is silent. "Can I ask you to please avoid mass layoffs?"

"Employees made redundant are offered retraining," says Martin. "In fact, retraining is part of our broader challenge. How do we create a 32,000-person startup?"

"How do we teach an elephant to dance...?" says Stephen.

"All employees are getting Lean and Agile training, and the opportunity to participate in PIEs," says Yumi. "Then there's our Boot Camp series – Digital immersion, Lean Startup, and Design Thinking. Hackathons are in the works to target core technology problems."

"Impressive," says Stephen. "What are your next steps, Yumi-san?"

"We need an Innovation Platform," Yumi answers.

"What's that?" Stephen asks.

"It's a space," Yumi answers, "where the organization isn't in our way."

Today's executive coaching session focused on 'Quality in the Process', and the Go See walk was in an SME Lending process. Martin drew out the process steps, noting, where possible, delays, defects, over-processing and other forms of waste. It wasn't easy – most of the work, and waste, was invisible. They also attended the team's daily huddle, during which Martin practiced 'humble inquiry', which the team seemed to appreciate. Back in the Lighthouse, Yumi questioned Martin to reflect on what he'd seen, gave homework, and asked for questions.

"Please help me understand the Innovation Platform concept," said Martin.

The Innovation Platform

"Our Aspiration is to go *Digital to the Core*," Yumi replied, "and our winning logic is:

1. *Digitize key client journeys.*
2. *Deploy new ways of working.*
3. *Simplify & modernize our IT and data architecture.*

The problem is, both run contrary to our culture. And so, we need a space where the organization is not in our way. Our Innovation Platform is a physical, financial, strategic, psychological and cultural *space* - where we can practice, learn and develop new offerings. At its heart is a physical space called a Learning Laboratory."

Yumi handed Martin a one-pager. "Think of the Innovation Platform as a house." [**See Figure 6.1**]

"The roof represents our Strategy," Yumi continued. "*Where are we going? How do we get there?* Everything is designed to support the roof. Our management system aligns, deploys and monitors the strategy. You'll recognize the elements – Lighthouse, daily team huddles, and operating rhythms. Our foundation is a community of pragmatic innovators, developing projects aligned with our strategy."

Martin pondered the image in silence. "What's an Innovation Council?" he asked.

"In effect," Yumi said, "it's an internal VC[1] comprising senior leaders who provide *metered* funding to high potential innovation projects, based on Innovation Accounting metrics. Client Experience Councils are similar and we'll introduce them as we scale our transformation. We use traditional accounting to run the business, and Innovation Accounting in our breakthrough work."

"I recognize the pillars – they're our strategic pillars. But there are things in each I don't understand. For example, what does 'end-to-end innovation framework mean? And I don't understand the stuff in the Data and Tech pillar."

"We'll return to this image repeatedly," said Yumi. "For now, let me introduce an idea that animates all our activities."

Hacker, Hipster, Hustler

"To sustain our Innovation Platform," said Yumi, "we need to build three core capabilities: client intimacy, agile software development, and Lean experimentation. This entails aligning three *methodologies* – Design Thinking, Agile, and Lean Startup. And three personalities or *mindsets*: experience designer, software engineer, and business person.

---

[1] Venture capital – a form of financing provided by firms or funds to small, early stage emerging firms deemed to have high growth potential.

Figure 6.1   APB's Innovation Platform

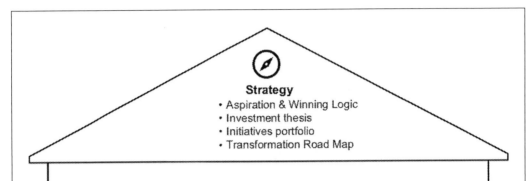

Strategy
- Aspiration & Winning Logic
- Investment thesis
- Initiatives portfolio
- Transformation Road Map

Performance (Management system)
- Transformation Lighthouse
- Operating Rhythm (management cadence)
- Innovation & Customer Experience Councils
- Innovation Accounting (aka Metered-funding)

new Ways of Working (nWoW)

- Leadership development
- End-to-end innovation management framework
- nWoW Academy: Design Thinking, Agile, Growth Hacking, Lean experiments
- Intrapreneurship program

Customer Centricity
(co-design with clients)

- Digitize key client & employee journeys
- New digital offerings
- Commercial pilots, new business models

Technology & Data

- Modular architecture to support constant Tech change & Fintech alliances
- Hybrid Cloud & Software as a Service for productivity, agility & cost
- Agile development and DevOps pipeline

Pragmatic innovators activity
- **Innovation Projects:** focused interventions, informed by strategy
- **Pragmatic Innovators network:** Mentorship, support community
- **Well-supported intrapreneurship** program that enables (some) employees to channel their passion and test their innovation ideas, within the confines of APB's objectives.

Source: Digital Pathways

Figure 6.2   Does It Wow, Does It Work, Can We Make Money?

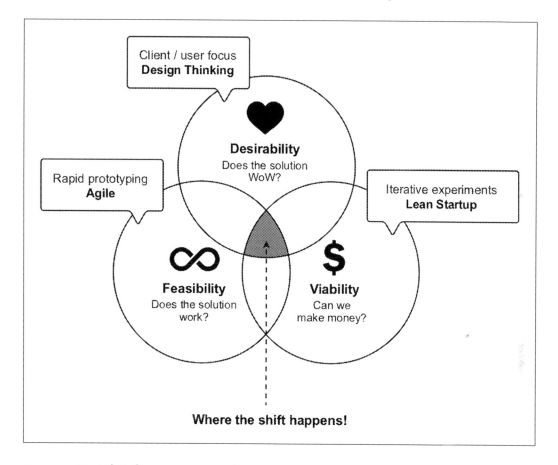

Source: Digital Pathways

We call them *Hipsters, Hackers,* and *Hustlers,* respectively. The magic is in their collaboration, which dissolves silos and creates *feasible, valuable,* and *viable* solutions to client problems."

Yumi gave Martin another one-pager. **[See Figure 6.2]**

Martin absorbed the image. *"Does it wow, does it work, can we make money?"* he said. "Let me see if I understand this. Stanley Phau is a classic hustler – he knows how to make money, but he doesn't really understand the client or technology. Mohan Bilgi knows technology but has major blind spots around the client and the business. And there are others who know the client, but don't know IT or how to make money."

"You've got it, Martin," said Yumi. "Our transformation hinges on integrating these disparate mentalities. It's hard to do – for a start, the personality types tend to be quite different. Then we have our silos and all the other blockers. In the longer term, we want to develop people who can comfortably wear all of these hats – generalists, in the best sense."

Martin rubbed his forehead. "It's a stretch. Banking culture and politics is about building empires and defending turf. Silos are highly specialized and don't easily share people or ideas."

Yumi nodded. "Talent is going to be a constraint. Sustained innovation requires people who are equally at home with business, design and technology. Finding the right Fintech partners will help – they're better at this than we are."

"We have plenty of good Hackers and Hustlers," said Martin, "but I'd say we're light in the Hipster department."

Yumi nodded again. "Hipsters at APB are scarce, under-used and under-valued. A hipster told me: *People think my job is picking landing page colors.*"

"Forgive my ignorance, Yumi," Martin said, "but what do they actually do?"

"Hipsters help design the entire client experience," Yumi answered. "Client pains, gains, jobs-to-be-done, the subtle and swift ups and downs in experience. we ignore these at our peril."

"Are the Design Thinking boot camps helping?" Martin asked.

"Yes, but slowly," Yumi answered. "We need to open up our hiring process and get more so-called 'bizarre' people in the door."

"*Stop hiring bankers…*" said Martin. "Now I think I understand why."

"Let me reiterate the key point," said Yumi. "We not only need Hipsters, Hackers and Hustlers working together, we also need to develop generalists who embody each mindset and can fluidly switch between them."

Despite all the challenges, green shoots of change continued to appear. With all the saved client-hours came improvements in TAT, quality and productivity. All the PIEs, Boot Camps, and Hackathons energized hundreds of employees from across Commercial Banking. Martin turned out to be a charismatic champion, attending endless kick-offs and team presentations, and communicating the core messages cheerfully. Yumi hired a professional journalist to communicate transformation news throughout APB.

Today's executive coaching session was focused on Lean and Agile methods and took place in APB's enormous IT division. These methods were still an anomaly across APB, a gap the Lean Digital team was working hard to address. To help, Yumi had pulled in Kenji Shioda, an old friend, and master Lean and Agile coach. Martin was proving to be a capable student. He did his homework and pre-reading, and always arrived ready to learn.

Martin and Yumi took in a couple of IT scrums. Each team had plans and metrics, and a reasonable grasp of client needs. There were improvement points, to be sure, including too much work-in-progress, and a weak understanding of bottlenecks. Problem solving was also weak and rarely got to the root cause. Flow was constrained as a result, and delivery delays were endemic. Martin was glad to hear they'd begun RCPS[2] training.

Growth Hacking

Back in the Lighthouse, Yumi gave Martin his homework and asked for questions.

Martin put his hands on his head. "What does a model innovation project look like? I believe we use the term 'Proof of Concept', no?"

"Let's use *Proof of Value* or *PoV*," Yumi replied. "By focusing on *value* we hope to avoid so-called innovation theater. Here's a model PoV trajectory. As usual, there's more here than you can easily absorb, and we'll continually refer to this image. **[See Figure 6.3]**

"You'll notice it's an end-to-end process that begins with Strategy," Yumi continued. "Our Digital Compass helps us filter and align PoVs. Selected projects follow clearly defined steps up the so-called hockey stick curve. They have to pass a number of tests:

- *Problem fit* – Do we understand the client's problem?
- *Solution fit* – Does our solution solves the client's problem?
- *Market fit* – Is the client willing to pay for our solution – *right now*?

Governance is a big deal. We're setting up our first Innovation Council, and I'm going to ask you to chair it. PoVs that pass muster will get a bit more money. Those that don't, will be shut down. We can't afford 'zombie' innovations."

"So *this* is our end-to-end innovation framework," Martin. "Let me test my understanding. To create 'feasible, desirable and viable' solutions, we form cross-functional Hacker-Hipster-Hustler teams. We test ideas early and often,

---

2 Root Cause Problem Solving.

Figure 6.3   Proof of Value (PoV) – Expected Trajectory

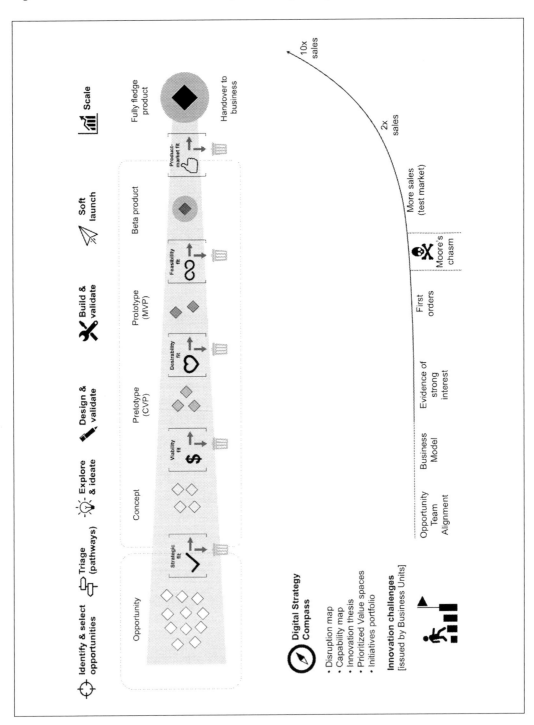

Source: Digital Pathways

and cull the losers. *Minimum Viable Product* is the minimum feature set that provides value to the client. *Moore's Chasm*[3] reflects the challenge of achieving market traction in the much bigger Early Majority. Getting up the hockey stick curve involves achieving Problem, Solution, and Market Fit."

"Crack on, Martin," said Yumi.

"That Innovation Accounting paper you sent makes a lot of sense," Martin went on. "We provide metered funding only to those PoV teams that meet agreed upon goals – which reflect their ability to *reduce* technical and market-related *risk*. By doing so, we're buying the right to purchase the innovation at a discounted price, as in a conventional option. We don't apply conventional valuation financial metrics like ROI[4] till the scaling phase. Otherwise, we'd never invest in anything."

"That's correct, with one proviso," said Yumi. "Innovation Accounting applies to *breakthrough innovation. Sustaining innovation,* by contrast, is often amenable to ROI and other traditional metrics. It's a judgement call."

"How do we bring disruptive innovation back into the business?" Martin asked.

"That's one of our biggest challenges," Yumi answered. "Some people say don't try to reform traditional banks. Instead, build a digital bank from scratch. Maybe we can prove them wrong. In fact, I believe both are possible. But that's a discussion for another day."

Martin was silent again. "Let's have that chat when the time is right," he said. "Let's get back to our end-to-end framework. H*ow* do you know you're getting up the growth curve? Traditional metrics like revenue and ROI are effectively zero. So what do you measure?"

"I like Dave McClure's so-called Pirate metrics,"[5] Yumi answered, "which form the acronym AARRR. They comprise two categories:

■ *Value* metrics
  • Awareness – (I hear about your product and find you)
  • Activation – (I'm interested enough to sign up)
  • Retention – (I come back)

---

[3] According to Geoffrey Moore, the marketer should focus on one group of clients at a time, using each group as a base for marketing to the next group. The most difficult step is making the transition between visionaries (early adopters) and pragmatists (early majority). This is Moore's chasm. https://en.wikipedia.org/wiki/Crossing_the_Chasm.

[4] Return on Investment.

[5] Tip of the hat to Dave McClure https://www.youtube.com/watch?v=irjgfW0BIrw.

- *Growth* metrics, typically
  - Revenue – (I buy something)
  - Referral – (I tell everybody about the product)

So how do you get up the growth curve? Use Value metrics to confirm Problem Fit and then Solution Fit. Use Growth metrics when you've achieved Market fit."

"How do you know you have Market fit?" Martin asked.

"When clients tell you, *I want this right now!*" Yumi answered. "In fact, there are three growth drivers:

- *Acquisition* – We advertise our product and get more people into our now-proven marketing funnel
- *Stickiness* – We get more revenue per client e.g. by cross-selling or up-selling
- *Viral* or word of mouth (WOM) – Our clients tell all their friends and family about it

All this is part of so-called 'Growth Hacking', which means creating viral growth using social media, product landing pages, Google AdWords, and other non-traditional marketing methods. Here's another one-pager showing what typically needs to happen to get us up the growth curve. The columns correspond to the steps in our innovation process, and the rows to the 3 H's." **[See Figure 6.4]**

Martin absorbed the image. "There's a great deal here I don't understand. But I'm starting to get what *Digital to the Core* means. I'm glad we're partnering with Fintechs and building an Intrapreneur Network. Last question: *who* do we partner with?"

"We'll have a good idea after next week's Innovation Festival," Yumi answered. "We've published our problem statements and are inviting Fintech bids."

Innovation Lab Crawl

Singapore Innovation Festival

Martin, Stephen, Andy, and Yumi were visiting their fifth Innovation Lab open house and having a grand time. They had driven all over Singapore

Figure 6.4   Proof of Value (PoV) – Key Activities

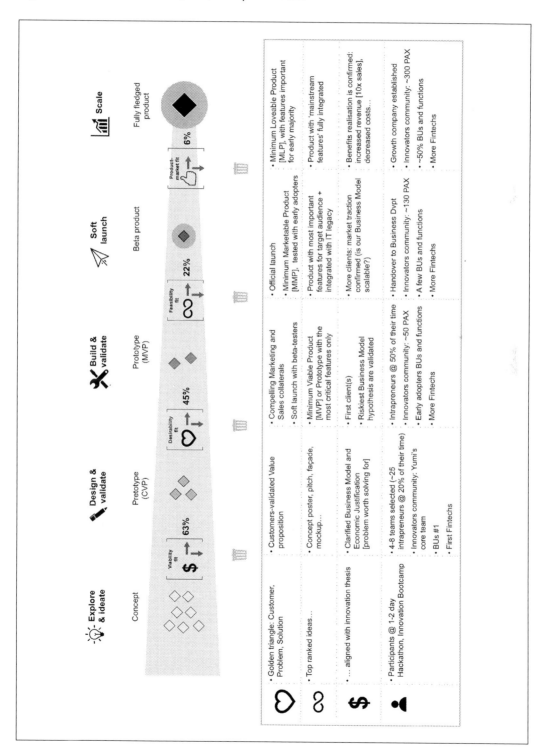

exploring the nooks and crannies of the startup ecosystem. Martin had played ping-pong with a robot, flown a drone covered with advanced sensors, explored several for-sale high-end homes wearing prototype AR glasses and tried to outwit chatbots. He had talked to FinTechs offering a broad range of services in payment, lending, cross-border money transfer, investment management, and insurance. He had met engaging entrepreneurs whose minds seemed to operate at the speed of light.

Martin was pleased to see how well Stephen and Andy were getting along. Martin admired their shared values and commitment to the greater good. Andy was helping Stephen educate the Board on Lean Digital basics and helping them better understand APB's activities.

"The FlowBase presentation is beginning in two minutes," said Yumi. "I'd like you to meet the founder, Asim Agarwal – an interesting fellow and a potential partner. Asim is a graduate of MIT's entrepreneur program[6], who managed to transform his thesis into a viable business." They walked over and found seats, just as the lights went down. A smiling gentleman walked to the podium.

"What if we could eliminate all the waste in banking?" Asim Agarwal began.

"There'd be nothing left!" somebody hollered, which drew knowing laughter.

Agarwal grinned. "Errors, delay, and never-ending hassle, that seems to be our daily reality in banking. But what if we really could streamline our back- and middle-office processes and free our people up to create value streams that delight the client? That's what FlowBase is all about."

Agarwal then demonstrated the FlowBase platform, a suite of apps including Fetching, Classifying, Refining and Analyzing. FlowBase, Agarwal explained, could fetch, classify and compare documents to identify differences, extract critical data, and identify abnormalities. FlowBase could process both internal and external databases, scan the Internet, extract meaning from text, identify potential fraud and fraudsters, and turn images into editable data.

Martin's eyes were wide. "If it works, Flowbase could transform our KYC and AML[7] processes," he whispered.

"I think we can cut KYC lead times by up to *90%*," Yumi replied. "Accounts Payable and Investments are other obvious applications."

---

[6] http://entrepreneurship.mit.edu/.
[7] Know Your Client, and Anti-Money Laundering.

Agarwal concluded his talk with a Q&A by taking questions and inviting people to play with the FlowBase platform on the monitors provided. Yumi walked over and was greeted warmly. Yumi introduced Martin and Andy. "An impressive presentation, Asim," said Martin.

"Thank you," said Asim. "We ran a PoV with APB a few years ago but it didn't go very well."

Martin raised an eyebrow. "Do tell."

"To be honest, it was a complete waste of time," Asim said. "Connecting to your IT system took forever. We wanted to try a cloud-based application, but your Compliance people shut it down. I still remember your Mr. Decker saying *sorry mate, you can't do that*. IT was also uncooperative with respect to connectivity, even though your mainframes are API friendly. Despite all this, we proved the concept and were ready to scale. That's when we ran into *Procurement*, who gave us a *100-page* contract. Mr. Decker told us getting to market would take 'at least 10 months' to get our PoV into production. And that's when I pulled the plug."

"Sorry to hear that, Asim." said Martin. "Things are in flux at APB and all that is going to change. Would you be open to discussing a serious project?"

"With respect, Martin, I'd have to think about it," said Asim. "We like to do things quickly. I can't stand this *I'll-get-back-to-you-in-three weeks* stuff."

※

Yumi, Andy, Stephen, and Martin had dinner together that night and reflected on all they had seen during Innovation Week. "I'm impressed with all the talent and energy," Martin said.

"Singapore is becoming a Smart Nation,"[8] said Stephen. "This is what we dreamed about at the Ministry of Finance."

"Did any of the FinTechs catch your eye?" Andy asked. "Any potential partners?"

"FlowBase could really help us with client on-boarding," said Martin. "I'm disappointed that Asim's APB experience was so bad. I'll give him a call. I also like QuickPay, the international money transfer group."

"I like SmartWealth's robo-advisor services," said Andy

"I like Connectivity Inc.," said Yumi. "Their platform connects legacy IT systems like ours with external partners using pre-packaged APIs and

---

[8] Singapore established the Smart Nation initiative in 2014 dedicated to better living through technology and innovation.

microservices, and related functionality. The Connectivity platform could give us a boost."

"Will that give Mohan heartburn?" said Martin.

"Digitizing client journeys requires both internal and external connectivity," Yumi answered. "Our legacy systems are spaghetti. We need to help Mohan."

The View from the Front Line

Late Friday afternoon: people are heading out of the office and onto the MRT.[9] Kenny Soh sees Martin and smiles. "Good to see you, boss."

"Good to see you too, Ken. It's been quite a week. I thought I'd drop by and check in with you. How are we doing?"

"Well, my team and I have just completed our second Process Improvement Event," said Kenny. "We spent three days finding and fixing process bottlenecks. All in all, it was a pretty good experience. Our biggest challenge is sticking to the new process."

"How were the facilitators?" Martin asked.

"Quite knowledgeable," Kenny said. "Marcus Kupper dropped in for our summary presentation. That's never happened before."

"Any feedback for me?"

"There seems to be a lot of activity everywhere," said Kenny. "The office is buzzing - everybody seems to be talking to everybody else. I think people like all the visual management. It makes it easy to see what's going on."

"Any further thoughts on our Aspiration and winning logic?" Martin asked. "Have we communicated well? Do they make sense?"

"Communication has been good," Kenny answered. "People like your videos. They really like your Town Hall meetings because you speak plain English and you're honest. They like it when senior leaders attend team huddles and PIE report outs, though it's still pretty rare. The winning logic makes sense to most people. We know we have to go Digital, but it's scary, as I said. We like your commitment to retraining and re-skilling. If you follow through, I think people will support the strategy."

---

[9] Mass Rapid Transit, Singapore's extensive subway and railway system.

CHAPTER 6 – STUDY QUESTIONS

1. Define the main elements of an Innovation Platform.
   a. Based on your experience, what are some of the obstacles to setting up and sustaining an Innovation Platform?
   b. What are possible countermeasures to each obstacle?
   c. Any personal experiences?
2. Describe the 3H model in your own words.
   a. Why do we need these personas to move up the hockey stick curve?
   b. In your experience, how do the three personas differ in personality, mindset, and training?
   c. What is the dominant persona(s) in your organization?
   d. What are the obstacles to bringing 3H teams together in your organization? Any possible countermeasures?
3. In your experience what are the major obstacles to bringing a breakthrough or disruptive innovation 'into the business'?
   a. What are the root causes of each obstacle?
   b. What are possible countermeasures?
   c. How do these obstacles differ for product versus service offerings?
4. Draw out a model PoV trajectory
   a. Describe at least five critical tests built into the process
   b. Does this trajectory apply to product as well as service offerings?
   c. In what ways might product and service offering PoVs differ?
   d. In your experience, what are common obstacles to getting up the hockey stick curve?
5. Describe your organization's current innovation (PoV) process
   a. What are the strengths and weaknesses?
   b. How might your organization improve?
6. Define Growth Hacking
   a. What are the obstacles to implementing Growth Hacking in your organization?
   b. How might your organization reduce these obstacles?

Chapter 7

Launching Our First Wave Innovation Projects

Core business improvement: Bringing tech and operations together

"I don't believe in failure. I believe in learning experiences."
— Don Norman (American researcher)

Video and Letter to All Employees

Putting the client in the center of all we do.

I've been your CEO for almost a year now and have had the opportunity to get to know you and our business a whole lot better. I'm honoured at the trust you've shown me and want to give you my sense of where we are, where we're going, and what needs to change if we're to achieve our aspirations.

Our clients' needs and expectations are evolving faster than ever before. To win in this new environment we need to put the client in the center of all we do. I see an APB of small, flexible, empowered, multidisciplinary teams focused on end-to-end client journeys. They have all the information and skills they need, especially digital skills, they develop deep empathy with clients, and learn fast through quick experiments.

Cooperation has to become our foundation. To prosper we need to connect internally and externally. We need to simplify and streamline our processes, which today are full of waste and hassle. We need to automate the boring and repetitive, so you can spend more time where you know you can add value. We need to invest in people to ensure your skills continually evolve and improve in tandem with client needs. We need to invest intelligently in technology and in strategic partnerships to ensure you have the tools you need to create a seamless, hassle-free client experience.

People and culture are the engine of our transformation. We're going to evolve our training and development so you can learn by doing, so you can grow and be successful in this new environment. We're going to develop new ways of working, and a simpler, more visual evidence-based management system. We're going to make decisions based on data, and solve problems by going to the root cause.

Our aspiration is to be recognized as the world's most client-friendly bank. We are committed to saving 10 million client-hours this year and are well on our way.

Our strategic focus areas, or pillars if you will, are 1) Digitize key client journeys, 2) Simplify and modernize our IT and data architecture, and 3) Deploy new Ways of Working. Our great enabler is Digital – we're going to go Digital to the Core and you're going to be banking's most digital savvy workforce. We have terrific activities in progress including Process Improvement Events, Digital Immersion sessions, Design Thinking Boot Camps and hackathons where you're learning to tackle difficult problems with our local ecosystem partners. Like many of you, I am not a digital native. It's all about learning by doing, it's all about growing together.

We have ambitious goals and an enormous challenge ahead. I have absolute confidence in you. We are going to grow together and succeed beyond any possibility of doubt. Thanks, and let's go out there and have some fun.

Martin

Finding Our Learning Lab Leader

Ola Cocina del Mar Restaurant, Marina Bay Financial Center

Oliver Chan strides into the restaurant, spots Yumi and Andy, and walks over to greet them. "So glad you could come, Oliver," Yumi says. "Please join us for a glass of wine and some tapas."

Oliver grins. "You've discovered my weakness."

"You've written a strong letter," says Yumi. "I want to chat in person before I talk to Martin Picard."

Oliver sits down and accepts a glass of wine. "I'm fed up with APB," he says. "Martin Picard says all the right things in his letters, videos and Town Hall meetings. But I'm trying to effect change, and I get shut down at every turn. My project is a no-brainer. Fifty million SGD – that's the size of the prize. But I have to get approval from thirty people, including ten IT system heads, and attend endless useless meetings. Six months later nothing has happened – *nothing*. Just more committees and more excuses. Writing to you is my last resort."

"You're one of APB's best product managers," says Andy.

Oliver shrugs. "I can join any number of companies. Why waste my time at APB?"

"What are the main blockers, Oliver-san?" Andy asks.

"Bureaucracy," says Oliver. "If I have a good idea, I want to talk to five people – not *25*. And then there's IT. All I get from them is excuses and deflection. *We already do this…We'd love to help you, but first we have to do a, b and c…What a great idea…Too bad we don't have any spare resources…blah, blah, blah.* What drives me crazy is that nobody owns, or can even *see*, the client journey. How can we prosper if we don't care about our clients?"

"The blockers are strong," Andy agrees. "To change APB, we will need more like you, not fewer."

"I'm tired of fighting, Mr. Saito."

"May I ask a favour, Oliver?" Yumi says. "Please don't submit your resignation letter just yet. Give me a month. Interesting opportunities are arising."

Oliver raised an eyebrow. "Okay," he says. "With all respect, I'll need something concrete." With that Oliver excuses himself, explaining he has to pick up his children from school.

"Well, what do you think, Yumi-chan?" Andy asks.

"I think we may have found our Learning Lab leader."

Martin was silent as Yumi summarized her chat with Oliver Chan. "He's one of our best, and he's desperate to leave," said Martin. "How many talented people are we losing? I'm confident we can fix our technology and process gaps. But how do we attract and keep our Oliver Chans?"

"We have to learn to work in a new way," Yumi said. "That's what our Learning Lab is all about. We're up and running, by the way."

"I saw the videos – impressive," said Martin. "Your reporter is doing a fine job communicating progress."

"The new Fusionopolis space has a good feel," said Yumi. "We've already run a number of Client Journey and Design Thinking boot camps there."

"What's our first innovation project?" Martin asked.

"Client on-boarding," said Yumi. "We want to fix the biggest pain points in the KY Tay journey.[1] FlowBase is on board - looks like you made an impression on Asim Agarwal. Marcus promised Asim he'd fix the IT and Procurement hassles."

"It's an efficiency innovation project, correct?" said Martin. "We're protecting our core business by fixing problems in the middle of a critical client journey."

Yumi nodded in agreement. "This project is a major challenge on its own. Our goal is to improve client experience and reduce unit transaction cost. The prize is juicy – on-boarding improvements are scalable. But there's much more at stake. The Learning Lab represents a test of our overall approach."

"Can you please explain?" said Martin.

"Can we work in a totally different way?" Yumi replied. "Can our silos, starting with Operations and IT, work together to improve core processes? Can we pull in and engage other silos? Can we adhere to a structured experimentation-based improvement recipe? Can we manage people in a different way? These are just some of the tests."

Martin pondered this. "Yumi, I fear the answer to many of these questions will be *no*."

"The Learning Lab's deeper purpose is to surface problems," Yumi answered. "We *want* them to bubble up, so we can learn and fix them."

Martin was struck, again, by the depth of APB's challenge. "That's a different way of thinking," he said. "We usually go to great lengths to hide problems. Anything I can do?"

"Our Learning Lab needs a Director," said Yumi. "We're looking for what Tim Brown[2] calls a T-shaped leader, meaning both leadership and technical

---

[1] See Figure 2.7.
[2] CEO of IDEO.

Figure 7.1 T-Shaped Profile for an Innovation Leader

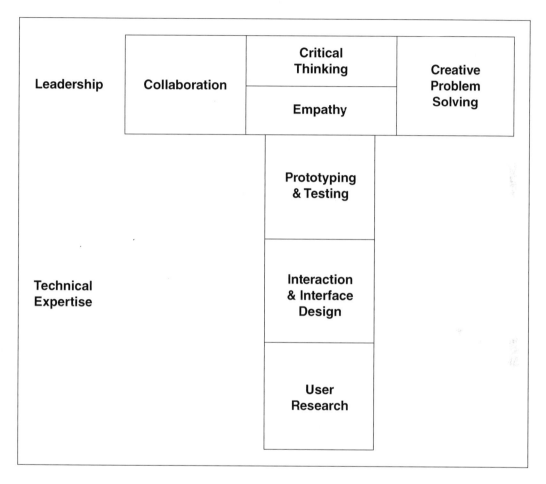

Source: Ideo

skills. **[See Figure 7.1]** Oliver Chan fits the bill. He has what it takes to manage cross-functional teams. Shall I offer him the job?"

"Giddy up," said Martin.

The Learning Lab Takes Shape

APB's Learning Lab took up an entire floor of Building 2A in the Fusionopolis research complex, about 15 minutes northwest of the CBD.[3]

---

[3] Central Business District.

Yumi liked the building's elegant curves, lush green spaces and proximity to the INSEAD[4] Asia campus, where she had many friends and colleagues. Martin had made his expectations clear. "No digital lipstick, no theater, no phony baloney. I want the Lab to embody our transformation."

Oliver Chan accepted the Learning Lab Director position. Working with Elina Gosh, he began to develop a workspace that would reflect Martin's vision. The Lab had floor to ceiling windows, and plants in abundance. There were no offices and few partitions. Worktables, laptops and whiteboards were everywhere. There was a little self-serve cafeteria, and a small, low stage to facilitate report outs. It felt a bit like a comedy club.

A central collaboration zone served as a mini-Lighthouse, providing an overview of what was happening at any given time. The Learning Lab's mantra was prominently posted: *Digital to the Core,* as was APB's winning logic:

1. *Digitize key client journeys*
2. *Deploy new Ways of Working*
3. *Simplify & modernize our IT and Data architecture*

Core metrics were tracked on a whiteboard, including client-hours saved, cash freed up, innovations commercialized, and new revenue generated per annum.

The Learning Lab hosted PIEs and a range of boot camps: Client Journeys, Lean Startup, and Design Thinking to start. There were Hackathons, Digital Immersion sessions, and Hack & Hires that sought to attract scarce digital talent. Some Hackathons focused on API development, and others paired APB leaders with local FinTech talent in problem discovery and solution development. The 'Imagineering' program featured a series of TED-like talks featuring prominent experts. Some activities worked, some did not. Yumi's response was consistent. "What did you learn, and how will you improve?"

Stephanie Shan set up an Innovation Council comprising C-suite executives, which Martin chaired. On 'Pitch Fridays', PoV teams would report out, as if they were startups reporting to a VC.

There were growing pains, as Martin had anticipated. The innovation mantra – ***Does it work? Does it wow? Can we make money?*** – was

---

[4] INSEAD is a graduate business school with campuses in Europe (Fontainebleau, France), Asia (Singapore), and the Middle East (Abu Dhabi). 'INSEAD' was originally an acronym for the French "Institut Européen d'Administration des Affaires" or European Institute of Business Administration.

prominently displayed, but poorly understood. Lean and Agile methods were unnatural to people accustomed to working in silos. Project teams struggled to form, storm and norm. Each day began with awkward stand-up meetings around ill-defined team boards. The teams gamely posed the core questions: *What's our current condition? What are our biggest problems? What are we doing about them?* But the data was weak, and the answers shallow.

Project teams often lacked the cross-functionality needed to get traction. Hipster insight was lacking, as was Hustler business acumen. Some Divisions sent unmotivated or cynical people. Other Divisions ignored support requests entirely. HR was slow to recognize the Learning Lab's activities, and participants often failed to receive credit. Oliver documented every hassle and shared it with Yumi who was quick to follow up.

All the while, Yumi, and with time, Martin, were coaching the senior team in Lean Digital fundamentals. "We'll teach you," Martin told them, "and you teach your direct reports. That's my expectation." A few senior leaders took to Lean Digital naturally, but most struggled. Despite his impatience, Martin tried to lead with a 'light touch', as Yumi advised. Fear shuts down thinking, she told him.

First Proof of Value

Four Months Later – Fusionopolis Building, One North Park, Singapore

Yumi, Martin, and Stephen Kwan took the Fusionopolis elevator up to the eleventh floor. They were attending the Client On-boarding PoV team's report to the Innovation Council. The PoV's focus was reducing the hassles Yumi described in her *'Did you know'* presentation. Martin was also keen to follow-up with Asim Agarwal on FlowBase's on-boarding experience. Had previous hassles been remedied?

Oliver and Elina were waiting for them in the leafy foyer. "Busy day," said Elina. "We have a couple of boot camps going." The visitors could hear a raucous team reporting out. Oliver gave them a quick tour. "The Client On-boarding PoV is entering its fourth month," he said. "They're having difficulty cashing out, as we'll see. Two more PoVs are kicking off in the two weeks – one focused on payments, the other on Identity Verification.

Both entail reducing internal and external hassle, and are based on AI and Blockchain,[5] technologies we need to understand."

"Sounds like you're getting traction," said Martin. "Are there any end-to-end innovations in the pipeline?"

"There's a promising SME lending project," Oliver answered. "We would digitize the entire SME lending process. Qualified clients could get small loans approved within 24 hours. Our FinTech partners haven't committed yet."

"They're waiting to see what happens with FlowBase," said Yumi.

"Looks like the Client On-boarding presentation is ready to go," said Oliver.

They walked over, welcomed Asim Agarwal and the Innovation Council members – Marcus Kupper, Stephanie Shan, and Stanley Phau. "How come Mohan and Richard aren't here?" Martin asked Oliver. "Richard never shows up," Oliver whispered, "and Mohan is dealing with an IT crisis."

Oliver thanked everyone for coming and asked Martin if he'd like to say a few words.

"Client on-boarding is a major pain point, as you know," said Martin, "and fixing it will give us a big boost. But there's more at stake here. This PoV is a test of our winning logic. Can we work in a Lean Digital way? Yumi-san, can you please remind us what that means?"

"Lean Digital," said Yumi, "you all know the main elements:

- Self-organizing, cross-functional teams working in an open, visual space; daily stand-up meetings and regular playback sessions with senior leaders, who quickly handle blockers
- A disciplined, end-to-end innovation process based on Lean experiments and data, and
- Three-step recipe – streamline the process, deploy smart automation, and harvest the benefits by scaling the new process and redeploying freed up team members." **[See Figure 7.2]**

"Thanks, Yumi," Martin went on. "Here's what I'm learning about our new way of working. When it comes to innovation, the goal is *not* perfection. That doesn't exist. As Yumi suggests, the goal is *learning*. Build-measure-learn. We're trying to surface problems here, so we can fix them and improve. Oliver, take it away."

---

[5] Distributed ledger technology.

Figure 7.2 Three-Step Recipe (to Improve Client Journey Rapidly)

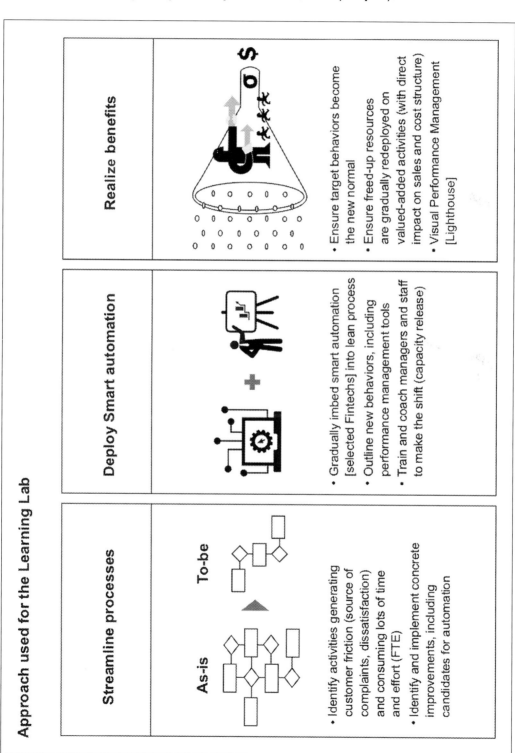

Source: Digital Pathways

"*Client on-boarding*," Oliver began, "was our first detailed Client Journey. To open a simple CaSA[6] in Singapore, a new-to-bank SME client has to:

- Provide 13 document sets
- Fill in a 46-page Account Opening pack, and a 7-page Channel Activation form, and
- Wait for 39 days (if they use the on-line portal) or 46 days (if they use e-mail)

We want to reduce all that delay and hassle, and improve productivity. The PIE teams have laid the foundation. We want to take it to the next level. Let me begin with an overview of the PoV process." **[See Figure 7.3]**

"What's the *size of the prize*?" Oliver asked. "In the Singapore market alone, each 10% improvement in Productivity is worth about $ 7 million SGD. We don't yet have a dollar value on client service improvements. **[See Figure 7.4]**
"Our overall approach," Oliver continued, "follows the Lean Digital recipe Yumi described earlier:

1. Streamline the process,
2. Deploy smart automation, and
3. Harvest the benefits

We began by creating a so-called Model Office running in parallel to the actual process, a very different approach for us. Operations and IT were heavily involved in this work. We freed up 10 people from the business, collocated them here, and put them to work reducing process hassles using dummy data." **[See Figure 7.5]**

"This is a complex image," said Stephen. "Can you help us understand the main ideas?"

"Our process improvements," Oliver replied, "involve screening and segmenting applications, and building quality into the process. We *screen* all incoming work. Some applications we reject out of hand. Incomplete or inaccurate applications, we send back. As a result, there's less junk in the system.

"Then we *segment* applications in terms of complexity. About 80% are 'simple cases', and these we 'fast-track'. We channel 'complex cases' into

---

[6] Current and Savings Account, see Figure 2.7.

Figure 7.3 Client On-Boarding PoV – Overview

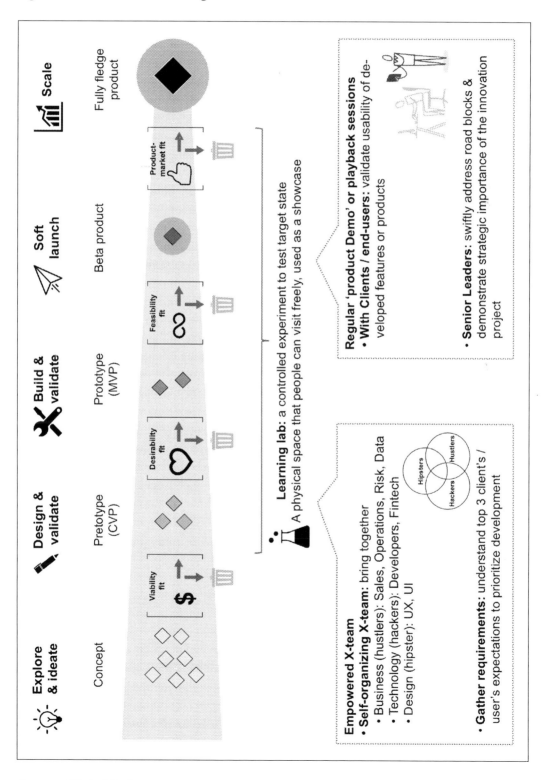

Source: Digital Pathways

Figure 7.4 Client On-Boarding PoV – Size of the Prize

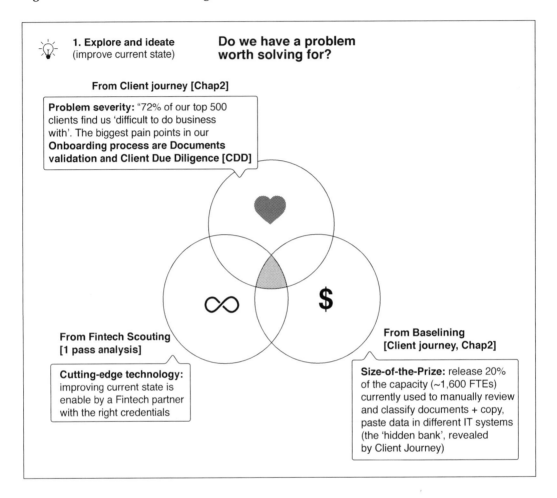

Source: Digital Pathways

the 'Expert Track'. We build quality into the process through daily cross-functional huddles and by standardizing core processes."

"Ah, this is what 'streamline the process' means," said Stephen.

"That's correct, Mr. Kwan," said Oliver. "Once we've streamlined the process, we pull in the FlowBase team and begin to digitize it. Asim, can you please describe the FlowBase capabilities we're using?"

"FlowBase uses Artificial Intelligence and Machine Learning to eliminate boring, repetitive work," said Asim. "We want to free up people for value-added work. Here's an overview of our core tools. I apologize for the complexity of the image. There's a great deal of functionality here."

[See Figure 7.6]

Figure 7.5   Client On-Boarding PoV – Model Office Concept

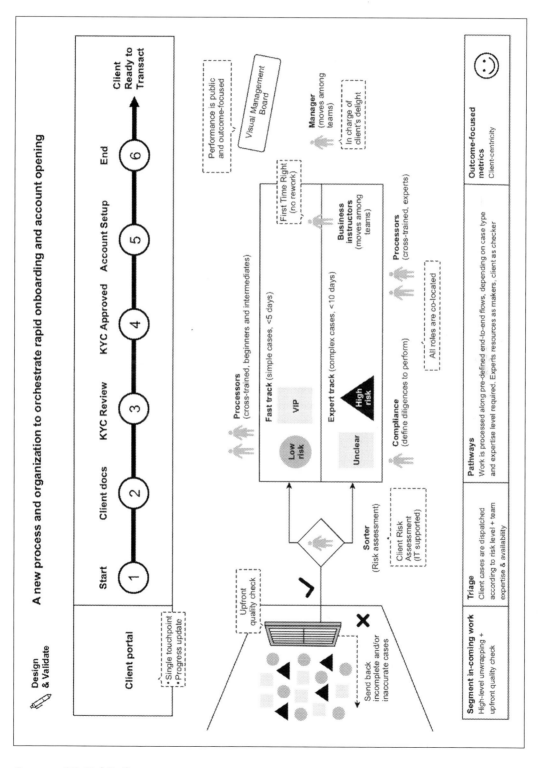

Source: Digital Pathways

Figure 7.6   FlowBase Capability – Do We Have the Right Fintech Partner?

Explore & Ideate

Do we have the right Fintech partner?

Can FlowBase help us partially automate our client onboarding process, to
- improve overall client experience
- reduce unit cost of transaction, e.g. significant manual effort associated with Client Due Diligence (and rework required to fix processing errors)

How to identify good candidates for automation?
- High volume, low complexity tasks
- Manual, paper-based transactions
- That generate significant level of errors, rework, delays...

Flowbase Functionality	Relevance for on-boarding journey
OCR — **Extract and classify unstructured data** • Turn images and/or pdf into editable data. • Turn those data into a structured document (rules based extraction)	• **Interpret scanned documents** (smart OCR)
Fetcher — **Extract and classify structured data** • Fetch data from external DataBases and consolidate them. • Analyse and extract meaning from text, using Natural Language Processing (NLP) and contextual search	• **Client Due Diligence (CDD)**, e.g. sourcing external information to perform Know Your Client (KYC) and its Business (KYB) + sanction search
Classifier — **Compare and classify documents** • Confirm difference (positive / negative) in documents	• **Compare outbound vs. inbound documents**, e.g. is client document signed, amended, complete?
STP — **Join-up different IT systems / data sources** • Auto-populate key fields in our systems • Straight-Through Processing (STP)	• **Partial automation of our KYC process**, e.g. pre-populate key fields for human operator to review and validate

Building internal capability on Artificial Intelligence [AI] is a strategic priority for APB
FlowBase is an AI-based platform that provides apps that are really relevant to
- digitize APB's operations (the Enter-Copy-Paste data factory)
- generate insights from our internal data (combined with external data fetching)

Source: Digital Pathways

"We use Fetcher, Classifier, and STP[7]," Asim went on, "for core documentation-related tasks. OCR[8] allows us to turn images (passports, scanned documents, photos…) into machine-encoded text. Doc Diff and Sanctions Search allow us to quickly identify abnormalities and screen out questionable applications."

"Here is our proposed design to improve client experience," Oliver said. **[See Figure 7.7]**

And here's how we tested it. We try to practice evidence-based management, which means clear goals, experimental design, and metrics. **[See Figure 7.8]**

"Now let's dig a little deeper," said Asim. "The next image is also complex, but it highlights the heart of our experiment. Can we deploy the five *circled* capabilities across the client on-boarding process? If so, we're on our way to breakthrough performance. Please note that Capability 5, pre-populating KYC[9] fields, is the key to harvesting the benefits of our work. **[See Figure 7.9]**

"So, what happened?" Stephanie Shan asked.

"We've had partial success," Asim answered. "As you can see, three of five capabilities have been deployed successfully. The good news is we should be able to deploy them in other client journeys. Unfortunately, pre-populating KYC is *not* one of them – at least not yet. We're disappointed, but not deterred. **[See Figure 7.10]**

"In summary," said Asim, "the parallel process we developed works well, but we haven't been able to harvest the benefits, at least not yet." **[See Figure 7.11]**

"Thanks, Asim," said Oliver. "Are there any questions or comments?"

"I really like the three-step Lean Digital recipe," said Steven. "I'm glad to hear that Operations and IT worked together on this. If we can master these three steps, there is no limit to what we can achieve."

"Operations team members enjoy the daily huddles and related coaching," said Marcus.

"Client Satisfaction shows the least improvement," said Stanley. "Why is that?"

Asim paused. "Oliver, maybe you can answer this one?"

"The few clients we talked to liked the quicker turnaround time," said Oliver, "but felt the process required too much 'clicking'. And that reflects

---

[7] STP = Straight Through Processing.
[8] OCR = Optical Character Recognition.
[9] Know Your Client (and its Business).

Figure 7.7   Proposed Design to Improve Client On-Boarding Experience

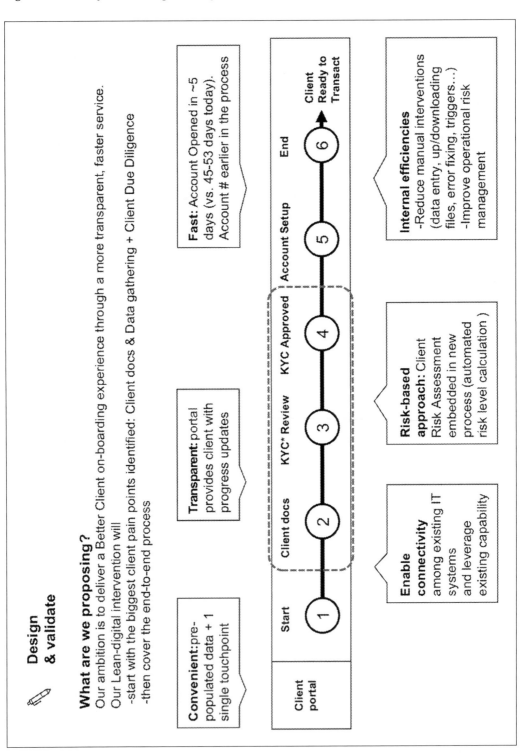

Figure 7.8 FlowBase Experiment Outline

Experiment outline

Problem Statement:
Can FlowBase help us improve client on-boarding experience, while reducing unit cost of transaction?

Build & validate
(Quantitative & qualitative)

1. Learning goals

What hypotheses do we want to prove / disprove?
- **Tactical:** Improve quality (reduce rework), increase productivity (reduce manual effort and error fixing)
- **Strategic:** Improve client experience (speed), while reduce unit transaction cost, with Lean-Automation

Are there other qualitative things to learn during this experiment?
- Build our internal capability and confidence
- Tweak internal processes to foster effective Fintech collaboration (test our Path to PoC process)
- Improve User experience to foster adoption of new solution and capture $ benefits

2. Experiment design
(How do we run this successfully?)

How long does the experiment run for?
3 months, including regular playback session with C-suite and user / client feedback

Who are the target participants?
All roles involved in clients' documents validation and Client Due Diligence (CDD)

How many participants do we need?
All processing roles + manager co-located @ Learning lab (n = 10)

How are we going to get them?
Secure commitment from Senior Executives and General Managers (n = 7)

How do we run the experiment?
Scope: In our PoC, we will test 5 FlowBase capabilities:

#1. Extract information from external databases (Automate Business Information Sourcing)

#2. Automate docs inbound / outbound comparison (Acct Opening pack)

#3. Automate data extraction (same inputs, different formats, e.g. passports)

#4. Run semantic analysis and **extract key data from Google searches** (Automate sanction searches, both on entities and individuals)

#5. Pre-populate fields @ KYC system

3. Validation criteria
(How do we know the test is a success?)

For each hypothesis, what are our pass/fail metric(s)?
- **Quality:** +50% (focusing on First Time Right case, i.e. no rework is needed)
- **Speed:** -50% Turn Around Time [proxy for Client Service]
- **Number of client touchpoints:** -50%

- Productivity: +20% capacity created [#cases /FTEs /week]
- Cost: -10% of current cost base (2,242 processing FTEs globally)

Source: Digital Pathways

Figure 7.9   The Heart of Our Experiment – Can We Deploy Circled Capabilities?

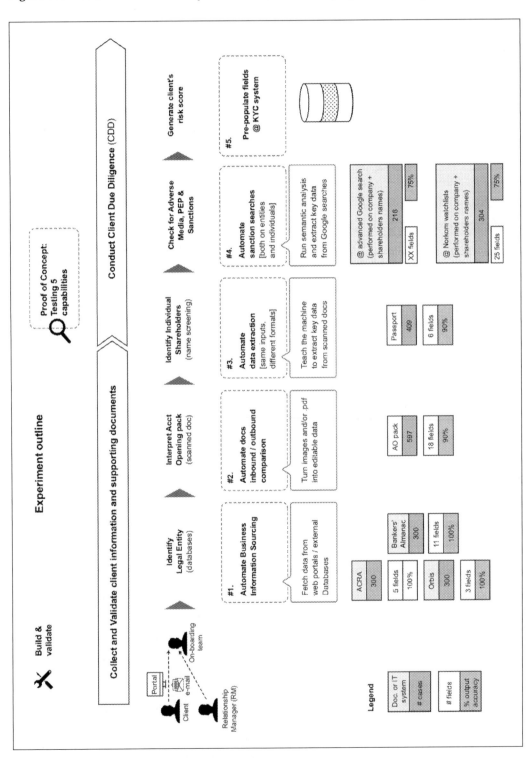

Source: Digital Pathways

Figure 7.10   FlowBase Experiment – Do We Have a Proof of Value (PoV)?

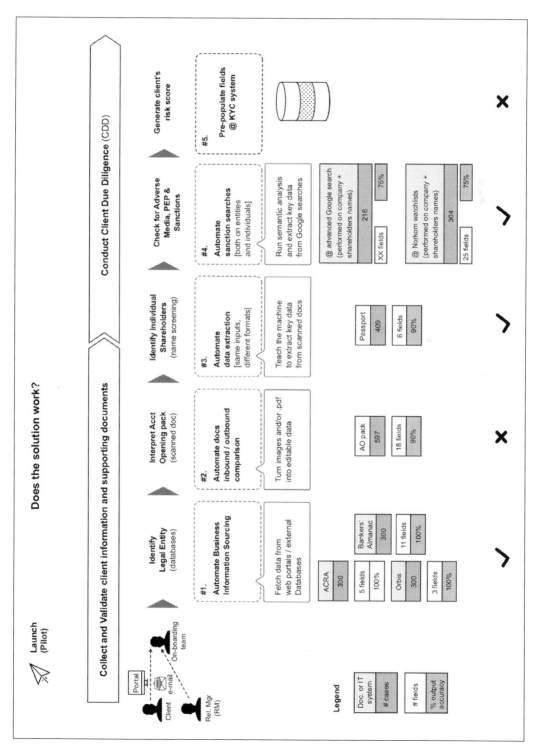

Source: Digital Pathways

Figure 7.11   FlowBase Experiment – Impact 90 Days into the Pilot (Singapore Market)

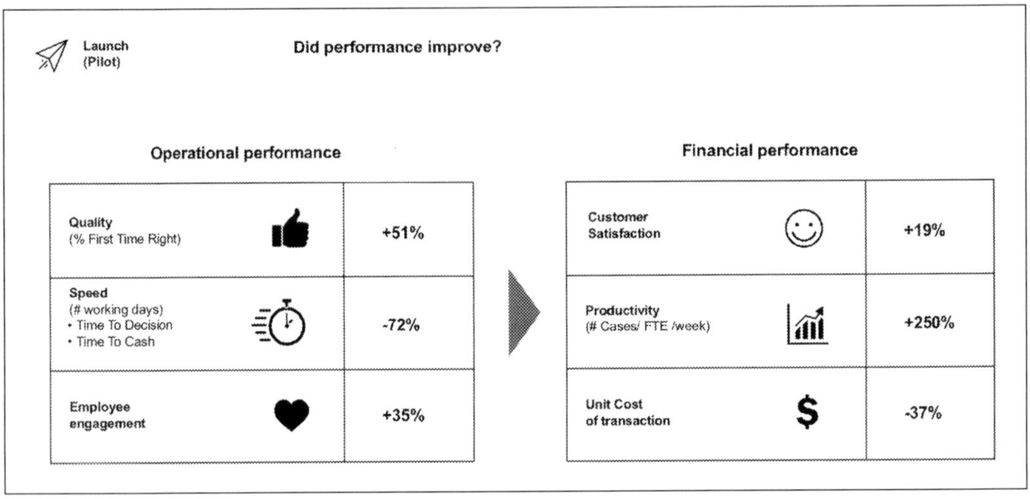

Source: Digital Pathways

the deeper problem: we don't have CX expertise, not really. I can fake it, but I'm not an expert."

"Why didn't you talk to more clients?" Stephen asked.

Oliver paused. "Relationship managers [RMs] were reluctant to give us access."

"I'm not sure I trust your data," said Stephanie. "Where did you get it?"

"We put together a SWAT team of number-crunchers," said Oliver. "Getting reliable data from our systems is difficult, so we created our own."

"Bad data seems to be a recurring theme," said Martin.

"There are three deadly data sins," said Marcus, "and we suffer from them all – data capture, quality, and breadth (end-to-end). I supported Oliver's request to put a data SWAT team together. We may also want to engage FinTech partners who specialize in demystifying data."

"Let's get back to FlowBase," said Stanley. "Why haven't you been unable to cash out?"

"We're not fully connected to internal systems," said Oliver. "I don't want to be misunderstood. IT has done a lot of good work for us, but they've been inconsistent. We've had good engineers but they keep getting pulled away into other projects."

"Mohan asked me to report that FlowBase will be fully integrated by month end," said Marcus. "He sends his apologies for the delay, and for not being here today. IT has been under great pressure lately."

"Glad to see Tech and OPS are working together," said Martin "That's something to build on. And the new process works reasonably well, we just can't plug it in. So, what have we learned?"

"Connectivity is a big problem," said Stephanie. "We have to deal with it."

"We have to fix our data problems," said Marcus.

"Silos remain a problem," said Oliver. "IT support has been inconsistent, and Compliance support is non-existent. Stanley, with great respect, to pull this off, we need you to send your best business people."

"I can do that," said Stanley, "and we'll make sure RMs support you better."

"We've *got* to have good CX designers, aka Hipsters," said Oliver, "especially for new offerings."

"Hipsters will help us with both CX and UX,"[10] said Yumi. "UX remains a big opportunity, and one that we'll take in PoVs to come."

"I'd like to hear from our Fintech partner," said Martin, "Asim, how has your experience been this time around?"

"Working with Oliver and the Learning Lab team is a pleasure," said Asim. "Thanks Marcus, the Procurement process is a lot better. IT support has been inconsistent, but, I think the constraint is capacity, and not motivation."

They went on like this for some time, opening up and speaking frankly. Yumi and Oliver summarized learning points, problems, and next steps. The Innovation Council members voted to continue funding the Client On-boarding PoV.

Lessons Learned

When they got back to the APB place. Martin asked Stephen, Marcus and Yumi to join him in his office for coffee. "What do you think?" he asked.

"Overall, I am impressed with the Learning Lab," said Stephen, "but it's not a priority for Mohan, Stanley, or Richard Decker."

"I think Stanley will come around," said Martin. "I'm more concerned about Mohan and Richard."

"Mohan is dragging his feet for some reason," said Yumi. "It's a problem. Our next major PoV depends entirely on connectivity. We'll be pulling in multiple Fintech partners. As for Richard, I'm no idea what's going on."

---

[10] User Experience.

"How do we ensure internal/external connectivity?" Marcus asked. "I don't think our legacy systems are up to it."

"We need to walk around our legacy systems, at least for now." said Yumi. "I have a Fintech partner in mind. We can turn this constraint into an opportunity."

"Mohan, Stanley and Richard are experienced people," said Stephen. "Why would they not support innovation work?"

"Nobody comes to work wanting to do a bad job," said Yumi. "Sooner or later we have to address thorny topics like incentive structure."

"Incentive structures can be hard to understand," said Marcus, "and even harder to change."

"It would take a report to the Compensation Committee and a Board level vote," said Martin

"In spite of everything." said Stephen, "I am encouraged. We've come a long way in the past year."

"Tech and Operations are working together," said Yumi. "Our PIEs are delivering results and the Learning Lab is getting stronger. We're starting to understand the three-step Lean Digital recipe. Culture and technology remain sore spots. And we're going to have to address our CX and UX gaps."

"We've improved Fintech on-boarding," said Marcus. "But our data problem comes up repeatedly."

"Data is the new superpower," Yumi said. "For the Client Onboarding PoV Oliver and team learned to create their own data, but that's not sustainable. For our next major PoV, we'll need to pull in Fintech partners who specialize in cleaning up, integrating and demystifying data. Which, of course, requires better connectivity."

"What is our next major PoV?" Stephen asked.

"An entirely new digital product in SME[11] lending," Yumi answered. "We're going to simplify and digitize an entire client journey. Qualified SME clients will be able do *everything* from their smartphone."

Martin raised an eyebrow. "Growth, end-to-end innovation – glad to hear it. I'm tired of playing defence."

"We can use the help," said Marcus. "SME lending is in trouble. My sense is it's going to take a lot more than Tech and OPS working together."

"We're surfacing important problems," said Yumi. "To pull off the next PoV, we're going to have to fix them."

---

[11] Small- and medium-size enterprises, which represent 99%+ of all businesses.

CHAPTER 7 – STUDY QUESTIONS

1. What is a 'T-shaped' leader?
   a. Do such leaders naturally exist in most industries? Explain your answer with examples.
   b. How does an organization attract and develop such people?
2. What is a Learning Lab?
   a. What makes for an effective Learning Lab? Any personal experience?
   b. What can hinder a Learning Lab?
3. What are the pros and cons of having a Learning Lab that's remote from head office, such as APB's Fusionopolis lab?
   a. What additional challenges can exist in a global, decentralized business?
4. What are the main elements of the Client On-boarding (FlowBase) PoV?
   a. What do you think of the PoV team's approach? Explain your thinking.
   b. Are they missing anything? Anything they could do better?
5. Define the 'three-step Lean Digital improvement process'.
   a. What are the technical prerequisites?
   b. What are the cultural prerequisites?
   c. What kind of leadership behaviour is required?
6. Describe a PoV with which you are familiar.
   a. What was the team trying to achieve?
   b. What was their overall approach?
   c. What experiments did they run, what happened and why?
   d. How well did the team practice evidence-based management? What might the team do to improve?
7. The PoV team is not getting needed support from important divisions, including IT and Compliance. What are possible reasons for this?
   a. How might you address these reasons?
   b. Are there any risk-averse functions in your organization that can block innovation? How might you address these challenges?
   c. Describe any relevant personal experience. Any reflections or learning points?

Chapter 8

Launching Our Second Wave Innovation Projects

End-to-end flow and a commercial pilot. Can we create entirely new digital products?

"If you're good at course correcting, being wrong may be less costly than you think, whereas being slow is going to be expensive for sure."

– Jeff Bezos

INSEAD Asia Campus, Knowledge Hub District, Singapore

Yumi, Martin, and Mohan Bilgi check in at reception and make their way through the leafy inner garden, past the koi pool and plant walls to the Leadership Development Center and room 3B, where Susan Tse Lau and Paul Dumont are waiting. Susan is Managing Director of Connectivity Inc., a Fintech focused on enabling innovation in major banks. Paul is her technical director. Yumi, who has worked with Susan in the past, makes the introductions.

"Thank you for coming," says Susan. "Rapid innovation can be a quantum leap for big banks. You have enormous challenges including legacy IT systems, demanding clients and regulators, and fast-moving

Fintech competitors. Our goal is to provide a modern software platform that enables innovation; a bridge, if you will, between where you are now, and an agile, flexible future. Paul has prepared a demonstration. He just returned from Belgium and may have some jet-lag."

Paul spends the next 45 minutes demonstrating Connectivity's platform, which includes pre-packaged APIs, microservices, and non-functional requirements specific to banking. Prospect management, client on-boarding and data management, signatures, dynamic pricing/discounting, fraud detection and other core services are available out of the box. Paul takes them through client case studies. "We want to enable open banking," Paul says. "We want to be the glue that connects your back, middle and front-end with your Fintech partners."

Mohan sits with his arms crossed, smiling politely. He asks perfunctory technical questions. "Connectivity is not the only thing," he says. "Stability and security are also important."

Martin and Yumi ask about different use cases, testing whether Connectivity has the experience and capability to support APB's more advanced PoVs. They're especially interested in the client and loan on-boarding modules. The group agrees to meet again, this time at APB, for a controlled live demonstration. "We'll need input/output access," Paul says.

"Yes, of course," Mohan says.

Connectivity Inc.

Mohan was silent in the Grab car back to APB Place. "I know this is uncomfortable for you," said Martin.

Mohan rubbed his eyes. "Paul and Susan made a good presentation. I can tell you're excited about it."

"Connectivity will enable QuickLoan," said Yumi, "and help us cash out the Client On-boarding PoV."

"Mohan, you don't seem happy," said Martin. "What's bothering you?"

Mohan took a deep breath. "My priority is preventing major system crashes – keeping the lights on, as we say. Preventing data breaches is a close second. Engaging with Connectivity Inc. is not going to help me do either. In fact, it may make things more difficult."

Mohan paused, as if weighing how much more he could say. "Look, my team and I don't even control our own budgets anymore – Operations does. And yet, we're pressured to launch more and more code into an unstable and leaky system. We're also pressured to 'open up'. Open banking is a nice slogan, but who gets blamed if the system crashes, or if there's a major data breach?"

Mohan was in full flow now. "Do you know the average tenure of an IT Director at APB? *Less than two years*. It's amazing I've survived this long. You want us to launch new code? You want us to open up? Okay, give us control of our budgets. Let us invest in open source mainframes and architecture. Let us hire people with the necessary skills."

"OPS[1] controls your budget?" said Martin. "I had no idea – that means you have accountability but no authority."

Mohan rubbed his forehead. "Now you know why I act defensive."

"Connectivity would enable our PoV launches," said Yumi, "but could also crash the system, and you'll be held responsible."

"Damned if you do," said Mohan, "and damned if you don't."

"When I took over as CEO, Mohan," said Martin, "I remember you were anxious to present a technology transformation plan – and I shut you down."

"You thought I wanted to build it internally, which is unrealistic," said Mohan. "In fact, I wanted to regain our IT budget so we could spend it on technology I felt we needed."

"That was unfair, Mohan, I apologize," said Martin. "But our problem remains: How to align the Operations and IT? The Board is open to changing incentive structures, but it'll take time. What do we do in the interim?"

"Let's cut a deal with Marcus," Yumi offered. "If we engage Connectivity, Operations has to support Mohan with the money and resources he needs to sustain the system. I'm sure Stephen Kwan would support such an arrangement."

Martin pondered this. "Mohan, could you prepare a list of what you need to ensure system stability and security?"

Mohan shrugs, "Do I have a choice?"

"Not really," Martin admits. "But I promise that I'll have your back. Please prepare that list."

---

[1] Operations.

"We still need a long-term solution," said Yumi. "Can I suggest we pilot so-called 'Two-in-a-Box' management? If you agree, for the coming year, Marcus and Mohan, and a select group of their direct reports, will have *shared* responsibility for their P & L[2]. Compensation and bonus will depend on how well we do across a range of operational and IT measures. Karen Hong has done a nice analysis and can share specifics with you."

"Sounds like you anticipated this problem," said Martin.

Yumi nodded. "The idea is to create a shared path. Either Marcus and Mohan both win, or neither wins. According to Karen, the upside would be very good for both. In return, Mohan, you have to make onboarding new Fintech partners a priority and support our PoVs with your best people."

Mohan looked at Yumi, then at Martin. "You would do this for me?"

"I'm open to a pilot," Martin replied. "I need to review the specifics with Karen Hong."

"Is Marcus okay with this?" Mohan asked.

"I haven't tested it with him," Yumi answered, "but I'm hopeful he'll be supportive. Two-in-a-Box would give you both a bigger budget and more authority, and hopefully eliminate some of the tensions you've been feeling."

Mohan looked out the window in silence, then back at Yumi and Martin.

Three Months Later, Executive Coaching Session, SME Lending Department

Martin and Yumi were concluding an executive coaching session on the Theory of Constraints.[3] They'd begun with a simple computer simulation, then walked the SME leading value stream. As usual, team members were capable, good natured, and doing their best in muddled processes. Martin was practicing 'humble inquiry'[4] and managed to glean important insight while respecting a team's work.

---

[2] Profit and Loss statement.
[3] A management paradigm developed by Eliyahu Goldratt and expressed in a series of books beginning in 1984 with *The Goal*.
[4] *Humble Inquiry, the Gentle Art of Asking Rather Than Telling* (San Francisco: Berrett-Koehler Publishers 2013), by Edgar Schein.

Demand, capacity, process cycle times, and bottlenecks – the fundamentals of process management – were not well understood. How would they know? Martin wondered. They've never been taught to think in such terms. He was glad that Yumi's team had deployed Process Management Lunch & Learns across Commercial Banking.

This was one of our best sessions, Yumi," Martin said. "*The maximum throughput rate is the bottleneck rate. Therefore, find and elevate the bottleneck.* It's clear and simple."

"And tricky in practice," Yumi added. "Bottlenecks can move around, especially where work standards are weak."

"On a different note," said Martin, "how is the Connectivity engagement going?"

"Connectivity Inc. is fully engaged," said Yumi, "and we're starting to see the benefits. The Client On-boarding PoV is fully integrated. By the way, thanks for talking to Stanley Phau. He gave us one of his 'high potentials', and she's really driving throughput and cost. Pilot area productivity has improved almost 30%. If we can scale across Commercial Banking, that represents over $20 million SGD."

"Full speed ahead," said Martin.

"Unfortunately not," said Yumi. "You've just learned the Theory of Constraints and know that bottlenecks can move. Well, that's what's happening. The bottleneck is no longer IT. Before we go live, Compliance and Procurement have to sign off. Without the former, we're not legal; without the latter, we can't scale across geographies. I suspect Compliance is exaggerating the legal risks."

Martin absorbed this in silence. "I need to have a chat with Richard Decker," he said. "On a related note, please tell me more about our QuickLoan PoV."

"QuickLoan is a new, entirely digital product," Yumi replied, "and it's our biggest test to date. Think end-to-end digital journey, world class UX and CX, and effective Fintech collaboration. Here's our target state: qualified SMEs can borrow up to $100,000 SGD within 24 hours, all from a smartphone."

Martin's eyes widened. "KYC, client qualification, and fund drawdown, all within 24 hours – that would be wonderful. This is higher level innovation aimed at growth, correct?"

"That's right," Yumi answered. "If you think back to our transformation model [Figure 5.4], it's a so-called coin and builds on our Efficiency innovations, or so-called 'diamonds'."

"QuickLoan is a big deal, then," said Martin. "What needs to happen for us to pull it off?"

"Shifting our mindset might be the biggest challenge," Yumi replied. "QuickLoan isn't about improving an existing client journey. It's about building a new *business*."

Martin pondered this. "What does that mean, in practical terms?"

"We have to start way upstream, with the client," said Yumi, "and we have to get very good at CX and UX. The Hipster, absent to date, has to fully engage with the Hacker and Hustler. We have to fully animate the 3H model – Does it wow? Does it work? - with Lean experimentation. Otherwise, QuickLoan will be a bust."

"Hold on," said Martin, "is it really that complicated? I would envision a simple recipe: Interview a number of SME lending clients. Learn their jobs-to-be-done and pain/gain points and then develop an offering that fixes them. What's wrong with that?"

"Your question goes to the heart of the matter," said Yumi. "QuickLoan is not about building features, it's about building *experiences*."

"Help me understand what that means," said Martin.

"It's about the commitment you made to *put the client at the center of everything we do*," Yumi said. "We call it Lean and Agile product development and it entails understanding the client journey at a much deeper level, and developing a terrific end-to-end experience. **[See Figure 8.1]**

"Lean and Agile product development is different from what we're used to. Here are the main elements:

1. **Client perspective:** We start by developing client personas and journeys. For QuickLoan, we've met and closely observed more than 40 SME clients and their journeys to identify 'jobs to be done', pain and gain points.
   • The client journey helps us visualize the *target experience* we want to deliver.
   • We translate jobs-to-be-done into *user stories*
2. **APB perspective:** User stories are translated into needed features. The sum of all features becomes the *Product Backlog*.
   • We prioritize features according to *value* (to the client) and *effort* needed to develop them.
   • The cross-functional team then agrees on which features they'll build in the next Sprint (normally a 2–4 week iteration). The selected features become the *Sprint Backlog*.

Figure 8.1   Refocusing on Our Clients with Lean-Agile Product Development

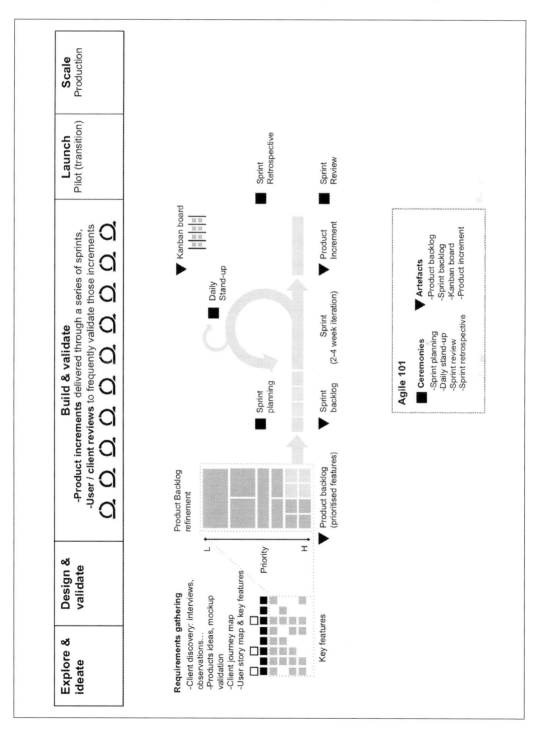

Source: Digital Pathways

- At the end of each Sprint, the team is expected to deliver a product increment, which is reviewed with selected SME clients. Senior leaders and stakeholders also regularly review results in our Lighthouse.

3. **Combined perspective:** All product features are reviewed and validated with our clients to ensure we're on target. To foster radical collaboration between Designers (Hipsters) and Developers (Hackers)**,** we run the Discovery and the Delivery tracks in parallel. We call this 'Dual Track Agile' and it's a practical way to integrate Lean UX and Agile/Scrum.

We iterate to value through *Lean experimentation*, which entails failing fast, cheap and often. We have to accept, going in, that we likely have little understanding of the client's actual problems, jobs-to-be-done or of possible solutions. Reviewing product increments in this way facilitates validation and allows for quick pivots when needed. It also reduces the risk of bad bets and preserves resources for the most promising ideas."

Martin put his hands on his head. "This is all very different indeed. But as you say, I promised to put the client in the center. We have to practice what we preach."

"Developing a new business is a higher level challenge," Yumi went on. "Here are some critical enablers:

1. *Technology*
   a. Connect internal systems and external partners using the *Connectivity* platform, harness microservices and APIs
   b. Use FlowBase for KYC, IDV[5] and client on-boarding
2. *Data*
   a. engage new Fintechs including i) *DataClean*, who specialize in cleaning, integrating, and drawing automatic insight from data, and ii) *JZero*, who specialize in integration, analysis and reporting of SME financial data
   b. Engage with providers of accounting software that SME clients use (e.g. *Fast Books*)

---

[5] Identity verification.

3. *People and Culture* – level up Lean and Agile management, especially Lean experimentation; consolidate Hacker-Hustler connection, and engage the Hipster; broaden scope to include CX and UX, as well as, revenue, productivity, TAT,[6] and cost

4. *Process capability* – map internal processes supporting the new client journey; take out the waste, digitize where possible; engage users to ensure good UX

5. *Management system* – better Fintech on-boarding; business leaders send their best people and commit to supporting the minimum business case; develop mini-Lighthouse process and supporting operating rhythms."

Martin looked out the window. "At times I feel overwhelmed. How can we possibly do all this?"

"What you're feeling is normal," said Yumi. "QuickLoan will, of course, run into problems. That's why we have a Learning Lab, and why we do Lean experimentation. To surface problems and learn our way up that hockey stick curve."

"Can you paint a picture for me?" Martin asked. "What does the QuickLoan PoV look like in practice?"

"Hipsters and Hackers run parallel, yet connected, sprints," said Yumi. "Hackers and Hustlers attend Hipster huddles, and vice-versa. Hipsters discover what the client values and translate it into sketches, mock-ups, wireframes, paper prototypes and other artefacts of the Design profession. Hackers build and test small increments of Code, which Hipsters validate in the next Design sprint. Once we've proven the product wows, and works, the Hustler takes the baton. We continue running Lean experiments till we build a viable business.

"Our PoV milestones reflect this process," Yumi went on. "Minimum *Lovable* Product, Minimum *Viable* Product, Minimum *Marketable* Product, and eventually, Minimum Viable *Business*."

Martin pondered some more. "When I first saw the '*Does it wow, does it work*' mantra," he said, "I assumed Hipsters, Hackers and Hustlers would work in their silos. But now I realize they're engaged throughout, and take the lead at different parts of the growth curve."

---

[6] Turn-around time.

"Crack on, Martin-san," said Yumi. "I hope other leaders are learning as quickly as you are."

"Each phase depends on the previous phase," Martin went on. "If the product doesn't *wow*, there's no point testing whether it *works*. If the product doesn't *work*, there's no point trying to build a *business*. The key is engaging the Hipster, Hacker, and Hustler throughout the process."

"Even better, let's develop people who can put on the Hipster, Hacker, and Hustler hat, as *needed*. That's our long-term HR challenge – developing such people."

"If not," said Martin, completing Yumi's thought, "our People system is going to become a constraint."

"Bingo," said Yumi. "In any event, Mohan and Stanley are finally sending us good Hackers and Hustlers. We don't have good Hipster capability yet, but our Design Thinking coaches and boot camps are helping."

"One last question," said Martin, "what are the attributes of a good experiment?"

"Focus, speed and learning," Yumi replied. "You decide on a *single* metric and do the *smallest* thing possible to learn. For example, if you're testing a software product, you do *not* need a working app – often a sketch of a landing page will do. If you're testing a physical product, let's say a new vegan food service, you don't need to invest in a restaurant. You can test your idea by renting a food truck, or by participating in a local food fair."

"Got it," said Martin. "Fail fast, fail cheap."

QuickLoan PoV – SME Lending

Three months later, APB Learning Lab, QuickLoan PoV Presentation

"It's Pitch Friday," said Elina Gosh. "Let me begin by welcoming our Innovation Council – Marcus Kupper, Stanley Phau, Mohan Bilgi, Stephanie Shan, and Martin Picard. Welcome also to Stephen Kwan and Yumi Saito. Finally, I want to acknowledge Takeshi Shioda, our Lean and Agile coach who has been so helpful to us. Today our focus is the QuickLoan PoV. Before we begin, I believe Martin has a few words."

"QuickLoan is our most ambitious PoV to date," said Martin, "and entails building a new digital business. All sorts of problems are going to bubble up. That's why we have a Learning Lab, so we can learn thereby and fix them. So let's not get too high, or too low. Let's learn our way up the growth curve."

Oliver thanked Martin, welcomed everybody, and launched into his presentation. "The QuickLoan team comprises members from the Business, Technology, Operations, Sales and Marketing, and from our Fintech partners: FlowBase, DataClean, JZero, FastBooks, and Connectivity. Long-term partnerships are essential for the Learning Lab's success. We've developed a new way of working with our external partners, which we call the 5Ps of Fintech collaboration. We believe the 5Ps provide a foundation for long-term collaboration." **[See Figure 8.2]**

"SME lending is a critical segment within Business Lending," said Oliver, "one of Commercial Banking's biggest divisions. What's our objective? Here's an overview of the challenge." **[See Figure 8.3]**

Figure 8.2   Effective Fintech Collaboration – Guiding Principles

⊘	**Purpose**	Fintech collaboration is a means to execute our Strategy. → **not a goal in itself!**
	Priorities	Focus only on growing our identified 'value spaces'. → **enablers, new products, new businesses**
	Process	Minimize administrative friction (procurement, legal, IT, data…) to scout, select and on-board the right Fintechs. → **become easy to innovate with**
🤝	**Partnership**	Offer attractive deal & fair rules of engagement to Fintech partners. → **beware of adverse selection!**
▮▮▮	**Performance Based decisions**	Measure progress & results often, enable 'fail fast cheap & often'. Be ready to pivot & restart. If it doesn't work, unplug. No drama - we tried. → **Champagne-based failure celebration** (What did we learn?)

Source: FutureFintech.io

Figure 8.3   SME Lending PoV – Challenge Overview

QuickLoan = 'controlled' experiment to
- Respond to bad performance in SME business segment [-12.5% in 2 years]
- Combat threat from Fintechs
- Build our internal **Lean-Digital** capability

FastLending initiative is designed to address the innovation challenge issued by Commercial Banking.

Key success factors identified to design, build and launch an impactful product:
1. **A rigourous end-to-end process to manage innovation**
2. **Effective Fintech collaboration**
3. **Agile Ways of Working**
4. **Systematic user/client validation**

SME lending Innovation challenge

- **For clients:** faster, more convenient and transparent, digital offering
  - Up to $100K unsecured lending
  - Application and decision <1 day
  - Fulfilment <1week

- **For bankers:** enhanced lending application process and tool
  - ~93,000 eligible customers
  - Simplify process process and co-locate roles
  - New portal, co-designed with selected key users

Source: Digital Pathways

"SME lending is down 12.5% the past two years," said Oliver. "We're trying to stop the bleeding. Here's our goal: *To develop, test, and launch a digital application in 14 weeks.* Target outcome: SME clients can secure loans of *up to $100,000 SGD* from a smartphone in *24 hours or less.*"

"What's the size of the prize?" Oliver continued. "The market is substantial and we only need a small part to meet our targets. If we can create something special, the upside is enormous. Doing so involves passing three tests. Is it desirable? Is it feasible? Is it viable?" **[See Figure 8.4]**

"So what does the QuickLoan PoV look like in practice?" Oliver went on. "Let's look at it from two perspectives:

Client perspective: We want to build a simple to use, fast and convenient digital application for Small-Medium Business lending ($100K unsecured)

APB perspective: We want to enrich our internal data sets by harnessing external data, so that we can expedite process step 3, *Know*

Figure 8.4   SME Lending PoV – Do We Have a Problem Worth Solving?

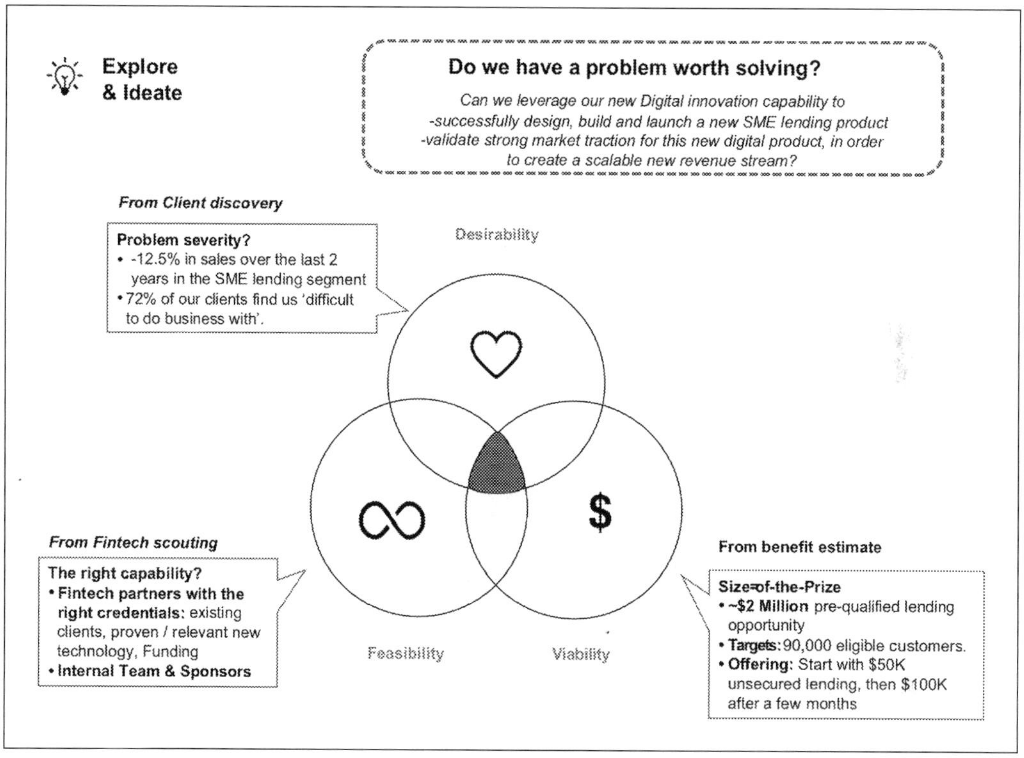

Source: Digital Pathways

Your Client and their Business (KYC-B), and process step 4, *Appraisal & Decision*. We can achieve this by collaborating with the Fintech *Data Clean* and the traditional *Accounting packages* used by our clients." **[See Figure 8.5]**

"Our team includes designers, developers and business analysts." said Oliver, "also known as Hipsters, Hackers and Hustlers. Our cross-functional teams work in time-bound sprints, usually one to two weeks in length. We have daily AM and PM stand-up meetings to track progress, highlight problems and agree on next steps. It's not easy, but we're learning as we go along." **[See Figure 8.6]**

"We started way upstream with the client. We had in-depth discussions with 41 clients and 12 bankers and gained 538 insights. We've launched 10+ prototypes, roughly one every few weeks. You know our mantra: *Does it wow, does it work, can we make money?* We're working our way up the

Figure 8.5   SME Lending PoV – What Are We Trying to Achieve?

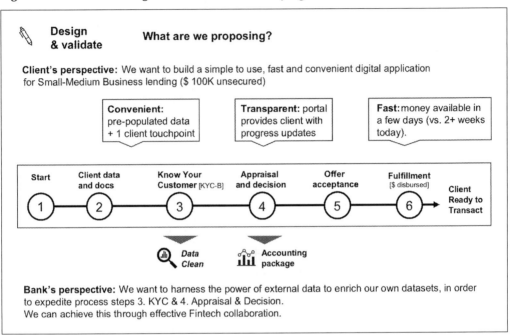

Source: Digital Pathways

Figure 8.6   Setting Up the Project X-Team – 3H Model

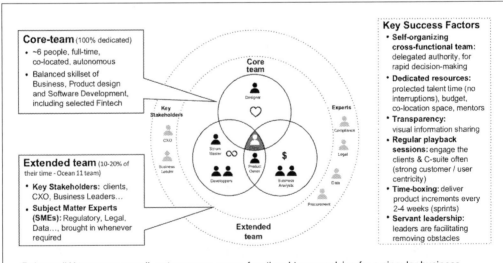

Source: Digital Pathways

hockey stick curve, from Minimum *Lovable* Product, to Minimum Viable Product and Minimum Viable Business.

"With respect to internal processes, we're following the Lean Digital recipe," said Oliver. "Streamline the process by taking out the waste and hassle, deploy smart automation, and harvest the benefits. We mapped our critical value streams end-to-end and aligned them with client jobs-to-be-done and pain points. Here's a picture of our new process. As you can see, we're using the Connectivity Inc. platform to integrate our Fintech partners."
[See Figure 8.7]

Figure 8.7   QuickLoan PoV – Does the Proposed Solution Work?

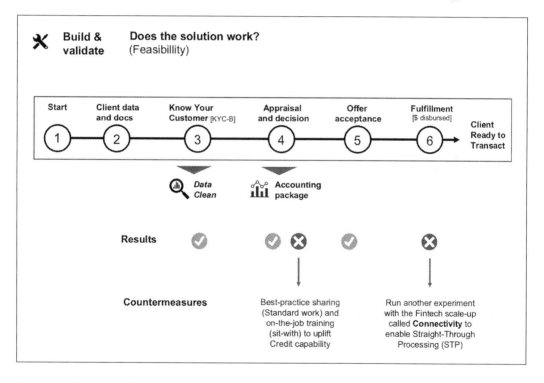

Source: Digital Pathways

"Let me also call attention to our Client Experience work," said Oliver. "We call it ease-of-use *testing*. Our Design coaches have been especially helpful. We're trying to observe and understand *how* our clients experience the application process. Do they find it intuitive, easy-to-use? What steps do they struggle with, and why? What steps make them happy and why? What impact does a given design tweak have?" **[See Figure 8.8]**

Figure 8.8   QuickLoan PoV – Does It Wow Our Clients? (Ease of Use Testing)

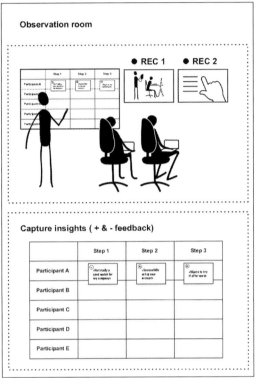

Source: Digital Pathways

"Now I'd like to demonstrate the latest iteration of our QuickLoan app," said Oliver. He spent the next few minutes demonstrating different user cases, easily navigating simple, elegant interfaces.

"That's pretty slick, Ollie," said Martin. "What are your results so far?"

"Here you go," said Oliver. "We're encouraged." **[See Figure 8.9]** "Can we trust your data?" Stephanie asked.

"Our DataClean and JZero partners meet the most stringent FI standards," said Oliver.

"What's your scaling plan?" Marcus asked.

"We're still waiting on Compliance and Procurement," said Oliver. "We may need Martin's help."

Martin put his hands on his head. "Can you talk about lessons learned, Oliver?"

Oliver nodded. "Here's a summary our team put together." **[See Figure 8.10]**

Figure 8.9   QuickLoan PoV – Can we Make Money? (Measuring Impact)

Launch (Pilot)

Impact delivered (a few months after the Soft Launch)

Operational performance

Quality (% First Time Right)	👍	+33%
Speed (# working days) -Time To Decision -Time To Cash	⏱	-87%
Employee engagement	♥	+39%

Financial performance

| Customer Satisfaction -Net Promoter Score (NPS) | ☺ | +19% |
| New business % sold through digital channel | $ | +24% |

| Productivity (# Cases/ FTE /week) | 📈 | +250% |
| Unit Cost of transaction | $ | -27% |

Source: Digital Pathways

Figure 8.10   Lessons Learned from the Soft Launch (Are We Ready to Scale?)

Launch (Pilot)

Lessons learned (from the Soft Launch)

What works?

- Pragmatic Innovators framework
  - Ensure members of the X-team share the same logic, speak the same language
  - Design Thinking + Agile + Lean experimentation = breakthrough results, in a few months
- Learning Lab = showcase new Ways of Working [nWoW], progress and results.
  - Have Senior leaders and staff visit the new environment often. Lab participants to answer their questions.
- Rapid prototyping **requires** visible and frequent sponsorship from the top

What must be improved?

- Market traction trumps everything!
  - Smart cannibalization > status quo
- Scaling is hard!
  - Anticipate early how to integrate PoC into IT legacy system + current operations
- End-to-end approach, from the beginning
  - Using client journey to accelerate reform of operating model (people, process, technology)
- Extend intrapreneurhsip program
  - Need a standard way to identify intrapreneurs [DNA test] and groom them to become our Change Ambassadors

→ What's next: How to replicate this proven approach in other Businesses, teams, markets, segments, internal processes... ?

Source: Digital Pathways

"And here are a few of my own:

- Start with the client and Design sprints,
- Engage Technology, Operations and the Business from the start,
- Think end to end, lean out the process then automate what you can,
- Make sure you have a good Lean and Agile coach,
- Work around legacy IT systems with Fintech partners (Connectivity Inc.),
- Work around Data problems with partners (like DataClean and JZero)."

"Here's a question for our Fintech partners," said Marcus. "How was your on-boarding experience? Did we follow the 5Ps?"

After a series of groans, jokes and droll faces, APB's Fintech partners said their on-boarding experience was 'okay, but not great'. Evidently, Compliance and Procurement still created hassles.

"Here's another question for our Fintech partners," said Yumi. "How well do APB team members practice Lean and Agile methods?"

More groans and funny faces. The Fintech partners put a nice veneer on it, but it was clear that rigor remained a problem at APB. As one joker put it, APB people have 'very good imaginations'.

"Why is Client Satisfaction lagging?" Stephen asked. "We have made it a point of emphasis."

"We're not very good at client empathy," said Oliver. "We did client interviews around problem, solution and market fit, but how well did we listen? Our interviews lack structure, and we like jumping to conclusions. Our Design Thinking sensei, Takeshi, is very good, but I don't think we've fully absorbed his teaching."

After some more questions and comments, the Innovation Board voted to continue funding QuickLoan. Elina thanked everyone for coming and asked for closing comments from Martin and Stephen.

"I'm encouraged," said Martin. "Problems are bubbling up, and we're starting to fix them. Thank you all for staying with it. QuickLoan is still an anomaly at APB, a seedling, vital and full of promise, but vulnerable. We have to nurture, and grow it. And to harvest its full potential, we have to scale it.

"Senior leaders, I need each of you to practice and teach what we're learning here – collaboration across silos and with Fintech partners, client empathy, end-to-end thinking, Lean experiments and new ways of working. QuickLoan is an important milestone, but even bigger challenges are on the horizon."

"I have seen Singapore grow," said Stephen, "from a small, vulnerable island of kampung villages into a confident and thriving country. My dream through all these years has been to see my country become an innovation leader, a truly smart nation. That's what I am beginning to see at Asia Pacific Bank. Thank you all from the bottom of my heart, and please continue."

"This is beginning to make sense, no?" said Marcus Kupper in the elevator.

"Conceptually, yes," Stephanie said. "Practically, I'm still not so sure about these numbers."

"I can accept the QuickLoan numbers," said Stanley Phau, "but we're cannibalizing our existing business. Has Martin considered the impact on jobs?"

"New ways of working, more PoVs, more risk…" said Mohan. "We're not a startup, we're a bank."

Treetop Walk,[7] Central Catchment Nature Reserve, Singapore

Yumi looks out across the forest and the still waters of MacRitchie Reservoir. "This is one of my favorite walks," she says.

They'd arrived early to avoid the heat and hiked an hour through MacRitchie park's lush forest. They'd seen macaque monkeys, squirrels and monitor lizards. Then they'd made their way to this free-standing suspension bridge spanning MacRitchie's highest points.

"I like it very much," said Andy. "It's hard to believe we are in Singapore."

The forest canopy around them is still wet with overnight rain. "There's a cannonball tree," says Yumi, "and a leopard tree."

Andy makes faces at the monkeys. "How is Asia Pacific Bank going?"

"We're making progress," Yumi replies, "but the backlash is building."

"People hate change," says Andy. "Where is the pushback coming from?"

"Compliance and Procurement mainly. Compliance is dragging its feet on both the client on-boarding and QuickLoan PoVs, which means we can't scale. Martin is working on it behind the scenes. He doesn't want to dampen the Learning Lab's enthusiasm."

"Not scaling the PoVs," says Andy, "means that APB's digital strategy has so far generated very little ROI. The year-end review may be challenging."

---

[7] https://www.nparks.gov.sg/gardens-parks-and-nature/parks-and-nature-reserves/central-catchment-nature-reserve/treetop-walk.

CHAPTER 8 – STUDY QUESTIONS

1. Mohan Bilgi says the IT team is torn between 'launching more and more code into an unstable system' and 'keeping the lights on'.
   a. Do similar tensions exist in your organization? Explain your answer.
   b. What are possible approaches to resolving this tension?
2. What does 'governance' obstacle mean?
   a. What are the governance obstacles in your digital transformation?
   b. What are the root causes of each obstacle?
   c. What are possible countermeasures?
3. What are the main elements of the QuickLoan PoV?
   a. How does the approach to QuickLoan differ from that of the Client On-Boarding PoV?
   b. What is the QuickLoan PoV missing? Anything they could do better?
4. Which client journeys in your organization do you think could or should be digitized?
   a. Explain your rationale
   b. What are the obstacles to digitizing these client journeys?
   c. What are the benefits?
5. What are the keys to effective Fintech engagement?
   a. How do you find possible Tech partners for your business?
6. How do you get up the hockey stick curve?
   a. What are some of the key milestones?
   b. What are some common challenges?
7. What are the main elements of Agile product development?
   a. What are some common challenges?
   b. What does Dual Track Agile management mean?

Chapter 9

Year-End Review at Asia Pacific Bank

The empire strikes back

"Some cause happiness wherever they go; others whenever they go."
— Oscar Wilde (Irish playwright)

Richard Decker's office, Asia Pacific Bank Place, 36th Floor

Richard Decker pours coffee. "So glad you could come, Yumi."

Antique prints cover the walls – temples, colonial buildings, the old port of Singapore…

"These are magnificent," says Yumi.

"Family heirlooms," Decker answers. "My family has been here for over 200 years. We arrived with Raffles."[1]

"What did you want to talk with me about?"

"I'm afraid I have some bad news," Decker says. "We'll have to scale back your Client on-boarding and SME lending PoVs. Both MAS[2] and Nancy Stark are quite clear on this."

"I beg your pardon," says Yumi. "You've talked to both our Regulator and Chief Risk Officer?"

---

[1] Sir Stamford Raffles (1781–1826), the founder of Singapore and British Malaysia.
[2] Monetary Authority of Singapore, financial services regulator.

Richard nods. "The rules are quite clear. We cannot use client data at scale – full stop. Nor is the Cloud acceptable. Lastly, electronic signatures won't do. We need wet signatures."

Decker takes a sip of coffee and looks up at Yumi. "Sorry to be the bearer of bad tidings."

Yumi knows that if these PoVs are shut down, so is APB's transformation. "Have you spoken with Martin Picard or Stephen Kwan?" she asks.

"Not to Martin, I thought you might do so on my behalf. As for Mr. Kwan, yes, I did provide him with a brief summary of the situation. I've also spoken with Mohan Bilgi who is fully aligned with our position."

"You seem quite pleased with yourself," says Yumi.

"Well, just trying to do one's job, protect the bank and all that."

"You know, Richard, I've seen this movie before…"

"But not at Asia Pacific Bank…"

"…and it doesn't end well for laggards," Yumi continues. "The jet is leaving the tarmac, with or without you."

"Perhaps it'll be leaving without *you*, dear Yumi."

Martin Picard's Office, Asia Pacific Bank Place, 37th floor

Martin listened in silence as Yumi summarized her discussion with Richard Decker. Martin had asked Nancy Stark, Chief Risk Officer, and Decker's boss, to join them, and she would be arriving in 15 minutes.

"I'm surprised Decker's taking such a big risk," said Martin. "It suggests that he has support at the Board level and among other senior executives. We have to be careful – he's well connected in Singapore and across East Asia, not to mention the City of London. You should also know that Richard lobbied aggressively for the CEO position. When that didn't go his way, he thought he'd get the Chief Risk Officer job, which was also vacant, but the Board decided to go with Nancy."

"I'm sure Decker is working behind the scenes," said Yumi. "He's likely to have enlisted Mohan Bilgi. Not sure what he's said to Stephen or Nancy. As you say, he has allies on the Board. My guess is he's orchestrating a showdown at our year-end review. It's less than a week away – there could be fireworks."

"I had a good chat with Stephen," Martin said. "He remains committed to our transformation but told me we need to have Nancy and MAS on board."

"We give Nancy regular updates," Yumi said. "No objections so far. As for MAS, their policy is all about openness and innovation.[3,4] Singapore has staked its future on becoming a financial innovation center."

"I'm not too worried about Nancy or MAS," said Martin. "My broader concern is Decker's influence on other senior leaders."

"We're getting pushback from Finance, Procurement, and, surprisingly, the Business," said Yumi. "Stephanie continues to challenge our data. Procurement, like Decker's Compliance group, has been slowing down PoV pilots in other markets. *'Before proceeding, we have to confirm everything with* each *Regulator'*. They're also playing games with our newer FinTech partners. Oliver Chan is furious, as you might imagine."

"What's the business squawking about?"

"The Learning Lab," Yumi replied. "They thought it was a one-and-done affair. They're telling us they can't spare their best people for continuous PoVs."

Nancy Stark arrived a few minutes later. Martin welcomed her and summarized the situation as he understood it. Yumi provided a quick summary of their overall approach, PoVs to date, including QuickLend, and the go-forward plan. "We're getting traction, and regaining the trust of our FinTech partners," she said. "Regulatory hassles and other major delays will set us way back."

Nancy listened in silence. She was an Aussie lawyer who'd grown up in a family restaurant on Lonsdale Street in Melbourne's Greektown. Her personal motto, prominently displayed in her office, along with photos of her now grown children, was: *Let's color within the lines, shall we?*

"I support your overall approach," said Nancy, "but Richard has raised important questions about using client data at scale and on the external Cloud."

"All our PoVs to date are running an on-premise Cloud," said Yumi, "as a compromise with Mohan Bilgi."

Nancy seemed puzzled. "That's not what Richard told me," she said. "On-premise Cloud is no problem."

[3] "Singapore: Banking on the Future", Dec 2017 Interview with MAS Managing Director, Ravi Menon http://www.mas.gov.sg/News-and-Publications/Interviews/2017/Singapore-Banking-on-the-Future.aspx.

[4] "Centre of Connectivity", Feb 2017 Interview with MAS Managing Director, Ravi Menon http://www.mas.gov.sg/News-and-Publications/Interviews/2017/OMFIF-Interview-with-Mr-Ravi-Menon-Managing-Director-Monetary-Authority-of-Singapore.aspx.

"To scale our PoVs," Yumi went on, "we'll need to use the external Cloud. Can you help us with that?"

"MAS is publishing a position paper next month," Nancy answered, "and I'm sure I can get a preview copy. Can I ask you to hold off on a full scale-up for a few weeks?"

Yumi nodded. "Going forward, Nancy, we'd like you into our work more directly. We'd like you to act as our business advisor, helping us with things like scaling new offerings in major markets."

"I'd be happy to help," said Nancy. "In fact, *you* can help me too. Risk management is changing so quickly that my team and I struggle to keep up. Most of us have attended Lean Digital Boot Camps and Lunch & Learns and enjoyed them. But we need to go farther. I'm intrigued by your work on automation, AI and Machine Learning. My gut tells me that Risk is going to have to do the same sort of thing."

"Why don't we schedule some time together in the Learning Lab?" said Yumi. "I'll introduce you to some of our partners. Maybe we can get a Risk-related PoV going."

"That would be great," said Nancy. "Contrary to popular opinion, the Risk team doesn't want to shut down innovation. We just want to prevent fraud and protect the individual client and business client's privacy. And we understand that we have to innovate too."

"Sounds like we're on the same page," said Yumi.

"I appreciate you, Nancy," said Martin. "Thanks for dropping by, and please let us know what happens with MAS."

After Nancy left, Martin said, "Well, that was a pleasant surprise."

"Especially compared to what's coming," said Yumi.

APB Digital Strategy Year-End Review

Board Room, Asia Pacific Bank Place, Level 37

"Welcome to our year-end Digital Strategy review," says Martin. "Digital is a core element of our corporate strategy and warrants a deep dive review. Special thanks to Stephen Kwan and all the other Board members in attendance. Let me begin by reiterating our Aspiration and Winning Logic.

"Our Aspiration is to become *Digital to the core,* and our winning logic is:

1. *Digitize key client journeys*
2. *Progressively simplify and modernize our IT data and infrastructure, and*
3. *Deploy New Ways of Working*

Any reflections or comments? Is our purpose and overall approach still sound?"

Richard Decker smiles, drumming his fingers on the table. He looks over at Mohan Bilgi, who looks down at his notebook. "There is broad agreement among Board members," says Stephen, "that our Aspiration is appropriate, and our winning logic sound."

"Very good," says Martin. "Now I'd like to ask Yumi to summarize our Digital activities and key results this year."

"Let me use a pipeline metaphor to frame our reflections," Yumi begins. "We want to assess not only *end-of-pipe* results, but also *process* metrics. These represent this year's final score, if you will, as well as, how well we played the game. Taken together, they provide important learning and insights into possible next steps. **[See Figure 9.1]**

"Our end-of-pipe results are mixed:

- Revenue, Commercial Banking – *Red*
  - Target: Increase by 20%
  - Actual: Increased by 3.1%
- Cost per Transaction, Commercial Banking – *Yellow*
  - Target: Reduce by 10%
  - Actual: Reduced by 5.6%
- Win Client Service – *Yellow*
  - Target: Gold
  - Actual: Silver
- Save Client-Hours – *Green*
  - Target: 10 million
  - Actual: 16 million

"Our process metrics are generally *Green*. We've made progress in each of our strategic pillars. Here are some highlights:

- We digitized Client on-boarding for 67 products
- APB PayLah! and Paynow for 12,500 SME Clients
- 154 Process Improvement Events

Figure 9.1 Digital Strategy Year-End Summary

Overview:
overall strategy & key pillars (below) are sound

	Target	Actual	Status	Comments
1. Revenue growth: business contribution from digital (digital channels and new offering)	+20%	+3.10%	X	Need to faster capture top-line impact derived from better client experiences and new digital offerings.
2. Cost reduction: financial ROI derived from Lean-Digital transformation initiatives (efficiency gains)	-10%	-5.60%	△	Strong activities have stanched bleeding. Now must get stronger, expand scope and accelerate
3. Technology stronger: connectivity partners, internal/external APIs	Win Cust Service Gold	Silver	△	We've turned corner - now accelerate
4. People & Culture turning	Save 10 MM customer-hrs	16 MM	✓	Keys: PIE program, digitization bootcamps, nWoW Academy

Goal: Our clients can reach us anywhere, anytime via smartphone

Goals	Activities	YTD Results Target	Actual	Eval.	Comments/Concerns	Next Steps/Learning Points
A. Get Digital to the Core	Digitize Customer On-boarding	50 products	50 products	✓		
	APB PayLah! - SME clients	15,000	12,500	△	Launch delays, now addressed	
	API connect - in-house systems	50	59	✓	Connectivity platform - fine enabler	
	API connect – external partners	50	85	✓	Massive reduction in paper systems	
B. Digitize critical the Client Journeys	Map critical Customer Journeys	65	52	△	On-boarding cycle times cut up to 50%	
	Build on-line access for SME customers	25%	31%	✓	Record Customer Sat levels	
	Enable on-line remittances	25%	37%	✓		
	Engage SME customers - BizPro App	24,000	36,900	✓	BizPro app close to inflection point	
C. Change culture through Leadership development program and new Ways of Working (nWoW) Academy to grow pragmatic innovators network	Rapid Digitization Boot Camps	96	127	✓	Learning Lab active, well received	Introduce Healthy Worker program
	Start-Up Exchanges	6	8	✓		
	API Hackathons	12	11	△	Accelerate API development	
	API partnerships	12	12	✓		
	Launch APB Academy in SNG (pilot)	240 students	480 students	✓	Employee trust & engagement improving	Accelerate
	Experiments	100	160	✓		

Legend: ✓ On target △ Watch out X Trouble

Source: Digital Pathways

- 127 Boot Camps – Digital, Essential 8 Technologies, Lean Startup, Design
- 11 API Hackathons, 12 API partnerships
- 8 Startup Exchanges
- 12,300 employees involved in innovation programs
- 160 experiments
- 34 certified APB Intrapreneurs
- 11 PoVs launched, with the following aggregated results:
  - Client experience: 40% improvement
  - Turn-around Time: 73% reduction
  - Productivity savings to date: $32 million SGD
  - First Time Right: 50% improvement

"We began with a deep dive into core Client journeys," Yumi resumes, "which helped us understand our blockers. We implemented a plan to close the gaps in technology, capability, management system and culture. We set up our Innovation Platform and Learning Lab, found an excellent Director, and built a solid team around him. We reached out and engaged Fintech partners. We now have a portfolio of 11 PoVs aligned with our Digital Strategy and Aspiration. With each PoV we build our muscles for greater challenges. Now I'd like to do a deeper dive on a handful of representative PoVs. Let's begin with Client On-boarding..."

Yumi concludes her review. "Any questions or comments?"

"I appreciate the clarity of your presentation," says Stephen. "It's refreshing to have frank discussions based on facts."

"Only one Green out of four," says Richard Decker. "A disappointing result, Yumi, wouldn't you say?"

"Our Growth and Cost results are the best in a decade," says Martin. "We have Reds because we set aggressive targets. I can live with that."

"Our in-process metrics are largely *Green*," says Marcus, "but our end-of-pipe results are *Red*. What does that mean?"

"It means two things," Yumi replies. "We have to accelerate our activities..."

"Hold on," says Decker. "I think it means we have the *wrong* strategy."

Yumi turns to Decker, "and it also means our blockers are holding us back."

"Oh really, Yumi," says Decker, "are we going to start scapegoating?"

"With respect, Yumi," says Stephanie, "I don't trust your PoV results."

"We've had this discussion a number of times, Stephanie."

"My books are audited, not yours," says Stephanie. "If there's something wrong, I'll be the one going to jail."

"As I've suggested, please give us a scorekeeper," says Yumi, "so we'll have numbers we can all agree on."

"I'll do that," says Stephanie. "But I have a related concern. Why are we moving so fast? We're causing tremendous disruption to our core business. Why don't we slow down and catch our breath?"

"I have a different concern," says Stanley Phau. "Many of these PoVs have the potential to cannibalize our existing business. What's going to happen to the people who lose their jobs? Are we going to fire people? Is that how we cash out?"

"Our policy is very clear," says Martin. "All employees freed up by process improvement will have the opportunity for retraining. You know that, Stanley. And how do we cash out? We do *more* with the same number of people."

"Well, right now it all seems theoretical to me," Stanley replies.

"I have an even more basic problem," says Richard Decker, shaking his head. "*Risk* ... risk of fraud, cyberattacks, financial contagion, and privacy breaches. As company directors, many of us face substantial *personal* liability. As Stephanie says, if something goes awry, we'll be the ones facing the Regulator. And how do we avoid our personal liabilities? How do we protect our Clients' data and privacy? The Regulator has been very clear. *No Cloud* and *no* scaling with Client data – *full stop.*"

The air is thick with tension. Board members are talking earnestly in hushed tones. Richard Decker gives Martin an almost imperceptible wink. Executives rub their eyes or pretend to look out the window. Stephen looks over at Martin and Yumi with concern. **[See Figure 9.2]**

Martin stands up. "I'm surprised by your comments, Richard. Your boss and our Chief Risk Officer, Nancy Stark, has received an advance copy of the latest MAS policy paper. I believe she shared it with you, but perhaps you haven't bothered to read it.

"Let me extract the salient points for you," Martin continues. "MAS policy has shifted; the Regulator is now encouraging Singapore's banking community to *accelerate* their journey to the Cloud and to open banking. In other words, the Smart City[5] is acting like a smart city."

"Look, Martin, I haven't read the paper," says Decker. "But the fact remains, we *cannot* open up to Fintechs in the way you're proposing without severe risk." Decker turns to Mohan Bilgi. "Isn't that right, Mohan?"

---

[5] The city of Singapore was chosen as the Smart City of 2018 at the Smart City Expo World Congress to recognize the most outstanding initiatives and projects in the urban innovation and transformation industry.

Figure 9.2   The Jaws of Culture

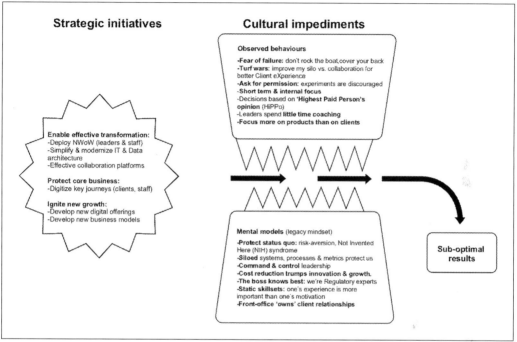

Source: Digital Pathways, adapted from Senn Delaney, Heidrick & Struggles

Mohan shifts awkwardly in his chair. "Actually, that's not true, Richard," he says. "I've been pleasantly surprised by our Fintech partners' risk management practices, which in many cases exceed our own."

Decker shakes his head again. "Well that's not what you've been telling the Compliance team."

"Leaving Risk and liability aside," Decker continues, "let me shine a light on another proverbial elephant in this room. *Return on Investment...* just where is it? We've spent a fortune hiring, staffing and training, and what do we have to show for it? Modest improvements in Revenue and Cost, which in my view are merely due to cyclical effects. I repeat, *where is the ROI?* As a shareholder and Director, I am frankly appalled at the wanton waste of precious resources."

The tension in the room is peaking. Board members fidget, and senior leaders look out the window some more.

"There's no ROI, Richard," says Yumi, "because you and the Compliance team have been blocking PoV deployment. We have world class results, but we cannot scale. Please explain why you're blocking the Client on-boarding and QuickLoan PoVs? The size of the prize is enormous. As a shareholder and Director, I would expect you to expedite them. Instead, you've been sitting on them for months now. *Please explain...*"

Decker is not used to direct challenges. "Well, I'm simply fulfilling my duties as a senior Risk and Compliance officer. I cannot sit idly as Asia Pacific Bank squanders the hard-won trust of its Clients and the Regulator. Nor can I allow APB to squander resources pursuing trendy endeavours with little hope of ROI."

"You don't get it, do you, Richard?" says Martin. "Despite all the coaching and training, you *just don't get it.* Our Digital activities are not about ROI, at least not yet. We're creating new *businesses.* We're buying profit *insurance.* We're protecting ourselves thereby, against future losses. Our intrapreneurs are like wild-catters in the oil and gas industry, drilling exploratory wells. Most of them will be dry, but now and then we'll hit a gusher. And why do we do this? Because we know that our existing wells are drying up."

Martin spreads his arms wide. "Board members, senior leaders and friends, in today's uncertain world, it's no longer safe to 'play it safe'. Doing nothing is the riskiest thing we can do. We've just taken our first steps on a long journey. Our PoV results are world class; once we scale the numbers will speak for themselves. After one short year, there's a palpable buzz across Commercial Banking, an energy that has been lacking in our company. Silos are dissolving, we're gluing our IT systems together and collaborating like never before. FinTechs are lining up to work with us.

"I know the obstacles are enormous. We've barely scratched the surface when it comes to Technology. When it comes to Culture, we don't know what we don't know. But the ship is already turning. Let me address the nay-sayers in this room. We are going to do this – with or without you. We are going to succeed beyond any possibility of doubt. If there is anybody who doubts this let them leave now."

The Boardroom was silent. Richard Decker is visibly flustered. Stephanie Shan and Stanley Phau look at one another in silence. Yumi gives Martin a barely perceptible nod.

"Thank you all for a difficult but necessary discussion," said Stephen. "I know emotions are running high. Let me speak on behalf of the Board. This is a journey we *have* to make. To our naysayers I ask, *what is the alternative?* Singapore's future hinges on the kind of transformation Asia Pacific Bank has embarked on.

"I am confident that APB's overall strategy is correct, and I know that my confidence reflects that of the Board. Nobody can predict where technology and the client will take us. Sometimes by walking we find out where we are going. We are going to continue on this great journey. Thank you all for your energy and commitment this year, and for your honesty today."

Asia Pacific Bank Place, Martin Picard's Office, 37th Floor

A few days later...

Richard Decker strides into Martin's office, nods at Martin and notices Stephen Kwan standing at the window. "Ah, Stephen, I didn't expect to see you here."

"Hello, Richard, glad you could join us," Martin replies. "Please sit down. Look, I'm going to be brief. You've lied about MAS policy around the Cloud and Open Innovation. You tried to manipulate Mohan into blocking our PoVs. There is strong evidence that you've actively hindered our client on-boarding and QuickLend PoVs, even though the Compliance team broadly supports them. All this amounts to sabotage, for which there is only one appropriate response. I expect your resignation by the end of the day."

Decker looks at Stephen Kwan, then at Martin. "Well, well, well, Martin," he says. "Never thought you had it in you. Dismissing our senior Compliance executive in a time of complex and growing risk, are we? Are you prepared to face the music at MAS? It'll be three months and they could reverse this decision. You *may* be forced to take me back. Imagine *that...*"

"I want you the hell out of here, Richard."

"Richard, it is time for you to go," says Stephen quietly.

CHAPTER 9 – STUDY QUESTIONS

1. Define 'Jaws of Culture'
   a. What are some of the core elements of the 'Jaws'?
   b. What are the root causes and possible countermeasures?
2. How do leading organizations protect digital transformation from the 'Jaws'?
   a. How effective have these measures been?
3. 'It's no longer safe to play it safe'.
   a. What does Martin mean by this?
   b. Is this true in your industry? Explain your answer.
   c. Do you have any relevant personal experiences?
   d. Explain Martin's 'wild-catter' metaphor.
4. *The best approach to digital transformation is to take the transformation outside the organization* (e.g. in a joint venture, or entirely new company).
   a. What are the pros and cons of such an approach?
   b. What would this look like in your organization?
   c. Which approach would be best for organization?

Chapter 10

How Do We Accelerate Our Digital Transformation?

Everybody wants to go to heaven, but nobody wants to die

When the winds of change blow, some people build walls and others build windmills.

Lao Tzu (Chinese philosopher)

Maison Ikkoku,[1] Bugis, Singapore

Stephen, Martin, and Yumi sink into their chairs. The bar is cool and empty this late afternoon. In the nearby mosque, the muezzin is completing the call to prayer. The bartender asks how they're feeling.

"A bit stressed," says Martin.

"Then you need something to calm the mind," says the bartender, going off to make bespoke cocktails.

"What did you think of our year-end review?" Yumi asks.

"I think we surfaced important problems," says Stephen. "I imagine our transformation will go easier now."

---

[1] http://www.ethanleslieleong.com/.

"It was a close thing," says Martin. "Without your support, Stephen, the outcome would've been different. We're lucky Mohan switched sides. Looks like we've gained his trust."

"Now that we have Nancy and Mohan on side," says Stephen, "I expect Richard will resign."

"I like how you handled Decker, Yumi," says Martin. *"Please explain..."*

"That's one of my father's expressions."

"What's next, Yumi?" Stephen asks.

"With respect, Stephen, I don't think things are going to be easier now. In fact, we're at the most vulnerable moment in our journey."

"Do tell," says Martin.

"Innovation fatigue is setting in," Yumi answers. "Our Lean Digital team has no more capacity, and we lack sustaining infrastructure. We need to resupply, and refocus for the next part of the journey."

"Let's talk more about this tomorrow," says Martin. "Today, let's celebrate an eventful year.

The drinks arrive, glorious creations reflecting their shared mood. They click glasses. *Yum seng*.

How Do We Accelerate?

Martin Picard's Office, One Month Later

Martin welcomes Yumi, Marcus Kupper, and Mohan Bilgi to his office. "Many transformations burn out about now," Martin begins. "So says our Sherpa, and I believe her. How do we avoid this fate, and how do we accelerate our transformation? That's why we're here today. I've asked Yumi to lead our discussion."

"We've scored some goals," Yumi begins, "and had some victories. People are on a high. The blockers, meanwhile, have gone underground and are biding their time. Innovation fatigue is setting in. Emotionally, there's nowhere to go but *down*. The Lean Digital team, meanwhile, is at maximum capacity. It's not big enough to take APB to the next level. All this is part of a broader problem: we lack sustaining infrastructure.

"To frame our situation let me introduce a metaphor: the innovation tree. **[See Figure 10.1]** To grow juicy fruit, we need good soil and a healthy trunk. The soil, of course, represents our culture, how we think and behave. The trunk represents how we work.

Figure 10.1   Digital Innovation Tree Metaphor

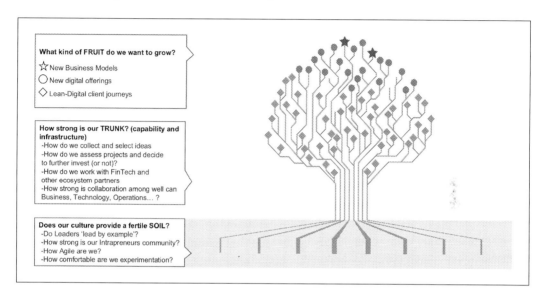

Source: Digital Pathways, inspired by Ed Essey @ Microsoft Garage

"So how do we accelerate our transformation?" Yumi continues. "We have to decide what kind of fruit we want, and we have to tend to our soil and trunk. What does this all mean?

■ What kind of *fruit* do we want to grow, and in what *mix*? Our options include: [per Figure 5.4]
   • Re-invent client journeys ('diamonds')
   • Launch new digital offerings ('coins')
   • Launch new digital businesses, ('stars', usually based on disruptive technology)
■ How healthy is our *trunk*? (Are our core systems in good shape?)
   • People system: mindset and skill set, for both leaders and staff
   • Work system: organization, processes and technology
   • Management System: Lighthouse (visual management), tiered huddles, operating rhythms, strategy development and deployment process
■ How innovation-friendly is our *soil*?
   • How well do leaders practice what they preach?
   • Client-focus, rapid prototyping and Lean experimentation?
   • Do we practice and reward agile Ways of Working?

Everybody wants the fruit, but not everybody wants to attend to the soil and tree."[2]

"Reminds me of an old blues song," says Martin. "*Everybody wants to go to heaven, but nobody wants to die.*"[3]

"So how do we enrich the soil and strengthen the trunk?" Marcus asks.

Yumi passes out a summary paper.

We have four levers to accelerate our digital transformation:
1. Deploy our Three Swimlane model across Commercial Banking
2. Expand our Pragmatic Innovator Network and kickstart our intrapreneurship program (InnoBox)
3. Improve Innovation Governance,[4] deploy Client Experience councils (focused on diamonds) to support the Innovation Council (focused on coins & stars)
4. Simplify and modernize our Technology stack and Data architecture

---

At first this may seem overwhelming. Please remember we'll implement it in stages, over a number of years, and that we'll have regular playbacks in the Lighthouse. Now let me elaborate on each element."

Accelerator 1: Deploy Our Three Swimlane Model across Commercial Banking

"Our transformation recipe is designed for scalability," says Yumi, "and, as you know, involves three swimlanes:

1. Leaders Development,
2. Pragmatic Innovators Network, and
3. Focused innovation projects, aligned with strategy.

Deploying it across all of Commercial Banking means more people involved, more pilot sites, more PIEs, Boot Camps, Lunch and Learns, Hackathons, and the like.

Here's what it looks like, as well as, a simplified overview of identified innovation projects." **[See Figure 10.2]**

---

[2] Hat tip to Ed Essey and our great discussion during San Francisco Lean Startup Conference 2019.

[3] The lyrics to a classic blues song. Here's Albert King's version: https://www.youtube.com/watch?v=Lb-EJEWRxlM.

[4] Effective innovation governance means getting better and faster at finding and funding the right projects, and culling losing ideas.

Figure 10.2   Deploy Three Swimlane Model across Commercial Banking

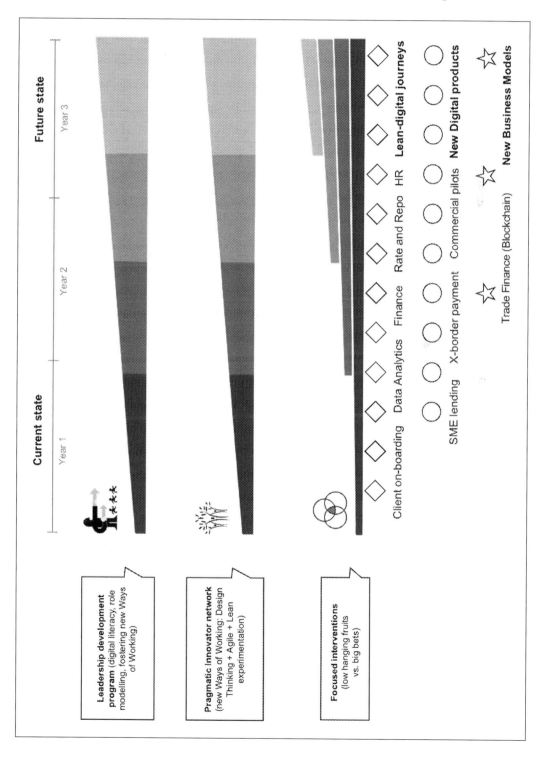

Source: Digital Pathways

Martin, Mohan, and Marcus absorb the paper in silence. "This is compelling, Yumi," says Mohan. "I like the concrete examples of diamonds, coins and stars."

"Our people understand the three swimlane model," says Marcus. "The Lean Digital team is good at deploying it, and we've had good results in our pilot areas."

Accelerator 2: Expand Our Pragmatic Innovators Network and Kickstart Our Intrapreneurship Program 'InnoBox'

Pragmatic Innovator Network – 'Team of Teams' Approach

"The Pragmatic Innovator Network, our middle swimlane, is a core infrastructure element," says Yumi. "We need more *intrapreneurs* on the ground, to serve as innovation coaches, and to help feed our innovation funnel.

Overtime, we want to supplement top-down innovation with homegrown, bottom-up ideas. Thereby, we'll tap into what my father calls our '*organizational genius*'. With time, the network will evolve into a 'team of teams', with the Lean Digital team at its hub."

Martin, Marcus and Mohan absorb this.

"It's a big stretch," says Mohan. "We've never asked our employees to do this before."

"I like the idea of an informal network," says Marcus, "but it's a big cultural shift indeed."

"We'll have to carefully screen network members," Martin says. "We want T-shaped[5] individuals with a strong sense of purpose and initiative."

"An army of Oliver Chans would be nice," says Mohan.

"I agree on all counts," says Yumi. "My team is working with HR to define our target profile, our Intrapreneurs DNA test, if you will. And also to ensure that innovation work is recognized when it comes to promotion. On a related note, we'll need to augment our budget to support intrapreneur 'Fellowships', comprising, say, six or eight rotating Lean Digital team positions. Each year we'll train and certify 'Fellows' and then redeploy them as coaches in their home departments."

---

[5] See Chapter 5.

"Will these be full time positions?" Marcus asks. "We can't afford more bureaucracy."

"Redeployed intrapreneur Fellows would spend, say, 20% of their time on innovation-related work," says Yumi. "We fill fellowship positions based on strategic need. Technology fellowships would be a priority, for example."

"This makes sense," says Mohan. "I'm especially interested in building DevOps capability."

"How do you make it easier for our people to develop their ideas?" Martin asks. "Suppose I'm a motivated young person with a great idea. I've been through our intrapreneur boot camps, and I understand the core methodologies. How do I get the funding, support and executive air cover needed to scale my idea? In today's APB, most bosses would say *forget it!*"

"And how do we create more coins and star innovations?" Marcus asks. "Diamond (efficiency) innovations are necessary, but they're not sufficient."

InnoBox Program: Enabling Innovators

"Great questions," says Yumi. "We've looked at a number of open source innovation methodologies. We particularly like Kickbox[6] which was invented by Mark Randall at Adobe. Employees with ideas receive a red box containing everything you need to get started. Employees pitch their ideas to a panel of senior leaders. If the data is persuasive, they get more money and support, as in the popular 'Shark Tank' TV shows. This is 'metered funding' at its most basic. Kickbox provides employees with money, time, training, and the permission to innovate. Here's how we're proposing to tailor it to APB."

"We call it *InnoBox*," says Yumi, "and as you can see, it's an end-to-end innovation process. We want to help our people turn promising ideas into successful businesses." **[See Figure 10.3]**

---

[6] Hat tip to Adobe and Mark Randall. www.Kickbox.org is the non-profit association and collaborative community of best practices that curates, distributes, and supports Kickbox, ensuring it continues to evolve as a shared resource.

Figure 10.3   InnoBox Intrapreneurship Program – Building Innovation Capability at Scale

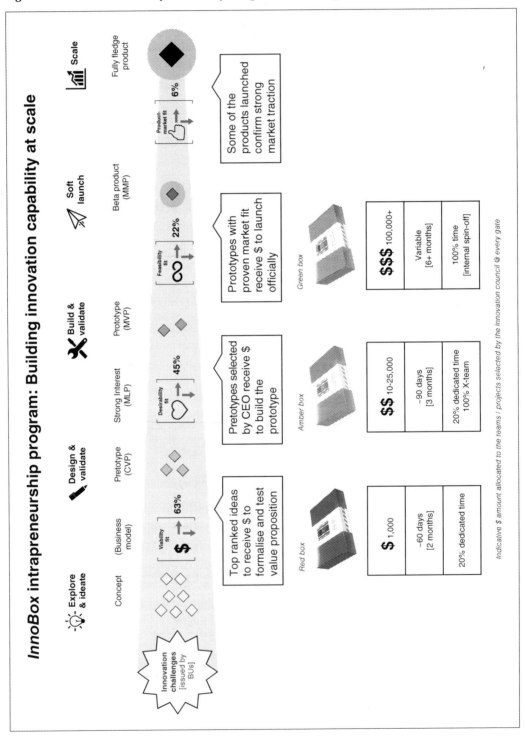

Source: Digital Pathways, inspired by Mark Randall's KickBox program @ Adobe

"Can you take us through each step, Yumi-san?" Martin asks.

The purpose of InnoBox program is to foster intrapreneurship and corporate innovation.

Our overarching goal is to create a movement, a community of intrapreneurs: we want to see more and more employees saying *'I am the CEO of my idea', 'I want to create my own startup within APB'*.

In order to generate fresh ideas, we organize regular events and collaboration opportunities with promising Fintech startups. In order to get ideas off the ground, we provide our employees and managers with a series of guided steps, access to seasoned mentors and other innovation service providers. Beyond training and support, we want to ensure that intrapreneurial talent within APB have a chance to bake their innovative ideas into the reality of customer development and market validation.

The InnoBox program is organized around the following milestones:

- **Start.** To focus effort and generate ideas to solve tangible business and/or client issues we need some *trigger events*. We typically start with innovation challenges issued by APB and/or a specific Business Unit. Employees can submit their ideas to address those challenges, as individuals or small teams.
- **The Red Box (explore and ideate, design and validate).** In order to remove friction to innovate, selected participants receive a Red Box containing
  - a pragmatic innovators playbook
  - a $1,000 prepaid card
  - the right to dedicate one day a week to their project.

Participants have 60 days to formalize their Business Model, clarify which problems to solve for which audience, design and validate their value proposition with their target customers or clients. This early stage prototype is often called a pretotype.[7] Are potential customers / clients willing to buy your proposition? The value proposition and testing data are pitched to the Innovation Council. Selected propositions (~45%) can proceed to the next step and receive an Amber Box.

- **The Amber Box (build and validate).** With evidence of market interest, participants receive additional funding (often $10,000+) and a stronger, more stable cross-functional team of Hustlers, Hipsters and Hackers. Each team has 90 days to build a prototype, often called Minimum Viable Product

---

[7] Hat tip to Alberto Savoia and his book "The Right It: Why So Many Ideas Fail and How to Make Sure Yours Succeed".

(MVP). The MVP and learning derived from customer / client testing are pitched to the Innovation Council. Working prototypes supported by evidence of early market traction receive a Green Box (~22%).

- **The Green Box (soft market launch).** A working prototype with the most critical features is often called Minimum Marketable Product (MMP). At that stage, the team receives additional resources (up to $100,000+ funding) to commercialize this 'Beta Product'. During the next 6 months, the selected teams are able to work full-time with the business to launch and scale their product.
- **Product-market fit (scaling).** Some Prototypes do confirm strong market traction. When that happens, those products can be "spun-out" into a startup within APB's innovation hub.

"We'll also protect people's availability (20% at the start), and provide mentoring and visible executive support."

"Enabling innovators," says Marcus, "is a powerful concept, but again, very different from anything we've done before."

"I like the idea, but need time to absorb it," Martin says. "Can you tell us more about accelerator 3?"

Accelerator 3: Improve Innovation Governance

"As you know, APB has two very different challenges," Yumi answers. "We have to protect our *core* business, and grow *new* business. These entail different types of innovation, and a different pace and governance.

1. *Protect core business:* involves efficiency innovation projects (diamonds), that provide quick and obvious ROI. These are usually so-called 'no brainer' incremental projects, and will be governed by *Client Experience Councils (CEC)*. The goal here is to free up cash to fund other innovations.
2. *Growing new business:* involves sustaining and breakthrough innovation (coins and stars), wherein we invest to learn through rapid testing with clients. These are often disruptive projects and involve risky investments in unfamiliar technologies, markets, products, and/r partnerships. Coins and stars will be governed by the *Innovation Council (IC)*. The overarching goal here is to reinvent ourselves and generate new sources of growth."

Martin, Mohan and Marcus are silent again. "This makes sense," says Martin finally. "Otherwise, the Innovation Council will become a bottleneck. How many CECs do you envision, Yumi?"

"I propose we deploy five CECs next year," Yumi answers, "each comprising business line leaders, and chaired by Martin. We want to encourage ownership and friendly competition."

"Five mini-Shark Tanks throughout Commercial Banking," says Martin. "I like the idea, but I don't think I can attend all the meetings."

"Marcus, Mohan or I can support the councils in your absence," says Yumi. "With time, we also want to pull in other senior leaders."

"We'll have to select Council members carefully," says Marcus. "And they'll need coaching..."

"I kicked this off by asking how to accelerate this thing," Martin says. "Looks like we have many arrows in the quiver."

Yumi nods and passes out a one-pager. "Here's another way of looking at our innovation journey. We started in the bottom-left corner and are evolving toward the top-right corner." This is a visual overview of APB's initiatives to strengthen and scale our nascent innovation ecosystem.
[See Figure 10.4]

The senior leaders absorb the image in silence. "A splendid image," says Marcus, finally. "Well done Yumi."

"I like it too," says Martin. "Let me change gears again. What's the plan around Technology?"

"Mohan and I have been working together on this one," says Yumi. "Mohan, can I ask you to present our thoughts?"

Accelerator 4: Levelling Up Our Technology

Open Banking

"Let's begin with 'Open Banking'," says Mohan. "Cloud, APIs, microservices, ecosystems – all the current technical discourse relate to this concept. Open Banking entails shifting:

- From a *closed* system wherein client data is kept in the bank (as in a vault),
- To an *open* ecosystem, wherein data is shared between ecosystem members (e.g. other banks, Fintechs, government agencies, utilities).

Figure 10.4   Scaling Our Innovation Ecosystem – Internal and External Collaboration

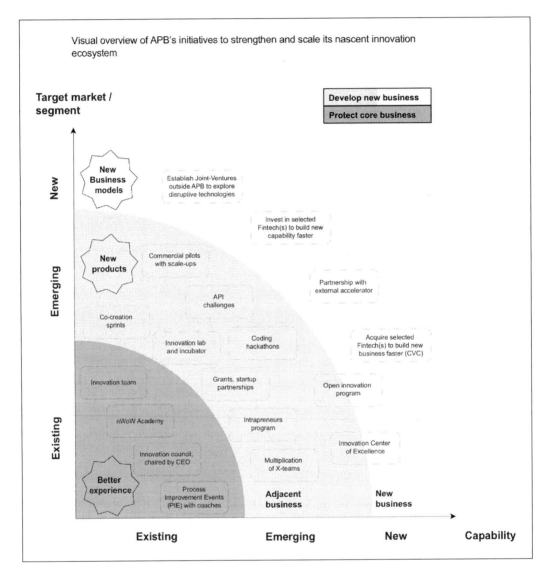

Source: Digital Pathways

We have no choice with respect to data-sharing - regulatory changes like PSD2[8] compel it, not to mention Tech innovation.

"So why is this important? We're a traditional bank operating in a closed system. We control our resources, assets and resources, and win by reducing friction and optimizing the entire value chain. Value for APB

[8] Pay Services Directive, legislation issued by the European Union.

is proportional to the *number of clients* we have. The model has worked for centuries, and in plenty of industries, it still works. But as you know Fintechs are attacking the juiciest parts of our value chain. And even more worrisome, a powerful new business model has emerged. Yumi, can you please elaborate?"

"Digital *platforms* operate under an entirely different logic," says Yumi, "and have devastated pipeline businesses in many industries. For example, when the iPhone arrived in 2007, the five major mobile-phone manufacturers – Nokia, Samsung, Motorola, Sony Ericsson, and LG – controlled 90% of the industry's global profits. They had all the classic strategic advantages: strong brands and product differentiation, strong logistics and operating systems, regulatory protection, large R&D budgets, and huge scale economies. And yet, by 2015, iPhone alone generated more than 90% of the global profits, while all but one of the incumbents made no profit at all.[9]

"How can we explain the iPhone's rise?" Yumi continues. "The answer is the *App Store* – a digital distribution platform, developed and maintained by Apple for mobile apps on its iOS operating system. The App Store allows users to browse and download apps developers create using Apple's iOS software development kit. Value created is proportional to the *number of users multiplied by the number of developers.*

"Apple conceived the iPhone as more than a stand-alone product or pipeline for services. The iPhone was a way of connecting app users and developers in a two-sided market – generating value for both. On its own, the iPhone on its own is essentially a pipeline. But when you connect it with the App Store, a digital marketplace, you have a platform." **[See Figure 10.5]**

"Uber's market cap exceeds that of General Motors," Marcus adds. "Airbnb's market cap exceeds that of any hotel chain. Yumi is right, APB is obviously vulnerable to big tech platforms. But not every platform is a winner. GE's Predix was a flop. Perhaps another time we can talk about why some platforms succeed and others fail."

Yumi nods. "For now, let's summarize our pipeline versus platform discussion. Pipeline growth/value logic is *linear.* APB, a classic pipeline, grows in proportion to the number of clients we have. By contrast, platform growth logic is *exponential.* Platform companies grow in proportion to the

---

[9] "Pipelines, Platforms, and the New Rules of Strategy", by Marshall W. Van Alstyne, Geoffrey G. Parker, and Sangeet Paul Choudery, *Harvard Business Review* April 2016.

Figure 10.5   Evolution from Closed to Open Banking

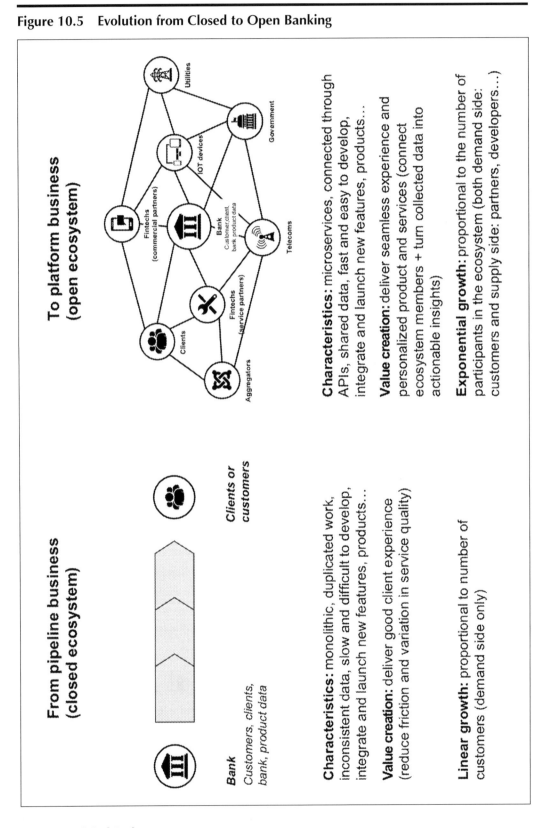

From pipeline business (closed ecosystem)

To platform business (open ecosystem)

Bank
Customers, clients, bank, product data

Clients or customers

Characteristics: monolithic, duplicated work, inconsistent data, slow and difficult to develop, integrate and launch new features, products...

Value creation: deliver good client experience (reduce friction and variation in service quality)

Linear growth: proportional to number of customers (demand side only)

Characteristics: microservices, connected through APIs, shared data, fast and easy to develop, integrate and launch new features, products...

Value creation: deliver seamless experience and personalized product and services (connect ecosystem members + turn collected data into actionable insights)

Exponential growth: proportional to the number of participants in the ecosystem (both demand side: customers and supply side: partners, developers...)

Source: Digital Pathways

size of their *network*, which in The App Store's case includes both users and developers. So, pipeline versus platform growth amounts to X versus X^2 – which is why successful platforms can dominate their markets so completely."

"Let's cut to the chase," says Martin. "What does this all mean for Asia Pacific Bank?"

"We're vulnerable," says Mohan. "FinTechs are attacking the juiciest parts of our value chain. Even more worrisome, Google, Alibaba, Amazon all have established platforms and strong relationships with tens of millions of customers. If and when they choose to enter our markets, we'll be in trouble. Google has already leveraged its platform to enter industries as diverse as mapping, mobile operating systems and home automation. For example, Google is competing directly with Siemens and Honeywell in home thermostats."

"The Fintechs are here," says Marcus, "and the Tech giants are coming. How do we respond?"

"Our options are as follows," says Yumi. "We can:

1. Develop and deliver our own products directly to target markets (also known as 'Specialized Banking').
2. Develop our own products but deliver them through preferred partners like Fintechs and utilities (also known as 'White Label Balance Sheet Operator'), and
3. Build our own platform and deliver a range of products, some homegrown, others provided by partners. Some call this Banking as a Service (BaaS).

All of these options depend on modernizing our Technology stack and data architecture. So how do we do that? Mohan, if you please..."

Open Architecture: API & Microservices

"To get into the game, we have to dramatically improve connectivity, both internal and external," says Mohan. "We want to be *easy* to work so that:

- Clients and customers enjoy banking with us,
- Developers (internal and external) and partners enjoy building apps and products with us,
- Intrapreneurs enjoy working with our rapid prototyping platform.

Figure 10.6   Target Technology Stack for Internal and External Connectivity

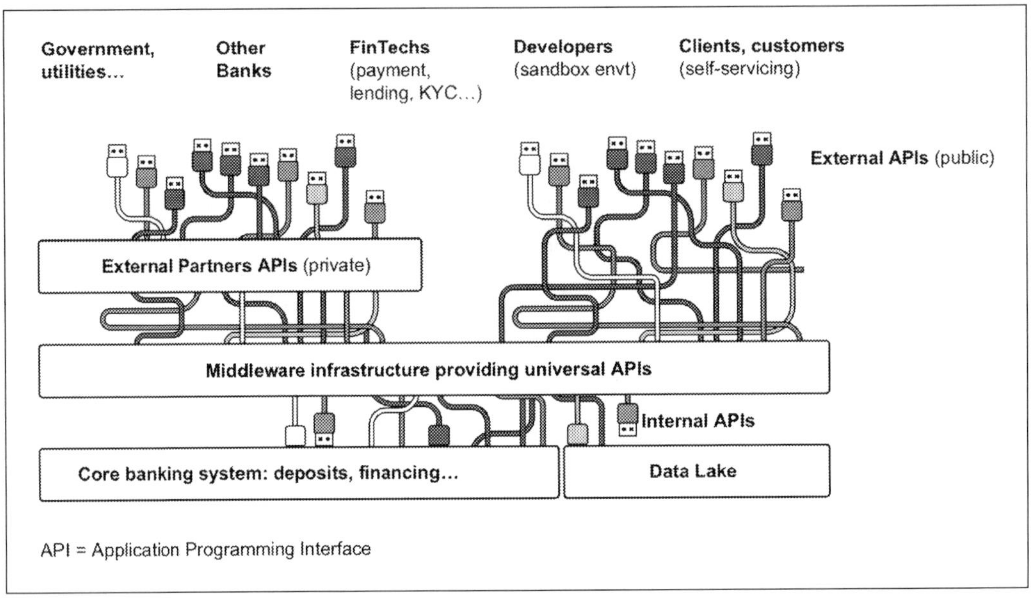

Source: Digital Pathways

In the short term, we'll continue to work with Connectivity Inc. and leverage their middleware system. Susan Tse Lau, their MD, and I believe we can quickly deploy a scalable API and middleware infrastructure. We'll connect everything using three types of APIs:

- *Internal API layer:* to provide our developers with easy access to our core banking system and Data hub. Expected benefits: efficiency, security, cost, and morale,
- *External* Private *API layer:* to help integrate our business with clients, suppliers, providers, resellers and other business partners. Expected benefits: lower transaction costs, security, and revenue through API monetization.
- *External* Public *API layer:* to help developers and external partners build new apps and digital products. Expected benefits: stronger ties with developers, access to a broader market, more innovation." **[See Figure 10.6]**

Mohan pauses. "Any questions?"

"Very clear, thank you," says Marcus. "How do we ensure that our current infrastructure doesn't slow us down?"

Hybrid Cloud and SaaS[10]

"We want to migrate to the Cloud in an orderly way," Mohan says, "though we'll likely have to keep *some* servers on premise. The Cloud confers many advantages in functionality, flexibility, speed and cost. Our migration plan entails stratifying all current applications and platforms according to (a) ease, and (b) benefits of migrating to the Cloud. We apply the so-called Six Rs[11] to prioritize the migration of our applications. Yumi, can you please elaborate?"

"The Six Rs are pretty straightforward," says Yumi.

"Here's what each R entails:

1. **Retain** – keep those workloads in-situ. Do not change them in any way, e.g. AS400 and unresolvable dependencies. This typically can represent 10% of our applications.
2. **Retire** – get rid of underutilised and/or obsolete applications. We will need to further explore this area but it typically can represent 5% of our applications.
3. **Re-host** – those applications require minimal re-engineering and can therefore be the first to migrate to the Cloud, e.g. IP, DNS, file path changes... This approach is often called *'lift and shift'*: it can typically represent up to 40% of our current workload and can deliver significant *'quick wins'*.
4. **Re-platform** – those applications require some changes to fully leverage cloud concepts such as elasticity, failover... This approach is often called *'lift, tinker and shift'*: it can typically represent up to 30% of our current workload, e.g. elastic database infrastructure, scaling and leveraging reserved resources.
5. **Re-factor** – those applications require significant re-engineering in order to run on the cloud, e.g. server-based application to serverless... This area can typically represent 10% of our applications.
6. **Re-purchase** – those applications are candidates for migration to Software-as- a-Service platform, e.g. moving from our homegrown CRM to Salesforce or MS Dynamics. It can typically represent up to 5% of our current workload and can significantly reduce the cost of expensive software licences."

---

[10] SaaS = Software as a Service.
[11] "Six Strategies for Migrating Applications to the Cloud", by Stephen Orban, AWS Cloud Enterprise Strategy Blog, November 2016.

"Mohan and I are working on a three-year Technology plan which we'll share in the next month."

"What do you mean by microservices?" Martin asks.

"Small, loosely coupled and independently deployable services," Mohan answers, "which enable speed and flexibility. Because services are fine, and protocols lightweight, they're a great way to modernize an application portfolio."

"So, you just deploy what you need," says Marcus, "and not the entire code monolith."

Mohan nods in agreement. "By the way, we're also planning learning visits to Cloud-native companies like Google, Amazon, Netflix, Apple, LinkedIn and Facebook. They're very gracious."

"These are going to be *learning* visits," Yumi adds, "and not the notorious 'Silicon Valley petting zoo' stuff. Each attendee will have learning objectives and will have to present what they've learned and how they'll share it."

Martin gives Yumi a thumbs up. "Can you tell us more about Data?"

Data Analytics

"APB data essentially comprises individual customer and business client information, interactions and transactions," says Mohan. "As we all know, our data is neither complete, nor end-to-end, nor of consistent quality. To use it we're having to overcome two blockers:

- Data resides in product silos
- Legacy IT applications that can neither communicate well, nor process large data quantities. Our systems are especially weak at processing unstructured data like video, speech, and images.

"Fintech partner projects," Mohan continues, "have helped enhance our AI and Machine Learning capability. For example, we've used external data to fill in our existing Data assets (e.g. system, application output file, document, database, or web pages directly associated with generating revenue). [**See Figure 10.7**]

"We're making progress on data collection, analysis, insight generation and decision-making," says Mohan. "We can now detect key patterns and relationships using multiple data sources (e.g. financial history, social

Figure 10.7   Data Assets Overview

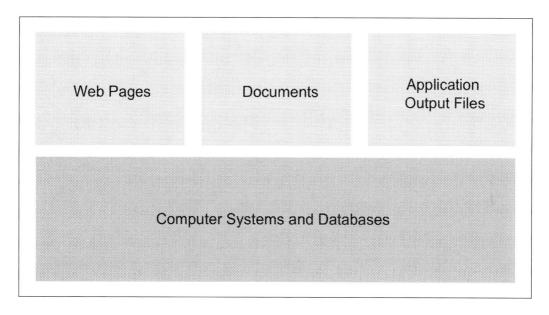

Source: Digital Pathways

media). We're starting to generate actionable insights testing them with clients. Our goal, of course, is to develop personalized experiences and products. We have to balance all this with respect for privacy and apply the highest international standards. Lastly, we've started to hire and develop top-shelf data scientists."

Building Engineering Muscle

"Technical expertise is a major constraint," Yumi says. "To build engineering muscle we're going to accelerate our Hack2Hires and Hackathons. We're also partnering with leading universities by offering promising engineers scholarships followed by job placements."

"HR has to become a source of competitive advantage," says Marcus.

Yumi nods. "Karen Hong and the HR team have done a good job at putting together our *new Ways of Working* (*nWoW*) Academy. The curriculum is modular and stackable. Participants systematically go through our *'Learn, Apply, Deliver'* cycle. We've designed a specific *Agile Developer* certification path, based on the so-called 'winning trio': Agile, DevOps, Cloud. Here's the overview." [**See Figure 10.8**]

Figure 10.8 *nWoW* **Academy – Overview of Agile Developers Certification Path**

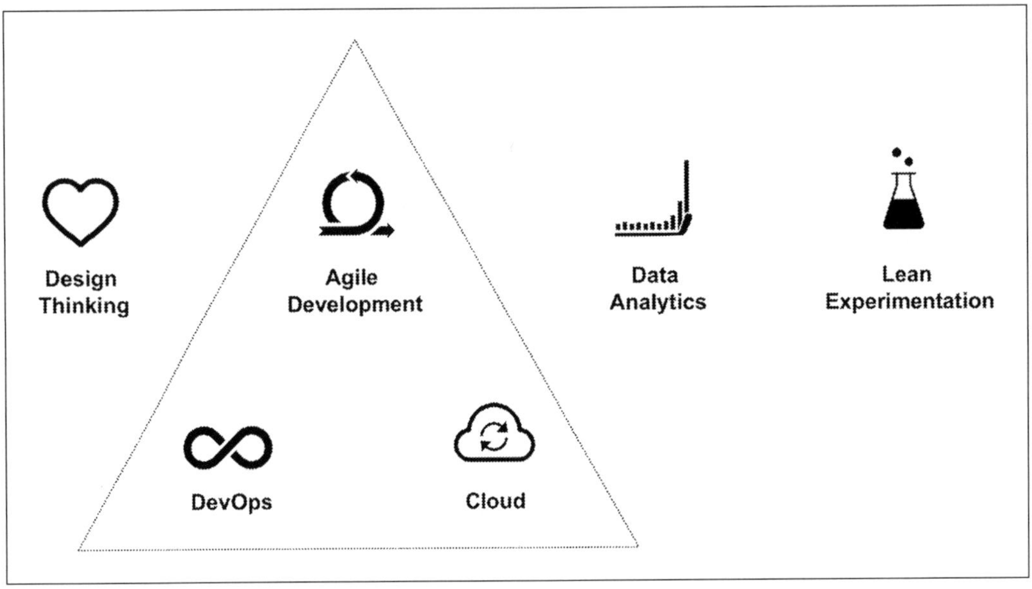

Source: Digital Pathways

"We've just talked about Cloud," says Martin. "How do Agile and DevOps fit in?"

"To level up our Technology," Yumi replies, "we have to break down walls, and two in particular:

■ **Wall of confusion**, between business and developers.
■ **Wall of conflict**, between IT Development and IT Operations.

Agile product development addresses the first wall. We need DevOps to take down the second." [**See Figure 10.9**]

"Please tell us more about DevOps,"[12] says Marcus.

DevOps: Right Mindset, Skillset, and Tool Set

"DevOps is about integrating IT silos, especially Development and Operations," Yumi replies, "so as to deliver features, patches and updates at the pace the business needs. Amazon releases code every ten *seconds* or so. We release new code every few *months*. That's not a knock on Mohan and the

---

12   A hat tip to our friend and colleague, Reuben Athaide, for many fruitful discussions on this topic.

Figure 10.9   How DevOps and Agile Dissolve Our Internal Silos

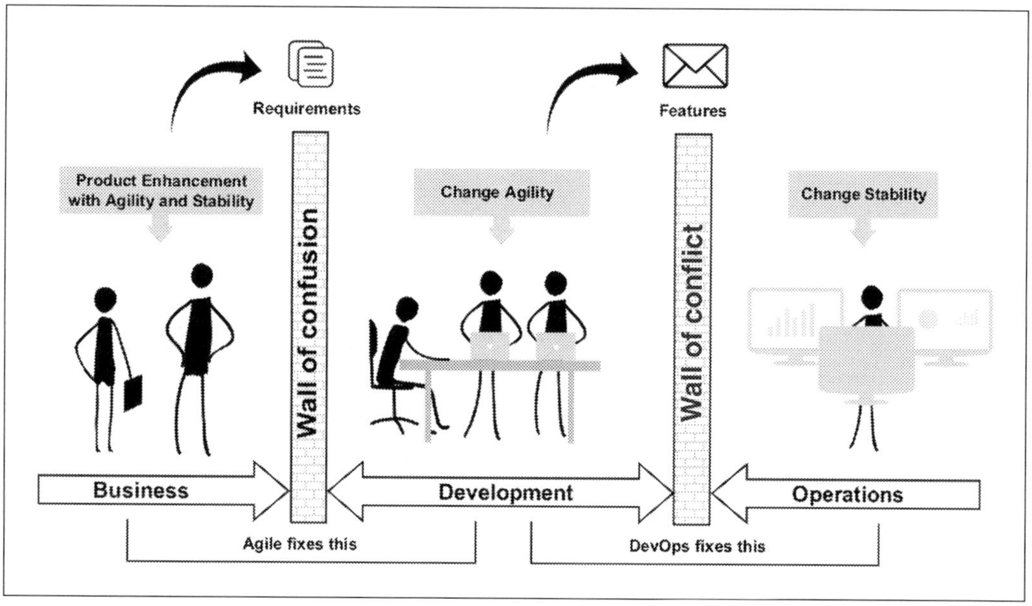

Source: Digital Pathways

IT team, whose focus has been keeping the lights on. But we have to shift our focus to speed, flexibility and client experience – while keeping the lights on.

"The DevOps *mindset*," Yumi says, "is expressed by the acronym CALMS:

■ *Culture of collaboration* – Lean and Agile methods, regular stand-up meetings, visual management
■ *Automation* – we automate boring repetitive tasks; in particular, we automate Quality Assurance (QA) testing
■ *Lean principles*:
  • End-to-end flow, from code development to IT Operations
  • Regular feedback from end users and clients, to ensure we deliver value
  • Continuous improvement, enabled by experimentation
■ *Measurement* – *telemetry* to continuously monitor IT performance. Measure what's important and use data to improve velocity and quality.
■ *Sharing* – reports, issues (with respect to code, system, applications and best practices), successes, failures, and lessons learned

"The DevOps *skillset*," says Yumi, "comprises both technical and leadership ability. We want to develop Hackers who also have CX and business skills, in accord with our 3H model. Such people are rare, as you know. To that end we're partnering with House of Digital, a coding school that incorporates our model."

Yumi pauses. "Any questions?"

"As usual, it's a lot to take in," says Martin. "This certainly builds on our work to date."

"It's definitely a multi-year plan," says Marcus. "We'll have to practice smart sequencing."

Yumi nods. "Mohan, would you mind describing the DevOps *tool set?*"

"Continuous integration and delivery," says Mohan, "are the essence of DevOps. That means we have to automate software development, deployment and monitoring. Some apps allow you to automate *parts* of the IT value chain. But as app complexity increases, so too does the need to automate the *entire* IT value chain. Hence the DevOps tool chain which, in effect, automatically builds quality into each step. We're just scratching the surface here, needless to say." [**See Figure 10.10**]

"DevOps is another big stretch," says Martin. "We're still learning Lean and Agile methods."

"So let me summarize," said Yumi. "How do we accelerate this thing?

1. Deploy our Three Swimlane model across all of Commercial Banking
2. Expand our Pragmatic Innovator Network and kickstart our intrapreneurship program (InnoBox)
3. Improve Innovation Governance,[13] by introducing Client Experience Councils (focus: diamonds) to supplement the Innovation council (focus: coins and stars).
4. Simplify and modernize our Technology stack and data architecture, and deploy DevOps to accelerate the delivery of high quality software.

Thereby, we'll improve our soil and trunk, so as to grow healthy fruit for a long time to come. We want to get to the point where improvement and innovation are 'no big deal'. They're just part of our day to day work. Any questions?"

"Right now it feels overwhelming," says Marcus. "I'm glad we're taking the long view."

"Everybody wants to go to heaven," says Martin, "but it's a hell of a lot of work."

---

[13] Effective innovation governance means getting better and faster at finding and funding the right projects, and culling losing ideas.

Figure 10.10   DevOps Toolset Overview

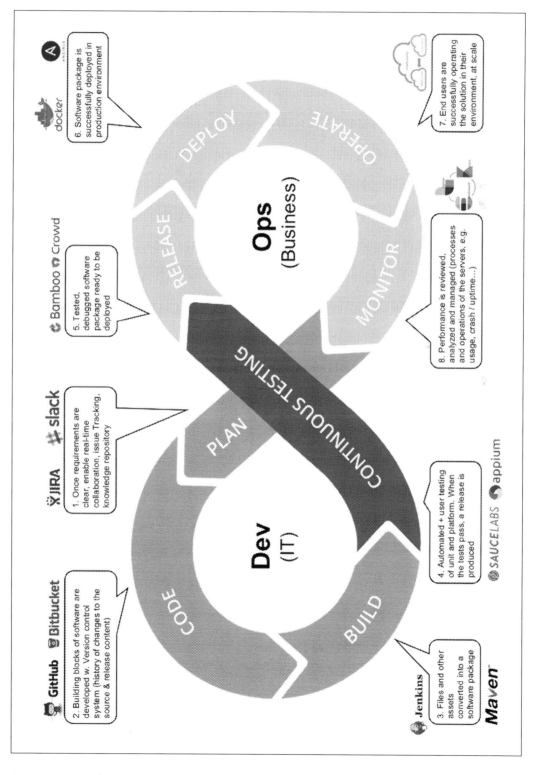

CHAPTER 10 – STUDY QUESTIONS

1. What does Yumi mean by 'innovation fatigue'?
   a. What are common symptoms of this condition?
   b. What are possible countermeasures?
2. Define the Innovation Tree metaphor
   a. What are the three possible kinds of fruit?
   b. How does the innovation tree link with 'a balanced portfolio of innovation projects'?
   c. What do the trunk and the soil represent in the Innovation Tree metaphor?
3. What is a 'digital platform' and how does it differ from a so-called 'pipeline' business?
   a. What advantages do digital platforms have over pipeline businesses?
   b. Are pipelines and platforms mutually exclusive or can they work together effectively? Explain your answer using examples.
   c. Is your organization predominantly a pipeline or digital platform business? Explain your answer.
4. What are the Four levers described by Yumi to accelerate APB's Digital Transformation?
   a. What are the characteristics and benefits associated with the 'Three Swimlane model'?
   b. How do the Pragmatic Innovators Network and InnoBox intrapreneurship program contribute to strengthening APB's innovation capability?
   c. With respect to Governance, why does APB distinguish between Client Experience Councils (CEC) and the Innovation Council (IC)?
   d. How does migrating to Cloud contribute to the simplification and modernization of APB's Technology stack and Data architecture?
5. What are the characteristics and benefits associated with the following?
   a. Application Programming Interface (API) & micro-services
   b. The 'Six Rs' to prioritize the migration of APB's applications
   c. Data Analytics capability
   d. Agile developers certification path
   e. DevOps toolset
6. Defining DevOps
   a. What are the main elements of DevOps?
   b. How can DevOps help an organization?
   c. What are the main challenges in adopting DevOps?
   d. What are possible countermeasures to each challenge?
   e. Any personal experiences?

Chapter 11

New Digital Ventures

What have we achieved, what have we learned, and what's next?

"Obstacles are those frightful things you see when you take your eyes off the goal."

– Henry Ford

Mr. Stork Rooftop Garden Bar, Andaz Singapore Hotel,[1] *Six Months Later*

Martin Picard sits down opposite Amy Tay. Sunlight glisters on Marina Bay and on the symphonic skyline. "It never gets old, does it?" says Martin.

Amy smiles. "Last time we were here I told you APB was 'slow, unreliable and expensive'."

"A phrase forever etched on my psyche," says Martin. "Your candour helped to wake me up. I'm grateful, Amy."

"I keep hearing good things about APB."

"We're entirely absorbed with Digital. The more we learn, the more we realize we don't know."

"I saw your Trade Finance presentation at the Fintech Festival," Amy says.

---

[1] https://www.hyatt.com/en-US/hotel/singapore/andaz-singapore/sinaz.

"We're part of a Blockchain consortium focused on APAC and Asia-Europe trade," says Martin. "Our Learning Lab is leading the development of the first use cases - digitizing documentation, and Letter of Credit[2] Turn-Around Time. The manual process takes 5 to 10 days, but our last pilot took *20 hours*. Our next Proof of Value is about Smart Contracts. We want to provide visibility at every stage of a very fragmented and complex international trade process. Big opportunity, big problems."

"You seem very engaged, Martin."

"We're facing the same problems we face at APB, but on a much bigger scale," Martin says. "And the countermeasures are very similar: alignment toward a shared purpose, shared standards, new technology, integrated systems, end-to-end thinking, client focus…If we pull it off, it's a game changer. They say it could boost global trade by up to 10%."

"KY International can't afford to be left behind," says Amy. "We'd like APB to be our Trade Finance partner, now and in the years to come."

Martin raises his eyebrows. Partnering with KY International on Trade Finance innovation would give APB's SME business a major boost and send a strong signal to the industry. "Would you be open to supporting our Smart Contract PoV?" Martin asks.

"That's why I'm here," says Amy.

Martin leans back in his chair. "This means a great deal to me. Thanks for trusting us again. And please give your father my regards. I miss him."

"He misses you too," says Amy, "and he's pleased APB is back on track."

"We have a very long way to go."

"Yes," says Amy, "but you are wide awake now."

It's a lovely cool morning and Yumi decides to walk the last few miles to the CBD and Asia Pacific Bank Place. She gets off the MRT at Raffles Place and makes her way along the Singapore River. The popular river cruises won't start for another few hours. There's the Parliament House with its prism-shaped top, and grand ceremonial driveway flanked by palm trees. There's Victoria Theater and Concert Hall – two pentagons and a clock tower joined by a common corridor, all in a sea of green parkland. There's

---

[2] Line of Credit, or documentary credit, a payment mechanism used in international trade to provide an economic guarantee from a creditworthy bank to an exporter of goods.

the white facade and clock tower of the Asian Civilizations Museum. And there beside it, Raffles' statue, standing on the spot where he first landed in January 1818. Yumi reflects again on his short, eventful life, so full of achievement yet darkened by tragedy.

Yumi crosses the Cavanaugh pedestrian bridge taking in the Fullerton Hotel's grey granite colonnade. Yumi loves standing here at night when floodlights turn the colonnade and bridge to gold. There's the extraordinary Marina Sands Resort, three gracefully tapering towers crowned by a three-acre SkyPark complete with swimming pools, gardens and jogging paths. There's Clifford Pier with its arched concrete trusses and splendid views of the bay. And there amid the steel, chrome and granite canyons of the CBD, stands Asia Pacific Bank Place.

Blockchain in Trade Finance

Asia Pacific Bank Place, 33rd Floor, Transformation Lighthouse

Martin welcomed Stephen Kwan and his fellow Blockchain Sub-committee members to the Lighthouse. This is our most ambitious PoV to date, Yumi told them. We're breaking new ground and want to keep you fully informed.

"Our innovations to date," Martin began, "have been Efficiency and Sustaining innovations, so-called diamonds and coins. All that hard work has prepared us for our first truly Disruptive Innovation, our first 'star'. We're building a *platform* business as part of a prominent Blockchain[3] consortium, focused on APAC and Asia-Europe trade.

"Our Blockchain-based Trade Finance PoV," Martin went on, "is a good example of how our new Open Banking ecosystem enables new business models. Oliver Chan will provide an overview, then we'll have a brief demonstration." **[See Figure 11.1]**

"We are keen to learn," said Stephen. "Congratulations, by the way, on reengaging with KY International. It's quite a coup for us."

"We're pleased," Martin answered. "Over to you, Oliver."

"Blockchain-based Trade Finance has enormous potential," Oliver said, "but faces significant challenges. We've learned that *alignment* of all the players, a big job, is essential. And so, we've spent a great deal of time

---

[3] Also known as Distributed Ledger Technology (DLT). The technology at the heart of bitcoin and other virtual currencies, *blockchain* is an open, distributed ledger that can record transactions between two parties efficiently and in a verifiable and permanent way.

Figure 11.1   Blockchain-Based Trade Finance – PoV Overview

Focus	Open account, Traditional trade finance Shipping logistics, Working capital optimization
Services	Pre / post-shipment, Digitized docs, Letter of Credit, Track & Trace, Supply Chain Finance (SCF)
Geography	APAC Europe-Asia
Client segment	Small and Medium Enterprises (SMEs) Mid-market
Technology provider + Distributed Ledger Technology (DLT) protocol	Work in progress
# Banks in the consortium	24

Source: Digital Pathways

with key clients, trying to understand their concerns, and validating their interest in the proposed solution. We've also spent alignment time with key stakeholders, both inside APB and within the internal trade ecosystem. Broad adoption of our platform, the so-called network effect, is another key success factor. In fact, our challenges are similar to the ones we've faced with earlier PoVs, though on a much greater scale:

- Understand the new technology at a basic level: What is Blockchain and what it can do for our Trade business?
- Align with partners toward a shared purpose,
- Manage uncertainty around use case cost/benefit ratios and payback times,
- Learn to apply the technology through Lean experimentation,
- Develop shared standards,
- Think in terms of end-to-end flow, and
- Make good investment decisions vis a vis other technologies.

As usual, we have to learn our way up the proverbial hockey stick. Here's a visual summary of how we're managing all the hurdles." **[See Figure 11.2]**

"How does Blockchain improve Trade Finance?" Stephen asked. "There is so much hype, I don't know what to believe."

Figure 11.2   Overcoming Barriers to Blockchain Adoption

Raise awareness (outreach)	Develop use case	Develop ecosystem within APB	Develop ecosystem within industry
• What is Blockchain? • What is Distributed Ledger Technology (DLT)? • Where can I find more? • How can Blockchain or DLT make a difference to my business?	• What is the use case for Trade Finance? • Is Blockchain / DLT the right fit for APB's use case? • What is the possible size of the prize? • What Blockchain protocol or solution best meets my business needs? • What about network effect?	• How do I get my clients and business partners to use my new Trade Finance platform ? • Do they see the benefits? • Is Blockchain / DLT apealling to them? • What Blockchain protocol or solution best meets my business needs?	• Can we leverage existing Blockchain consortia? • How do we choose the right one? • Are there industry Best Practices, Standard Operating Procedures? • Can we adopt some of them to save time and reduce risk? • What about network effect?

Source: Digital Pathways

"The main benefits are speed, cost, security and transparency," Oliver answered. "Conventional Trade Finance is expensive, complicated, error-prone and *invisible*. Imagine a game comprising:

- *Multiple parties* – e.g. Buyers, Suppliers and their banks, intermediary banks, Regulators, shipping and receiving organizations
- *Large number* of contracts
- Dozens of *error-prone documents* – Commercial, Transport and Regulatory documents, e.g. Bills of Lading, Letters of Credit
- Small errors (e.g. typos) can stop the process in its tracks, and
- Parties are *in the dark* – nobody can see the entire board, so to speak

In such a game, transactions are full of delay, cost and hassle. Everybody loses." **[See Figure 11.3]**

Figure 11.3   APB Trade Finance Use Case – Current State: Slow, Opaque, Cumbersome Process

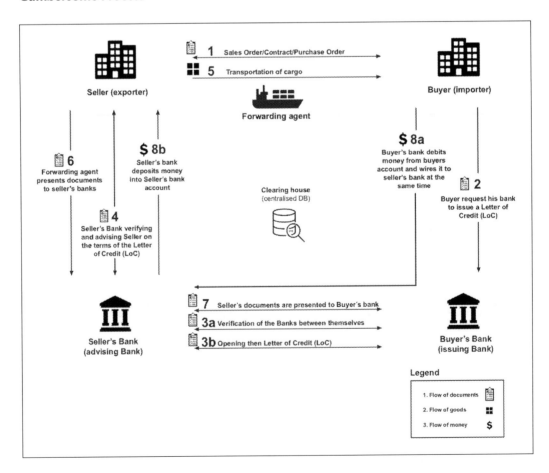

Source: Digital Pathways

With our Blockchain-based Trade finance platform, things are quite different. We all see the same things and in real time. For example, say I'm the Buyer's bank. Before I can pay the Supplier, I need to know things like:

- Have the goods arrived, and are they in the right condition?
- Has the Supplier satisfied applicable trade, security and financial laws?

Blockchain answers such questions for all the players in real time. I can easily issue and validate the Letter of Credit. I can pay the Supplier, the goods are released, and everybody is happy." **[See Figure 11.4]**

Figure 11.4   APB Trade Finance Use Case – Target State: Quick, Clear, Frictionless Experience

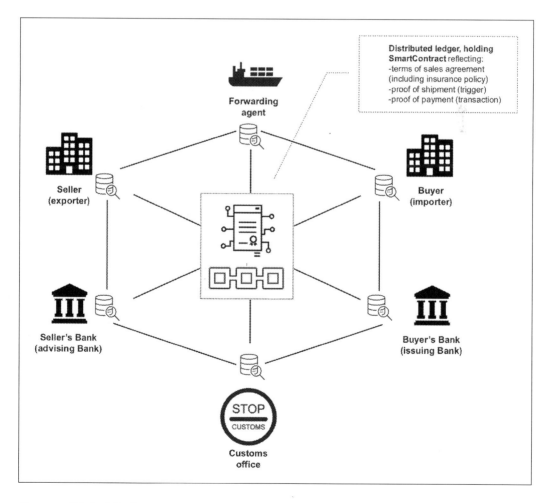

Source: Digital Pathways

Figure 11.5   Smart Contracts

1 Buyer and seller formalize their agreement into a contract.

2 The terms of this sales agreement is translated into lines of codes to create a self-executing contract. Smart contracts are designed to automatically execute, control or document legally relevant events and actions, accordings to the terms of a contract / agreement.

3 The smart contract is put into a distributed, decentralized blockchain network. This represent a reliable, single source of truth that can be accessed by the stakeholders involved in the operation (buyer, seller, banks, customs, forwarding agent…)

Source: Digital Pathways

"Moreover," said Oliver, "I can automate payment using so-called Smart Contracts, another key Blockchain application." **[See Figure 11.5]**

"What about security?" Stephen asked.

"It's virtually impossible to hack into and change information in a blockchain," Oliver answered. "Fraud is another matter. Blockchain *cannot* detect fake information. For that we need Data Analytics, which can help to identify fraud and forgery."

After further discussion, Oliver summarized the expected benefits of the Blockchain-based Trade Finance PoV. **[See Figure 11.6]**

Oliver then asked the Blockchain team to demonstrate applications developed to date, and to summarize their learnings and next steps. The presentation concluded with a spirited question and answer session. Martin thanked Oliver and the Blockchain team and asked for closing comments.

Figure 11.6   Blockchain-Based Trade Finance Platform – Benefits Overview

Performance metric		Traditional trade-finance model (centralized ledgers)	Blockchain-based model (distributed ledger)
	Speed (transaction settlement time)	Slow	Fast
	Transaction cost	Low	High
	Security and data integrity	Low, due to propensity for failure and fraud	High, due to robust cryptography and added transparency
	Effort 1 – Documentation management	High, due to large number of documents to manage and reconcile	Small, due to only one document to manage and reconcile
	Effort 2 – Data integration and validation	High, due to significant number of intermediaries (correspondent banks, forwarding agents, customs…)	Small, due to DLT enabling simplified integration
	Effort 3 – Confirmation of payment	High, due to manual confirmation of payment of seller's documents have been validated	Small, due to automatic payment triggered by Smart Contract

Source: Digital Pathways

"Blockchain represents a revolution in Trade Finance," said Stephen, "and I am glad that APB is in the middle of it. We do not shy away from difficult challenges. I commend Oliver and the Blockchain team for their fine work so far. I believe I speak for my fellow Board members when I say, *full speed ahead.*"

Reflections 18 Months into Our Transformation

Board Room Asia Pacific Bank Place, 37th Floor

Martin welcomes the senior leadership team. "We're 18 months into it. We've generated good results across Commercial Banking and are making good progress in other areas of APB. It's a good time to hit the Pause button and reflect. *What have we learned so far? What are our biggest challenges going forward?* I've asked Yumi to kick off our discussion."

Yumi puts a one-pager up on the screen. "To fully harvest the benefits of all our hard work, we need to apply what we've learned in

Commercial Banking across all of APB. We call this a Challenge – Cause – Countermeasure (3C) analysis.

"Here are our key challenges in CB to date, in my view:

- *Why have few sustaining or disruptive innovation projects turned into scalable businesses?*
- *Why does developing an intrapreneurial mindset require so much effort?*
- *Why does building in-house Digital innovation skills take so long?*
- *How do we strengthen our collaboration platforms?*
- *How do we move away from opinion-based decision making?*

And here are the causes of each, and the countermeasures we've applied, with mixed success." **[See Figure 11.7]**

"I don't want to be misunderstood," says Yumi. "Such challenges are normal at this point, and our pragmatic innovators framework is a sound response. But we need to take stock and adjust as required. So what do you all think?"

"I think it's an accurate assessment of our current condition," says Marcus Kupper. "Commercial Banking has come a long way, but we're still lagging behind our Digital competitors."

"I would add IT Architecture to our Challenges," Mohan Bilgi says. "Despite our progress, we still have major gaps in our IT stack and capability. The combination of Agile, DevOps and Cloud has definitely enabled rapid prototyping at scale. But APB's new ways of working are still foreign to many people."

"I also have no argument with this paper, Yumi," says Stephanie Shan. "I too would add to the Challenges. We're not good at Innovation Accounting or at innovation governance in general." Many are still confused as to why Efficiency projects (diamonds) need to be managed differently than Sustaining (coins) and Disruptive (stars) projects.

The discussion goes on like this for almost an hour. The senior team has become more open and relaxed since Richard Decker's departure. Yumi will reflect the senior team's feedback in her next iteration.

Martin then asks for personal reflections, which the senior team will summarize in a Lessons Learned document and reference in the years to come.

Figure 11.7 APB Transformation – Challenge | Causes | Countermeasures (3Cs)

Observed challenges	Root causes	Countermeasures
Few scalable Businesses	• Fragmented innovation process, not end-to-end. • No clear, structured pathway to turn best ideas into businesses	**Consistent, end-to-end, stage-gate process** • Validate with clients and users at each step: Explore & ideate, Design, Build, Commercialize (launch and scale) • Market traction trumps everything else → **Minimum Viable Companies (MVCs) > Minimum Viable Products (MVPs)**
Intrapreneurial Mindset?	• Inconsistent Intrapreneur support program • Are we on-boarding right people?	**InnoBox: engaging, outcome-focused Intrapreneurship program** • Guide intrapreneurs through journey to MVC, help them succeed • Intrapreneurs DNA test: onboarding the right people • Ensure they have enough time to dedicate to their innovation project → **Intrapreneurship program to feed our innovation funnel**
Digital Innovation Skills?	• Intrapreneurs often lack core innovation skills • Inconsistent language & logic, little guidance	**Pragmatic Innovator Framework** • Curriculum: integrate Design Thinking, Agile, Lean Startup & Growth Hacking • Training: workshops, bootcamps, e-learning; use same language & logic • On-demand mentoring → **Strengthen internal capability (to achieve transformation goals)**
Collaboration Platforms?	• Internal: Business, Tech and OPS tend to focus on silo performance, not client outcomes • External: Fintechs often find us 'difficult to work with'. Is our value proposition compelling for the best Fintechs?	**Bring together Hustlers, Hackers and Hipsters (3H teams) + engaged Fintechs (5Ps)** • Learning Lab: both controlled experiment & showcase • Small X-functional teams, building & test product increments. • Validate with short Sprints, frequent user & customer feedback → **Radical collaboration to build what people want, fast**
Opinion-based Decision-making	• Highest Paid Person's Opinion (HiPPo) vs. data generated by experiments & client feedback. • Test & Validation are weak	**Culture of Lean experimentation** (fail fast, often) • Experiment to generate ad hoc data and validate key assumptions • Get comfortable with failure and frequent course correction • Metered funding: require validated learnings before investing further → **Fact-based decisions**

Source: Digital Pathways

What Have We Learned?

"*Legacy* technology need not be a constraint," says Mohan. "Cloud technology isn't a problem, it's a vital business enabler. We don't have to build everything internally. Partnering with Fintechs can be faster and cheaper. To attract smart partners, we have to be easy to innovate with. Building the Tech & Ops platform was a personal revelation, especially after we pulled in Designers and began rapid validation with clients."

"*Experiences, not products*," says Marcus. "Being client-centric means understanding the client's problems and designing end-to-end experiences. And that means breaking down silos, Oceans 11 management and using very different metrics than we've in the past."

"*Digital* is the job of the bank," Stephanie offers. "Digital is not a department, channel or separate competency. Digital is what everybody in this room does."

"The Compliance team is a business partner," Nancy Stark puts in. "I'm gratified that you understand Compliance is *not* trying to kill innovation. In fact, we're happy to go to bat for you with the Regulator. Innovation is about pushing the envelope, after all."

"Open banking," Mohan says, "which means developing APIs for internal and external connectivity so we can strengthen our core, create distribution channels, and launch new ventures."

"*Artificial Intelligence* and *Data Analytics*," Yumi says. "We need to level up our Data Science and AI capability. At present, we're not fully capable of delivering insight-powered experiences and customized propositions. Our Data assets are substandard. Our work with FinTech partners like DataClean is an effective temporary countermeasure. Longer term we have to build our own Data muscle."

"We have to stop hiring *bankers*," says Martin. "Otherwise, we'll never solve these kinds of problems.

"*Human Resources* has to become a competitive advantage," Karen Hong puts in. "Digital talent is a critical gap. Our pilot with DigitalSG coding school is one example of how we might move forward. Practical digital experience and a 3H mindset are essential, but hard to provide."

"*Strategy deployment* has to be quicker and more flexible," says Marcus. "Our Digital Innovation Compass process is okay, but we're slow at deployment. Except for our Lighthouse process, our operating rhythms are inconsistent."

"*Fintech on-boarding* needs to be smoother," Mohan says. "Our ecosystem reputation is improving, but many Fintechs remain wary of working with us."

"*Metrics* for a digital age," says Stephanie. "Market share, ROI and other traditional metrics can be misleading. We have to get used to metrics like Speed to Market, Client and User Experience, Productivity and cost per transaction. Just as our Innovation Board is focused on traction measures for a given PoV, we need to focus on traction measures for our broader investment portfolio."

"*Blockchain* and other breakthrough technologies," Mohan adds, "we have to get good at them either directly or through partnerships."

"We have to be *ambidextrous*," says Marcus, "which means running a 'zero defect' culture in our core business, and an experimentation driven culture in new emerging business."

"An excellent list, thank you," says Martin. "Now I'd like to ask our Sherpa to tie it all together for us. Yumi, how does all this fit together? Can you paint a picture of the future for us?"

What's Next, Yumi-san?

We've stopped the bleeding. Now let's reinvent ourselves

"Are we a sunrise or a sunset organization?" Yumi begins. "We've stopped the bleeding, and laid the foundation for some growth. Is that enough for us?"

Yumi's words hang there, a challenge.

"Our goal isn't just survival," says Marcus, "it's *reinvention*. Our PoVs to date are aimed at efficiency and a return to growth. But they're also the foundation for breakthrough innovation - like Blockchain-based Trade Finance."

"In for a penny," says Nancy, "in for a pound. We've come too far to stop now."

"*Digital to the Core* means reinventing ourselves," says Stephanie. "Other companies have done it. Why not Asia Pacific Bank?"

"We have no choice," says Karen Hong. "Banking's traditional *hub and spoke* model is being disrupted. We've just highlighted a wide range of learning points. My question is, what are the *main* elements of reinvention?"

Figure 11.8   Amazon's Flywheel (Virtuous Cycle)

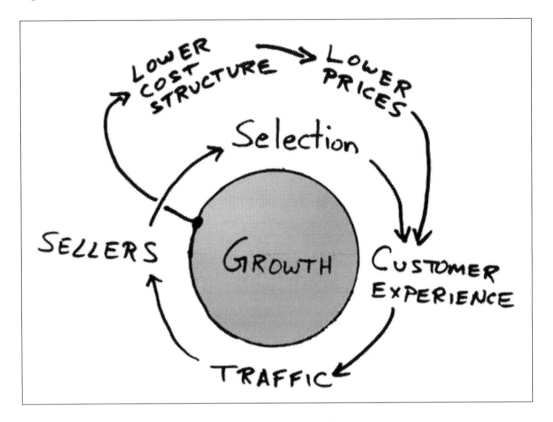

Source: Amazon (famous napkin sketch from Jeff Bezos)

"We have to make the shift from pipeline to *platform* company," says Yumi. "Data Analytics, Artificial Intelligence and Blockchain are also important elements. To what end? Our Clients are stressed, overburdened and time-poor. If we can make their lives easier, we'll succeed. That's what motivates me, that's why I'm here."

Yumi walks to the whiteboard and starts drawing. "Amazon's flywheel is a good example of what I'm talking about. **[See Figure 11.8]**

A flywheel is a mechanical device that stores rotational energy. How does Amazon turn the wheel? By reducing friction and creating a hassle-free experience. Great CX means more shoppers, which means more sellers. More sellers mean lower cost and higher selection, which means more shoppers - a virtuous cycle. That's our model."

"I find this all intimidating," says Stanley. "How can we possibly compete with Amazon, Alibaba and Google?"

"Let's apply the technology available," Yumi answers. "There is *no* reason not to do so. We've proven we can transform our legacy systems, and our mindset. We're applying leading edge methods, and launching sophisticated new offerings. We're quicker and more engaged with our clients, and ecosystem. Leading companies are reengaging with us. We're leading a major consortium and developing new business models.

"And we have innate strengths which Big Tech may never have. People trust us with their money and know we won't lose it. We know how to manage *risk* and have been doing it successfully for a very long time. Lastly, despite the ethical lapses of some banks, people believe we'll do the right thing for them and their families.

"We are a *sunrise* company," Yumi continues, "and, as you suggest, our goal is reinvention. Let's learn from Amazon, Alibaba and Google. Let's continue to level up our IT architecture and capabilities. Let's migrate to the Cloud in a thoughtful, orderly way. Let's accelerate with respect to APIs and microservices, and fully commit to open and multi-channel banking. Let's apply DevOps and Data Analytics, as well as we've applied Agile, Lean Startup and Design Thinking. Let's expand our data pool by partnering with telcos, utilities, and platform companies. Let's commit to making our clients' lives easier."

A Remarkable Journey

Martin concludes the meeting with a few thoughts of his own. "We're on a remarkable journey," he begins. "We began with the client's point of view and a frank, painful self-assessment. We found a Sherpa who knows the mountain, won't lie to us, and won't let us lie to ourselves. Our Sherpa has helped us define our Aspiration and the plan to achieve it.

"We've faced our blockers head on; we haven't flinched from the stark realities of culture, capability, technology and the rest. Instead, we developed an overall approach that works and that we can scale across our organization. We set up an Innovation Platform and embraced an entirely different way of working, incompletely and ineptly at times, but with sincerity and good spirit. And we've innovated like never before. We began with humble Efficiency innovation projects, also known as Process Improvement Events or PIE. We ran several Sustaining Innovation projects, associated with new products and services. And now we're also testing new business models. Each phase has prepared us for the next phase of the journey. Our PIEs have laid the foundation for digitizing key client journeys, which has given us the strength and stamina to tackle disruptive technology and new ventures.

"We are, I repeat, on a remarkable journey. Let's not get too high or too low. This is a marathon and stamina is everything. I have absolute confidence in you. We're going to be fine, and we'll have fun along the way.

"Last thing," says Martin. "The past few years we've learned many new ideas, methods and vocabulary: nWoW, Design Thinking, Agile, Lean Startup, DevOps and so on. This was all necessary. Going forward, let's not get hung up on buzzwords, and let's not get too doctrinaire about it all. In the long run, it's all about working together better to help the client."

The View from the Front Line

Kenny Soh's team launches into their morning huddle. Martin, Yumi and Marcus Kupper stand quietly in the back, next to Kenny. "I let my team members run the huddle," he whispers.

Kanya Arom leads the huddle and begins with a succinct overview of the team's current and future work. She summarizes target versus actual results across core metrics, and so-called 'Watchouts' (abnormalities and potential problems). "Am I missing anything, Kenny?" Kanya asks. Kenny gives her a thumbs up. "All right then," says Kanya. "It's going to be a great day - let's go out there and have some fun."

After thanking Kanya and the team, Martin, Yumi and Marcus spend a few minutes with Kenny. "Martin tells me you're his secret weapon," says Yumi.

Kenny grins. "Martin and I go way back so I guess we feel we can be honest with each other."

Martin makes a face. "Sometimes a little too honest…"

"I imagine you've seen a great deal of change at APB over the years," says Marcus. "How do the past few years compare?"

"We've had our ups and downs," says Kenny. "Years when our growth seemed unstoppable, and other times, like the GFC[4] or now in the

---

[4] Great Financial Crisis of 2008 – 2009.

COVID-19 era, when we seemed at risk of going under. But I've never seen internal change like we've had the past few years.

"*Digital to the Core* is still scary for us. But the team understands we have to change. We appreciate all the PIEs, Boot Camps, and Hackathons, and the opportunity to learn. To be honest, we're a little tired now and need to catch our breath.

"We appreciate Martin and the senior team being honest with us and using plain language. We like how you shared APB's aspiration and winning logic, and where our team fits in. And you know what? The more I learn about this Lean Digital stuff, the more I realize that underneath it all, it's just common sense. We're learning how to work together better, and how to get closer to our customers, both internal and external."

"That's a good summary," Yumi says. "Any advice for us?"

"Keep us in the loop," Kenny says, "and treat us with respect."

CHAPTER 11 – STUDY QUESTIONS

1. What is Blockchain?
   a. What other applications might Blockchain have?
   b. In your experience what are the biggest obstacles to Blockchain adoption?
2. What breakthrough technologies are most relevant for your organization and industry?
   a. Explain the impact of each technology on your organization's offerings and operations.
   b. What can your organization do to prepare for and harness these disruptive technologies?
3. According to Yumi, what are the key challenges to scaling their transformation across Asia Pacific Bank?
   a. What do you think of Yumi's root causes and proposed countermeasures?
   b. Is Yumi missing any important points?
   c. Do you have any examples from your experience?
4. What are the key challenges to scaling a transformation across your organization?
5. Martin asks the senior team, 'What have we learned?'
   a. Are the team's learning points realistic?
   b. Are they missing any important learning points?
   c. Are there any personal experiences you can draw on?
6. Martin asks Yumi to provide her views on 'what's next' in financial services.
   a. Do you agree or disagree with Yumi's reflections? Explain your rationale
   b. Are there any important factors and developments that Yumi is missing?
7. What are the top five lessons you have learned reading this book?
   a. Draw them out using as few words as possible.
   b. How are you going to apply these lessons in your work?

Appendix A

Singapore Places Featured in *Harnessing Digital Disruption*

Here are Singapore places and neighborhoods featured in the book. If you get a chance to go, you should take it.

Chapter 1. The Elephant and the Greyhounds

① Mr. Stork Rooftop Garden Bar, Andaz Singapore Hotel
https://www.hyatt.com/en-US/hotel/singapore/andaz-singapore/sinaz/dining
② Port of Singapore, TUAS Expansion
https://www.mpa.gov.sg/web/portal/home/port-of-singapore; https://www.singaporepsa.com/

Chapter 2. Mapping Client Journeys to Grasp the Real Situation

③ Singapore Central Business District
https://www.myguidesingapore.com/regionalinfo/central-business-district;
https://www.visitsingapore.com/walking-tour/culture/
running-route-in-the-central-business-district/
④ Akane Restaurant, Japanese Association Singapore
http://www.jas.org.sg/index_en.html
http://www.jas.org.sg/dining/akane/akane_en.html

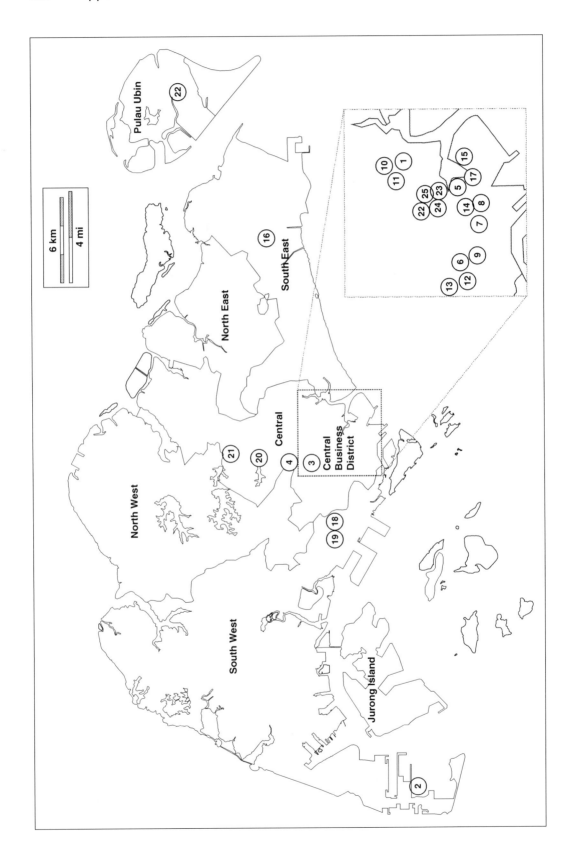

Chapter 3. Understanding Our Blockers

⑤Fullerton Hotel
https://www.fullertonhotels.com/fullerton-hotel-singapore

⑥Duxton Hill Neighborhood
https://en.wikipedia.org/wiki/Duxton_Hill
https://www.vogue.com/article/
a-guide-to-duxton-hill-singapore-neighborhood

⑦Telok Ayer Street
https://www.tripadvisor.com/Attraction_Review-g294265-d324751-Reviews-
Telok_Ayer_Street-Singapore.html

⑧Lau Pa Sat Food Hawker Center
http://www.laupasat.biz/
https://www.hotels.com/go/singapore/lau-pa-sat

⑨Brasserie Gavroche
https://brasseriegavroche.com/

Chapter 4. Finding True North with Our Digital Strategy Compass

⑩Maison Ikkoku
https://www.ethanleslieleong.com/

⑪Bugis Street and Kampong Gelam
https://www.visitsingapore.com/see-do-singapore/places-to-see/
kampong-gelam/
https://www.hotels.com/go/singapore/bugis-street-market

Chapter 5. Fostering Innovation in a Risk-Averse Culture

⑫Straits Clan Cafe
https://straitsclan.com/clan-cafe

⑬Bukit Pasoh and Chinatown
http://www.chinatown.sg/index.php?fx=precinct&g1=precinct&g2=2&g3=3

Chapter 6. Embracing New Ways of Working

⑭ Tower Club
https://www.tower-club.com.sg/

⑮ Marina Bay Sands Hotel
https://www.marinabaysands.com/

⑯ Singapore Fintech Festival @ Expo
https://www.fintechfestival.sg/

Chapter 7. Launching Our First Wave Innovation Projects

⑰ Ola Cocina del Mar Restaurant, Marina Bay Financial Center
https://ola.kitchen/

⑱ Fusionopolis Research Complex
https://www.jtc.gov.sg/industrial-land-and-space/Pages/fusionopolis.aspx

Chapter 8. Launching Our Second Wave Innovation Projects

⑲ INSEAD Asia Campus, Knowledge Hub District
https://www.insead.edu/campuses/asia

⑳ Treetop Walk, Central Catchment Nature Reserve
https://www.nparks.gov.sg/gardens-parks-and-nature/parks-and-nature-
reserves/central-catchment-nature-reserve/treetop-walk

㉑ MacRitchie Reservoir Park
https://www.nparks.gov.sg/gardens-parks-and-nature/parks-and-nature-
reserves/macritchie-reservoir-park

㉒ Pulau Ubin Island
https://www.nparks.gov.sg/gardens-parks-and-nature/parks-and-nature-
reserves/pulau-ubin-and-chek-jawa

Chapter 9. Year-End Review at Asia Pacific Bank

The empire strikes back

Chapter 10. How Do We Scale Our Transformation?

⑩ Maison Ikkoku
https://www.ethanleslieleong.com/

⑪ Bugis Street and Kampong Gelam
https://www.visitsingapore.com/see-do-singapore/places-to-see/
kampong-gelam/
https://www.hotels.com/go/singapore/bugis-street-market

Chapter 11. New Digital Ventures

①Mr. Stork Rooftop Garden Bar, Andaz Singapore Hotel
https://www.hyatt.com/en-US/hotel/singapore/andaz-singapore/sinaz/
dining

Parliament House, Singapore
https://www.parliament.gov.sg/

Asian Civilizations Museum
https://www.nhb.gov.sg/acm/

Raffles Statue and landing site, Singapore River
https://www.visitsingapore.com/see-do-singapore/history/memorials/
sir-raffles-statue-landing-site/

Victoria Theatre and Concert Hall
https://www.vtvch.com/

③Central Business District
https://www.myguidesingapore.com/regionalinfo/central-business-district

Official Guide to Singapore

https://www.visitsingapore.com/en

Appendix B

List of Figures

Asia Pacific Bank's Organization Chart (Main Characters)

Chapter 1. The Elephant and the Greyhounds

1.1 What Is Fintech?
1.2 Potential Impact of Fintech on APB's overall Business
1.3 Impact of Fintech on APB's Payment Business
1.4 Collaborating with Fintech – Why It Makes Sense on Paper
1.5 Collaborating with Fintech – Why It Is Difficult in Practice

Chapter 2. Mapping Client Journeys to Grasp the Real Situation

2.1 APB's Transformation Lighthouse
2.2 Yumi's First 30-Day Plan
2.3 Senior Leader's Deep Dive – Rules of Engagement
2.4 Client Journey Map – Core Elements
2.5 Client Persona – CEO of Tay International Retail Group
2.6 Three-Week Work Plan to Wow APB's C-Suite
2.7 Client Journey – KY Tay International Retail Group

Chapter 3. Understanding Our Blockers

3.1 Understanding APB Blockers through Three Systems
3.2 Understanding APB Skill Gaps (People System)
3.3 Surfacing APB Core Beliefs (People System)
3.4 Understanding APB Process and IT Landscape (Work System)
3.5 Understanding APB Technology Platform (Work System)
3.6 Enabling Effective Strategy Execution at APB (Management System)

Chapter 4. Finding True North with Our Digital Strategy Compass

4.1 Our Winning Logic
4.2 Strategy Pillar One: Digitize Key Client Journeys
4.3 Strategy Pillar Two: Deploy New Ways of Working
4.4 Strategy Pillar Three: Simplify & Modernize Our IT & Data Architecture
4.5 Our Digital Strategy Compass
4.6 Aligning Innovation Projects with Strategic Objectives

Chapter 5. Fostering Innovation in a Risk-Averse Culture

5.1 Lean-Digital Transformation Road Map – Think Big, Start Small, Scale Fast
5.2 Lean and Agile Ways of Working
5.3 APB Innovation Value Spaces
5.4 Three Swimlanes for a Sustained Transformation

Chapter 6. Embracing New Ways of Working

6.1 APB's Innovation Platform
6.2 Does It Wow, Does It Work, Can We Make Money?
6.3 Proof of Value (PoV) – Expected Trajectory
6.4 Proof of Value (PoV) – Key Activities

Chapter 7. Launching Our First Wave Innovation Projects

7.1   T-Shaped Profile for an Innovation Leader
7.2   Three-Step Recipe (to Improve Client Journey Rapidly)
7.3   Client On-Boarding PoV – Overview
7.4   Client On-Boarding PoV – Size of the Prize
7.5   Client On-Boarding PoV – Model Office Concept
7.6   FlowBase Capability – Do We Have the Right Fintech Partner?
7.7   Proposed Design to Improve Client On-Boarding Experience
7.8   FlowBase Experiment Outline
7.9   The Heart of Our Experiment – Can We Deploy Circled Capabilities?
7.10 FlowBase Experiment – Do We Have a Proof of Value (PoV)?
7.11 FlowBase Experiment – Impact 90 Days into the Pilot (Singapore Market)

Chapter 8. Launching Our Second Wave Innovation Projects

8.1   Refocusing on Our Clients with Lean-Agile Product Development
8.2   Effective Fintech Collaboration – Guiding Principles
8.3   SME Lending PoV – Challenge Overview
8.4   SME Lending PoV – Do We Have a Problem Worth Solving
8.5   SME Lending PoV – What Are We Trying to Achieve?
8.6   Setting Up the Project X-Team – 3H Model
8.7   QuickLoan PoV – Does the Proposed Solution Work?
8.8   QuickLoan PoV – Does It Wow Our Clients? (Ease of Use Testing)
8.9   QuickLoan PoV – Can we Make Money? (Measuring Impact)
8.10 Lessons Learned from the Soft Launch (Are We Ready to Scale?)

Chapter 9. Year-End Review at Asia Pacific Bank

9.1 Digital Strategy Year-End Summary
9.2 The Jaws of Culture

Chapter 10. How Do We Scale Our Transformation?

10.1   Digital Innovation Tree Metaphor
10.2   Deploy Three Swimlane Model across Commercial Banking
10.3   InnoBox Intrapreneurship Program – Building Innovation Capability at Scale
10.4   Scaling Our Innovation Ecosystem – Internal and External Collaboration
10.5   Evolution from Closed to Open Banking
10.6   Target Technology Stack for Internal and External Connectivity
10.7   Data Assets Overview
10.8   *nWoW* Academy – Overview of Agile Developers Certification Path
10.9   How DevOps and Agile Dissolve Our Internal Silos
10.10 DevOps Toolset Overview

Chapter 11. New Digital Ventures

11.1 Blockchain-Based Trade Finance – PoV Overview
11.2 Overcoming Barriers to Blockchain Adoption
11.3 APB Trade Finance Use Case – Current State: Slow, Opaque, Cumbersome Process
11.4 APB Trade Finance Use Case – Target State: Quick, Clear, Frictionless Experience
11.5 Smart Contracts
11.6 Blockchain-Based Trade Finance Platform – Benefits Overview
11.7 APB Transformation – Challenge | Causes | Countermeasures (3Cs)
11.8 Amazon's Flywheel (Virtuous Cycle)

Acknowledgments

From Pascal

I'm grateful for all the people who helped to make this book a reality, and I acknowledge them here.

Steve Blank, Alex Osterwalder, Ash Maurya, Gene Kim and other pioneers whose work has inspired us. All my mentors over the years whose kindness and generosity I can never repay. All our reviewers, whose time and care have helped to make a better book. The growing number of organizations around the world that are in the midst of heart-felt Digital transformations. I'm lucky enough to work with some of you. Hopefully, this book will make the journey a little easier. My co-author, Digital Sherpa and friend, Laurent Simon, from whom I have learned so much. My dear wife, Pamela, and our children, Eleanor, Katie, and Matthew.

From Laurent

Writing this book was quite an adventure: harder than I thought but truly rewarding. I will never forget the emotional roller-coaster associated with finalizing the book in the midst of the COVID-19 crisis...

I would like to start by expressing my sincere gratitude to my co-author, mentor and friend, Pascal Dennis. Without your talent and dedication, Pascal, this adventure would not have been possible.

I would like also to thank my wife, Eiko-san, for her unconditional love, many talents... and for the nice book cover too ;-) Additionally, my special thanks to Daria Romanova, artist extraordinaire, who helped turn our doodles and drawings into amazing illustrations.

From both of us

This book wouldn't have been possible without the organizations—large and small—that allowed us to test, validate and refine our Pragmatic Innovators approach, over the last five years.

We're grateful to the Digital@INSEAD community and the www.FutureFintech.io open collaboration platform, which have served as a splendid *Learning Laboratory*. What a pleasure to bring together the most progressive startups, large organizations, regulators and investors to test new ways of working and incubate scalable innovations.

We would also like to thank *Messrs Ravi Menon*, Managing Director of Monetary Authority of Singapore (MAS) and *Kok Yam Tan*, Deputy Secretary of Singapore Smart Nation & Digital Government for the strong support to Digital Innovation in Asia.

Finally, we want to thank our engaged and insightful readers: we love you guys!

Please continue to reach out and share your questions, real-life stories, lessons learned and (sometime crazy) ideas…

Index

Note: Page numbers in italics refer to text within figures, those followed by n refer to a note with its number.

Accelerators, 161–162
  data analytics, 176–177
  DevOps, 177–181
  Innobox Program, 164–168
  Innovation governance, 168–169
  IT system, 170–175
  Three Swim Lane model, 162–164
Adobe, 165
Agarwal, Asim, 98–99, 106, 110, 117
Agile, 11, *91*, 134; see also Lean-Agile working
  Developers Certification, 177–178
  software development process, *59, 60, 74, 78, 89, 90, 179, 181*
AI (artificial intelligence), 110, 114
  capability, *116*, 194
Amazon, 42, 178, 196

Ambidextrous organization, 79–80, 83, 195
API (Application Program Interface), 42–43, 61n4, 169–174, 192
Apple, 171
ASEAN plus Six, 61
Aspirations, 19, *62*
  Digital to the Core, 55–57, 83–84
  sharing, 199
  visual management, *20*, 44
Automation, *80, 111,* 179

Banking, 10–11, 14, 95, 128
  Banking as a Service (BaaS), 173
  commercial banking, 25–31, 162–164
  impact of Fintech, 5–7
  open banking, 64, 129, 169-173–173, 185, 194

  specialized banking, 173
  traditional, 170-171, *191,* 195
Behaviors, 37, *62*
Beliefs, 37–38, *39*
Benefit realization, *111*
Beta Business, 83
Bilgi, Mohan, 53, 91, 145
  DevOps capability, 164–165
  innovation, 123, 149, 151, 155, 168-169, 170-173
  IT system challenges, 43, 47, 128–130, 192, 194
  open systems, 61, 173–176
Blockchain, 110, 185–191, 195
  consortium, 184, 185
Blockers, 34–36, 105, 197; see also Resistance to change
  blockchain adoption, *187*

Blockers *(continued)*
  cultural, 105, *155*
  data analytics, 176–177
  management system, *36*, 44–46
  people, *36*, 37–40, 91–92
  walls, 177, *178*
  work system, *36*, 40–44
Boot Camps, 61, 81, 88, 92, 108
Bottlenecks, 42n3, 93, 100, 131, 169
Budgets
  control of, 129–130
  innovation, 65, 84, 164
Business people, see Hustlers

CALMS mindset, 179
Capability map, *62*
Chan, Oliver, 185
  blockchain, 188–190
  client on-boarding, 109–110, 112, 114, 122–123
  engagement, 105–108
  Quickloan, 110, 136–142
Client Experience Councils (CEC), 89, *90*, 168
Client journey, 18, 21, *22*, 76; see also FlowBase platform
  on-boarding, 30, 109–115, 117–118, 123
  core elements, *24*
  digital innovation, 56, *58*

IT system, *44*
KY Tay International, 26, *29*, 30, 106
product development, 132–134, 141–142
Clients
  Client Persona, *27*, 132
  data, 148, 149–150, 154
  experience, 46, 53, *62*, 92, 141–142, *142*
  focus on, 84, 89, *90*
  needs, 1–3, 5, *57*, *58*, 132, *133*
  satisfaction, *36*, 144
Cloud computing
  hybrid cloud, 149, 175–176
  migration to, 43, *74*, 175–176, 197
  resistance to, 99, 154
Coaching, 15, 92–93, 136
  cascading, 73, 109
Coins, 72, 76, 79, 131
  governance, 168-169, 192
  Three Swim Lane model, 81–82, 161–164
Collaboration, *78*
  Fintech and banks, *10*, *12*, 64, *116*
  5Ps of Fintech collaboration, *137*, 144
Commercial Banking, 6, 137-138; see also On-boarding
  client research, 25–31
  transformation, 46, 92, 162–164, 191

Competitors, 55, *62*, 64, 196–197
Compliance, 154
  resistance to change, 99, 131, 142, 144, 145, 147–148
Connectivity, *41*, 42–43, 123, 124
Connectivity Inc, 99–100, 127–128, 134, 141, 174
Consensus, 21, *22*
Constraints, Theory of, 130–131
Control, 11, 19, 47; see also Budgets
Core Business, 5–6, 63, 72, 169
Countermeasures, 19, 184, 192–193
Cross-functional teams, 19, 109, 110, *140*; see also 3H teams
Culture, 3
  challenges, 77, 78, 92, *155*
  as enabler, 135
  gap, 37–40, *62*
  mindset, 37–40, *62*, 89, 132, 179
  parallel cultures, 13, 79–80, 83, 89
Current and Saving Account (CASA), 26, *27*, *29*, 52–53, 112
Customers, see Clients

Data, 44, 134; see also IT system
  analytics, 43, 176–177, 190, 194, 197

architecture, *60, 90,*
173–174, 192
assets, 122, 124, 176,
177
client data, 148,
149–150, 154
DataClean, 142, 194
Decker, Richard, 47–48,
55–56
attitude, 52, 151
resistance to change,
61, 65–66, 99,
123, 131, 147–148,
153–157
Deep Dives, 23, 26
blockers, 47
client journey, 52–54
digital transformation,
83–84
Year-End review,
150–154
Designers, see Hipsters
Design Thinking, 11,
74, 89, *91*; see also
Agile; Lean Startup
Desirability, *91*, 93,
139
DevOps, *60, 74,* 165,
178–181, 197
Diamonds, 72, 76,
131
governance, 168-169,
192
Three Swim Lane
model, 81–82,
161–164
Digital Strategy Compass,
61–63, 66, 75, 79,
94, 194
Disruptive innovation,
64–65, 81, 83, 95
Disruption map, *62*

Distributed Ledger
Technology (DLT),
see Blockchain

ease of use testing,
141–142, *142*
Ecosystems
closed, 169, *170*
development of, *187*
Fintechs, 18, 43, 195
nascent Innovation,
169
open, 64, 169, *170, 185*
startup, 98
Efficiency innovation, 64,
81, 83
Employees, see People
Enablers, 44, 104, 135
Ethnographic research,
21, 25
Experimentation, *74*
on-boarding, 117,
119–122
ease of use testing,
141–142, *142*
embedded in culture,
79, *80,* 83, 89, *193*
product development,
134
SME lending, *138*

Fail Fast, 38, 136
Feasibility, *91,* 93, *139,*
141
Financial management,
3, 7, *143*, 153–154
Innovation
Accounting, 65, 83,
89, 95
ROI (Return on
Investment), 64, 65,
83, 95, 145, 155

Fintechs, 4, 171–173
on-boarding, 134-135,
195
compared to banks,
10, 12, 30, 194
evaluation, *116*
5Ps of Fintech
collaboration, 137,
144
impact on banking, 3,
5–7
and risk, 154–155
FlowBase platform,
98–100, 109, 114
experimentation, *116,*
117, *118–122*
Flywheel (virtuous
cycle), *196*
Fraud, 98, 150, 154, 190

Ghosh, Elina, 18, 26, 53,
108, 109, 136
Governance, 15, 46,
192
importance of, 65,
93
parallel systems, 162
Growth, 72, 168
engine, *62, 63,* 64
hacking, 81, 93–96
marketing, 37
metrics, 96

Hackathons, 18, 88, 92,
108, 177
Hackers
in 3H teams, 14, 132,
134–136, 139
mindsets, 78, 89,
91–92
HiPPo Management, 38,
193

Hipsters
  in, 3H teams, 14, 132,
    134–136, 139
  lack of, 109, 123
  mindsets, 78, 89,
    91–92
Hockey stick curve, 81,
    93, 95, 135, 140-141,
    187
Hong, Karen, 48, 61, 130,
    177, 195
Hoshin Kanri, 9n8, 61
HR system, see People
    system
Hustlers
  in 3H teams, 14, 132,
    134–136, 139
  lack of, 109
  mindsets, 78, 89,
    91–92

Infrastructure, 160–162
  IT, 4, 76, 174–175
  Pragmatic Innovators
    Network, 162–165
Innobox Program,
    165–167, *193*
Innovation, 64–66, 72
  aligned with strategic
    objectives, *63,* 79,
    162–164
  disruptive, *62,* 64–65,
    95
  fatigue, 160
  framework, 93–95
  mantra, 108, 135-136,
    139, 141
  nascent ecosystem,
    169
  platform, 88–90
  portfolio, 61, *62, 63,*
    66, 81

sustaining, 80–83
theater, 6, 93
Tree Metaphor, 160–
    162
Value Spaces, 79–80
Innovation Accounting,
    65, 83, 89, 95
Innovation Council
  client on-boarding, 123
  QuickLoan, 136, 144
  role, 15, 65–66, 89, *90,*
    93, 108, 168
Innovator network,
    81–84, *90, 143,*
    162–167, *193*
Intrapreneurship
  mindset, *193*
  training program, *59,*
    66, 81, 84, 164–167
IT system, 37, *44, 60,*
    170-175; see also
    Data
  API (Application
    Program Interface),
    42–43, 174, 192
  connectivity, *41,*
    42–43, 123, 124, 156
  infrastructure, 4, 76,
    174–175
  security, 128–129
  Six Rs of IT stack
    review and renewal,
    175–176
  weaknesses, 30–31

Jaws of Culture, *155*

kaizen, 64
KickBox, 165–166
Kupper, Marcus, 48,
    164–165
  concerns, 65

involvement, 100, 124
support, 145, 192, 194
Kwan, Stephen, 46–49,
    52–54
  Chairmanship, 83–84,
    87–88, 98, 112, 114,
    151
  and Singapore, 46, 99,
    144-145
  support, 123–124, 129,
    157, 185
KY Tay International, 2,
    5, 184
  Client journey, 26, *29,*
    30, 106
  Client persona, 27

Lau, Susan Tse, 127, 174
Leadership
  development program,
    38, 59, 81, 82,
    162–163
  of Learning Lab,
    105–107
  senior management,
    15, 23, 73, 84, 144
  T-shaped leader,
    106–107, 164–165
Lean-Agile working, 9,
    77–78, 108–109,
    132–136; see also
    Agile; Product
    Development
Lean Banking, 30–31
Lean Digital projects, 9,
    72, *80,* 81; see also
    Experimentation
  executive coaching,
    34, 109
Lean digital road map,
    73–77
Lean IT, 76

Three-Step Recipe,
110–112
Lean Digital Team, 26,
67, 73, 164–165
Lean Management
fundamentals, 75
Lean Startup, 11, 89,
91; see also Agile;
Design Thinking
Learning Lab, 107–109,
124, 135, *143*, 149
client on-boarding, *113*
leadership, 105–107
location, 84, 89
Learning points, 194–199
Legacy systems, 43, 46,
100, 124, 176, 194
Lending, see QuickLoan

Management system, 35,
36, 135, 161–162
gaps, 40, 44–46, *62*
operating rhythm, *45*,
90, 194
'Two in a Box'
management, 130
MAS (Monetary Authority
of Singapore), 7,
147–149, 154
Metrics, *119*, 195
client experience, 46
financial, 3, 83, 95–96,
143
performance, 21, *28*,
191
strategy pillars, 151–
153
Microservices, 173–174
Mindset, 37–40, *62*, 89, 132
DevOps, 178–180
MNCs (MultiNational
Companies), *57, 58*

Model Office concept,
112, *115*
Moments of Truth, 25,
26n4, *36*, *74*
Moore's Chasm, 95
Multi-channel banking,
197

Network effect, 186, *187*
New business models,
63, 64, 167, *170*–173
New Ways of Working
(nWoW), 11, *38*,
59, 72, *90*; see also
People system
training program, 177

Obeya, 18–19n1
Oceans 11 management,
13, 77–78, 194
Omni-channel (multi-
channel) banking,
197
On-boarding, 30, *44*, 56
FlowBase platform, 99,
117–118
problems, 5, 30
Proof of Value (PoV),
109–115, *121*, 123
Open architecture,
173–174
Open banking, 64, 129,
169–173, 185, 194
Operating rhythm, *45*,
90, 194
Organization structure,
45, 78

Pain points, 88
identification of, 21,
28, *29*, 30
and IT systems, 42

People, 11, 135–136
reaction to innovation,
66–67, 100, 198–199
retraining, 67, 88, 100,
154
People system; see
also New Ways of
Working (nWoW)
as competitive
advantage, 177-178
development
programs, *59*, 81,
164–167, 177–180
HR surveys, 37, *39*
skills gap, 35–37, *38*,
42, *62*, 194
Performance metrics, 21,
28, *191*
Phau, Stanley, 48, 91,
123, 131
concerns, 145, 154
Picard, Martin, 1–3, 9
acceleration of
change, 185, 191
coaching, 15, 109
and front line people,
66–67, 100, 103–105,
198–199
and key managers, 47–
49, 54–55, 123–124,
128–129, 157
problem identification,
1–8, 11, 13, 30–31,
51–52, 87–88
progress reviews, 150–
151, 154, 197–198
Pillars, strategic, 56,
58–60, 75, 76, 104
metrics, 151–153
Pipeline businesses, 171,
196
Pirate metrics, 95–96

Platform businesses, 171,
196
Policy Deployment, 9
Pragmatic Innovators
Network, 81–84,
90, 143, 162–167,
193
Pretotypes, 166–167
Processes, 30
bottlenecks, 42n3, 93,
100, 131, 169
capability gap, 35,
40–42
design, 40, 64
parallel, 112, 117
performance, *44,* 76,
151
streamlining, 106, *111,*
112, 114, *115,* 135,
141
weaknesses, 37, 98
Process Improvement
Events (PIEs), 67,
75–76, 92, 100, 108,
124
Product development,
81–83, *97,* 131–136,
143, 168-169,
185–191
ease of use testing,
141–142, *143*
product features, 132,
134
Project management, *28,*
77, 109
Proof of Value (PoV),
93–94, 153
Blockchain-based
Trade Finance, *186*
on-boarding, 109–115,
121, 123
key activities, *97*

Quickloan, 135,
136–145
Prototyping, 5, 89, *91,*
166–167
Pushback, 145, 149

QuickLoan, 128, 131–
132, 135, 149
Proof of Value (PoV),
136–145
QuickPay, 99

Regulation, 7, 147–149,
154, 194
Reinvention, 195, 197
Resistance to change,
65, 123–124, 151,
153–157; see also
Blockers
pushback, 145, 149
Retail Banking, 6, 55
Retraining, 67, 88, 100,
154
Rigor, 40, 144
Risk, 7, 11, 154–155,
156
management, 150, 197
market risk, 65
personal liability,
153–154
Roadblocks, 19, *20*
ROI (Return on
Investment), 64–65,
83, 95, 145, 155
Root Cause Problem
Solving (RCPS), 19,
30, 37, 93

Saito, Andy, 8–9, 105–106
coaching, 13–14, 15,
34, 51–52
pushback, 145

Saito, Yumi, 8–9, 71–72
client research, 25–26,
30–31
coaching, 15, 72–73,
92–93, 109
engagement, 3–5,
9–11, 13–15
and key managers,
47–49, 106, 123–124,
128–130, 148–151
new business
development,
134–136
progress reviews, 151,
153, 162, 191–192,
195–197
transformation plan,
14–15, 18–23, 84
Scaling, *143,* 150
API (Application
Program Interface),
174
importance of, 142,
145, 155
innovation capability,
165–167
innovation ecosystem,
169, *170*
Three Swim Lane
model, 162–164
Security, 128–129, 154–
155, 190
Shan, Stephanie, 48
concerns, 53, 65, 66,
145, 153–154
Innovation Council,
108, 110
support, 56, 87,
194–195
Silos, 10–11
IT/data, *41,* 176-177,
178-179

persistence of, 91–92, 123

working together, 15, 44, 106, 117, 156, 194

Singapore, 8, 33–34, 184–185, 202

financial innovation, 96, 98–99, 144-145, 149, 154, 156

Fintechs, 18, 183

meeting venues, 51–52, 71–72, 87

port of, 2–3

Six Rs of IT Stack review and renewal, 175–176

Size of the Prize, 23, 112, *114,* 138

Skills; see also New Ways of Working (nWoW); People system

gap, 35–37, *38,* 42, *62,* 194

IT skills, 37, 176–180, 194

Smart Contracts, 184, 190

Smartphones, 2, 124, 131, 138

iPhone, 171

Smart sequencing, *62,* 73, 76, 79, 180

SmartWealth, 99

SMEs (Small Medium Enterprises), *58,* 130

lending, *57,* 88, 110, 124, 131, 136–145

Social media, 96, 177

Soft Launch, *94, 144,* 166–167

Software as a Service (SaaS), 175–176

Software development, see Agile

Software engineers, see Hackers

Soh, Kenny, 66–67, 100, 198–199

Sprints, 19, 75, 132–135

Stark, Nancy, 48, 147–150, 154, 194

Stars, 72, 76, 79

governance, 168-169, 192

Three Swim Lane model, 81–82, 161–164

Strategy, 6

aligned with innovation, *63,* 79, 162–164

Digital Strategy Compass, 61–63, 66, 75, 79, *94,* 194

Digital to the Core, 55–57, 75, 83–84, 96, 108, 199

formulation, 54–61

Pillars, 56, *58–60,* 75, 76, 104, 151–153

Year-End Review, 150–154

Strategy Deployment, 9

Sustaining innovation, 64, 80–83, 92, 95

Tay, Amy, 1–2, 25, 26–27, 183–184

Teams, 13, *113*; see also 3H teams

balanced X teams, *140*

cross-functional, 19, 109, 110

huddles, 34, 36, 44, 198

SWAT teams, 14, 122

Technology gap, 42–44

3C Analysis (Challenge-Cause-Countermeasure), 192–193

3H teams, 14, 132, 180, *193*

mindsets, 78, 89, 91–92

Three-Step Recipe, 110–112, 117

Three Swim Lane model, 81–83, 162–164

Touch Points, 25, 26n4, *36, 74*

Toyota, 8, 46

Trade Finance, 185–191

Transaction costs, 55

Transformation Lighthouse, 18–21, *90,* 108

Transformation roadmap, 73–77

Tree Metaphor of Digital Innovation, 160–162

Trust, 3, 43, 197

T-shaped leader, 106–107, 164–165

'Two in a Box' management, 130

Uber, 171

Value metrics, 95–96

Value spaces, *62,* 66

Value streams, *45,* 46, 64

Venture capital, 15, 89

Viability, *91,* 93, *139*
Virtuous cycle, *196*
Visual management, 19–21
core enabler, *44*
effectiveness, 26, 100
knowledge gaps, 35

Walls, Confusion and
Conflict, 177, *178*
Waterfall approach, 47,
77, *78*

White Label Balance
Sheet Operators,
173
Winning Logic, 75,
150–151
defining, 19, 52, 56–57,
62, 67
innovation platform,
88–89
testing, 110
Workstreams, *28*

Work system, 35, *36,*
40–44, *62,* 161–162;
see also New Ways
of Working (nWoW)

Year-End review, 150–154

Zebra management, 48, 54
Zero-defect culture, 13,
79, 83
Zero-risk culture, *80*

Printed in the United States
By Bookmasters